D0855388

Test-Driven Database Development

Net Objectives Lean-Agile Series

Alan Shalloway, Series Editor

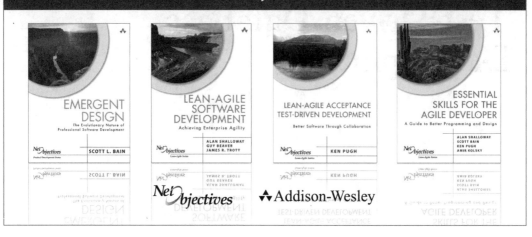

Visit **informit.com/netobjectives** for a complete list of available publications.

The **Net Objectives Lean-Agile Series** provides fully integrated Lean-Agile training, consulting, and coaching solutions for businesses, management, teams, and individuals. Series editor Alan Shalloway and the Net Objectives team strongly believe that it is not the software, but rather the value that software contributes – to the business, to the consumer, to the user – that is most important.

The best – and perhaps only – way to achieve effective product development across an organization is a well-thought-out combination of Lean principles to guide the enterprise, agile practices to manage teams, and core technical skills. The goal of **The Net Objectives Lean-Agile Series** is to establish software development as a true profession while helping unite management and individuals in work efforts that "optimize the whole," including

- The whole organization: Unifying enterprises, teams, and individuals to best work together
- The whole product: Not just its development, but also its maintenance and integration
- The whole of time: Not just now, but in the future – resulting in a sustainable return on investment

The titles included in this series are written by expert members of Net Objectives. These books are designed to help practitioners understand and implement the key concepts and principles that drive the development of valuable software.

Make sure to connect with us!
informit.com/socialconnect

 | |
Addison Wesley | informIT | Safari

ALWAYS LEARNING   PEARSON

Test-Driven Database Development

Unlocking Agility

Max Guernsey, III

✦ Addison-Wesley

Upper Saddle River, NJ • Boston • Indianapolis • San Francisco
New York • Toronto • Montreal • London • Munich • Paris • Madrid
Cape Town • Sydney • Tokyo • Singapore • Mexico City

Many of the designations used by manufacturers and sellers to distinguish their products are claimed as trademarks. Where those designations appear in this book, and the publisher was aware of a trademark claim, the designations have been printed with initial capital letters or in all capitals.

The authorz and publisher have taken care in the preparation of this book, but make no expressed or implied warranty of any kind and assume no responsibility for errors or omissions. No liability is assumed for incidental or consequential damages in connection with or arising out of the use of the information or programs contained herein.

The publisher offers excellent discounts on this book when ordered in quantity for bulk purchases or special sales, which may include electronic versions and/or custom covers and content particular to your business, training goals, marketing focus, and branding interests. For more information, please contact:

U.S. Corporate and Government Sales
(800) 382-3419
corpsales@pearsontechgroup.com

For sales outside the United States, please contact:

International Sales
international@pearsoned.com

Visit us on the Web: informit.com/aw

Library of Congress Cataloging-in-Publication Data

Guernsey, Max, 1978-
  Test-driven database development : unlocking agility / Max Guernsey.
    pages cm
  Includes bibliographical references and index.
  ISBN-13: 978-0-321-78412-4 (pbk. : alk. paper)
  ISBN-10: 0-321-78412-X (pbk. : alk. paper)
  1. Database design. 2. Agile software development. I. Title.
  QA76.9.D26G84 2013
  005.1--dc23
                                2012047608

Copyright © 2013 Pearson Education, Inc.

All rights reserved. Printed in the United States of America. This publication is protected by copyright, and permission must be obtained from the publisher prior to any prohibited reproduction, storage in a retrieval system, or transmission in any form or by any means, electronic, mechanical, photocopying, recording, or likewise. To obtain permission to use material from this work, please submit a written request to Pearson Education, Inc., Permissions Department, One Lake Street, Upper Saddle River, New Jersey 07458, or you may fax your request to (201) 236-3290.

ISBN-13: 978-0-32-178412-4
ISBN-10: 0-32-178412-X

Text printed in the United States on recycled paper at RR Donnelley and Sons in Crawfordsville, Indiana.

First printing, February 2013

Editor-in-Chief
Mark Taub

Executive Editor
Chris Guzikowski

Senior Development Editor
Chris Zahn

Managing Editor
Kristy Hart

Senior Project Editor
Lori Lyons

Copy Editor
Paula Lowell

Indexer
Tim Wright

Proofreader
Sarah Kearns

Editorial Assistant
Olivia Basegio

Cover Designer
Chuti Prasertsith

Compositor
Nonie Ratcliff

This book is dedicated to my wife, Amy Bingham,
who is largely responsible for my being the man I am today.

Contents at a Glance

Contents

Foreword

I've been a Test-Driven Development practitioner for many years and have also been writing, lecturing, and teaching courses on the subject as part of my duties at Net Objectives. A question that often arises during classes or conference talks is this: TDD seems ideal for business logic and other "middle-tier" concerns, but what about the presentation (UI) tier and the persistence (database) tier?

My answer, typically, has been to point out that there are two issues in each case:

1. How to manage the dependencies from the middle tier to the other two, so as to make the middle tier behaviors more easily testable

2. How to test-drive the other layers themselves

For issue #1, this is a matter of interfaces and mock objects, design patterns, and good separation of concerns in general. It is a matter of technique, and the TDD community has a lot of mature, proven techniques for isolating business logic from its dependencies. A lot of time is spent in my courses on these "tricks of the trade."

But when it comes to issue #2—test-driving the user interface and the database themselves—I've always said that these are largely unsolved problems. Not that we don't know how to test these things, but rather that we don't know how to test *drive* them, to write the kind of isolated, fast, granular tests that good TDD requires. We have to be satisfied with more traditional testing when it comes to these other layers of the system; this has been my traditional answer.

As far as I know, this is still true for the UI. But when it comes to databases, Max Guernsey has figured it out.

In my book *Emergent Design*, I talk a lot about the parallels between systems design and evolutionary processes in nature. If you think of your source code as the "DNA" of the system and the executable as the "individual organism," it really fits. The DNA is used to generate the individual. To make a change to the species, the DNA changes first, and then the next individual generated is altered. Nature does not evolve individuals; it makes changes to the species generationally. This is much akin to the code/compile/run nature of software. We throw away the .exe file, change the source code, and the compiler makes a new, different, hopefully better executable. Because of this, the source is king. It's the one thing we cannot afford to lose.

Max's insight began, at least in my conversations with him, with the notion that databases are not like this. If the schema is akin to the DNA, and thus an installed, running instance of the database (with all its critical enterprise data) is an individual, we cannot take nature's cavalier attitude toward it. The schema is easy to re-create—you just run your DDL scripts or equivalent. But a given, installed, "living" database contains information and knowledge that must be preserved as its structure changes.

Because of this, the paradigm of evolution does not fit. In databases, the individual is paramount. We cannot simply throw it away and re-create it from altered DNA. Nature, again, does not *evolve* individuals. But there is a natural paradigm that works. It is *morphing*. It is the way an individual creature transitions from one life phase to another—tadpole to frog, for example. In examining this insight and all of its ramifications, Max has developed a truly revolutionary view about databases: how to create them and change them and, at long last, how to test-drive them. His approach gives the database practitioner the fundamental clarity, safety, and leverage that a TDD practitioner enjoys.

This book is a ground-breaking work. Max has discovered the Rosetta stone of database development here, and if you follow him carefully, you will leave with a far more powerful way of doing your job when it comes to the persistence tier of your system. You will have the knowledge, tools, and overall approach that make this possible.

—Scott Bain
Senior Consultant, Net Objectives

Preface

This book applies the concepts of test-driven development to database development.

Who Should Read This Book

The short answer is "anyone who wants to learn how to do test-driven development of a database and is willing to do the hard work to get there." The long answer follows.

This book is aimed primarily at programmers who are in some way responsible for the development of at least one database design. A secondary target is people who think of themselves primarily as database developers who are interested in adding test-driven development to their process.

That is not meant to in any way diminish the value of the second group of people. The techniques in this book build on principals and methods that, at the time of this writing, are gaining widespread acceptance among the former group and still struggling to gain traction with the latter. That's not to say that things won't change—I hope they will—but this book would have spun out of control if I tried to take on all first principles from which it is derived.

The goal of this book is to help people apply the process of test-driven development to the new domain of database development, where the forces are different if only slightly.

If you read the book and are able to sustainably drive development of your database through test, it's a win both for you and for me. If you start using the principles to port over other techniques, such as pattern-oriented development, then the win will be doubled. If you start porting what you learn there back into any other domain where long-lived data is involved, such as the development of your installers, then the win is greater still.

What Needs to Be Done

To serve this goal, I start by establishing why test-driven development works. I then look at why it has so much trouble gaining traction in the database world. Mind you, it's not that I think database development is basically untested, but my experience has shown me that it is not sustainably tested nor is it test driven.

The main problem that makes database testing hard is the absence or misplacement of the concept of a class. Even the most "Wild-West-style" modern language still supports the idea of having classes and instances.

Database engines either pay lip service to this by having classes of data structures or do nothing whatsoever to establish truly testable classes. The reason for this appears to me to be that people generally haven't recognized what the true first-class object of the database world is: the database itself. So the first step is to establish a class of databases.

Change is central to the test-driven development process. You are constantly changing design to support new needs and to support the testability of an expanding feature set. One of the forces that makes test-driven development harder to adopt and to sustain is that change is seen as more dangerous in database designs than in other kinds of design.

If you mess up a design change in your middle tier, you might have to roll back. If you mess up a design change in the data tier, you could erase valuable knowledge stored therein. The solution is to test not only what your database does but also how it is changed.

Another problem that faces databases in regard to changing design is that the coupling between a database and its clients is weakly enforced. The possibility exists to make a change to a database's interface and not discover that you've broken a downstream application for a very long time. That risk can be mitigated by using your class of databases to harden the relationship between a database design and its clients.

Creating a strong class of databases with a controlled way of changing things solves the basic problems in the database world that stand in the way of TDD. That is, it gets developers up to the early '90s in terms of support for modern practices.

To get into the twenty-first century, you have to go a bit further. To that end, I help you understand that the scope of a test should be verification of a behavior. I support that by defining what a behavior is in the context of database development.

Enabling Emergent Design

I also show you how to maximize long-term maintainability by limiting a database's scope to what you need right now and using the techniques in this book to make it easy to add more features later. That is, I'll help you give up the fear you tend to associate with not planning a database's design far in advance.

No process is perfect and, even if it were, none of the people executing it would be. Despite all your efforts to avoid them, mistakes will be made. If you are doing true test-driven database development, most of the time a mistake will come in the form of a behavior not expressed in your test suite. I'll show you how best to correct an error.

Knowing how to develop and write tests for a class of databases while keeping their designs as simple and problem-appropriate as possible will bring database development into the twenty-first century—just one short era behind modern object-oriented development.

Modernizing Development

The final phase of modernizing database development to support a test-driven process involves adopting and adapting what I call the "advanced" object-oriented methodologies.

Getting a grip on design at the class/database level is the first phase. If you have a choice between one big database design and two smaller ones, you should choose the pair of smaller ones. If the database technology isn't in a place to permit that, use composition to place two logical database instances inside one physical database instance.

Another important activity is refactoring. You need to keep a database's design problem-appropriate for its entire life. That means the design must start out small, but it also means that it needs to change shape as you cover more and more of the problem space. I'll show you how to refactor database designs in the context of a test-driven process.

That will be everything you need to do test-driven database development for a typical, new database design. The remainder of the book is dedicated to helping you "wrangle" databases that were born in an untested context, deviating from the process in a controlled and testable way, and adapting the process to non-database applications.

Doing test-driven database development will not be easy—not at first. If you've already obtained a firm grip on "regular" test-driven development, this should come as absolutely no surprise. No matter how quickly you pick up new skills, TDD will take longer than anything else.

It costs so much because it is worth so much. When you finish this book, you'll have a theoretical understanding of test-driven database development. One, three, or even eighteen months later, you will have mastered it.

After mastering it, you'll be able to frequently, rapidly, and safely change your database designs with confidence. You'll be able to build just what you need, just when you need it. As a result, database improvement can become a fluid part of your software development process. In addition you'll be able to keep the design of your database clean, simple, and fast.

Chapter-by-Chapter Breakdown

Here's a chapter-by-chapter breakdown of what this book covers.

In Chapter 1, "Why, Who, and What," I explain why I wrote this book, who should read it, and what the real roadblocks to TDD are in the context of database design. I wrote this book because true test-driven development hasn't really gained any traction in the database world. I am targeting people who think of themselves as software developers and also must work with database designs. The biggest problem in the database development world is that there is no clear concept of a class, which is a central element of traditional TDD efforts.

To build a class of databases, you need to keep a permanent record of the exact set of scripts that are run on a database and to have a clean way of tracking which ones have already been run. A little infrastructure allows you to ensure that every instance of a class of databases is built exactly the same way. In Chapter 2, "Establishing a Class of Databases," I show you how to do exactly that.

Many things go into having a sustainable TDD process for a database design. The first step is to define a basic TDD process to which you can later add deeper, more data-oriented activities. In Chapter 3, "A Little TDD," I show you how to do some simple test-driven development against a class of databases.

In Chapter 4, "Safely Changing Design," I show you how to overcome one of the big obstacles: the risk associated with change. Introducing change frequently frightens a lot of people. The root of that fear is that databases store a lot of valuable stuff, and losing some of the data on account of a hastily made change is unacceptable in most environments. The fear and the risk can both be vanquished by testing not only the behavior of your database, but also the scripts that build or modify it.

Databases are the most depended-upon things in the software industry and modifying one's design can have unforeseen consequences. At the heart of this problem is massive, infective duplication that many simply accept as "natural." In Chapter 5, "Enforcing Interface," I show you how to control the cost of a rapidly evolving database design by eliminating that duplication.

As far as the TDD process is concerned, tests specify behaviors in objects. The question then becomes "What is a behavior in the context of a database?" In Chapter 6, "Defining Behaviors," I set a pretty good scope for a test by answering that question.

Having the scope of a single test well defined gives you the freedom to explore the larger topic of what kinds of database designs are conducive to change and which ones are difficult to maintain. In Chapter 7, "Building for Maintainability," I show you that keeping a database light, lean, and simple is a better path to supporting future needs than attempting to predict now what you will need months from now.

"Sure, this is all great if you never mess up," one might say, "but what happens when we do?" In Chapter 8, "Error and Remediation," I show you techniques that allow you to deal with any unplanned changes that might find their way into your database design.

In Chapter 9, "Design," I make recommendations about how to design a class of databases for maximum testability. I then go a little further and show how to apply object-oriented design concepts to classes of databases.

Tests are frequently plagued by unwanted coupling. Dependencies between behaviors create ripple effects and single changes end up causing dozens of tests to fail. In Chapter 10, "Mocking," I show you how to isolate behaviors from one another by building on the design techniques shown in Chapter 9.

The better your test coverage and the more rapidly you can introduce change, the more frequently you are going to modify design. In Chapter 11, "Refactoring," I demonstrate how to alter the design of your database while preserving behavior.

No process is complete unless it includes a mechanism to ingest software developed before its introduction. In Chapter 12, "Legacy Databases," I cover one of two ways to take a database that was developed with databases that weren't developed using the practices in this book by gradually covering them in tests.

Chapter 13, "The Façade Pattern," covers the other option for dealing with a legacy database. When employing the Façade pattern, you encapsulate a legacy design behind a new, well-tested one and gradually transfer behaviors from the old design to the new.

I would be crazy if I tried to sell this as a "one-size-fits-all" solution to the problem of bringing TDD to the database development world. The practices herein will work for a lot of people without modification. However, some people operate under conditions to which the first thirteen chapters of this book do not perfectly fit. In Chapter 14, "Variations," I cover some of the adaptations I've seen people apply in the past.

Finally, in Chapter 15, "Other Applications," I demonstrate a number of ways that the various techniques in this book can apply to data persisted by means other than a database. Some examples of these other storage mechanisms are file systems, XML documents, and the dreaded serialized middle-tier object.

Downloadable Code

You can download the code used in this book by going to
http://maxthe3rd.com/test-driven-database-development/code.aspx

Acknowledgments

There are numerous influences behind this book ranging back over nearly a decade.

First thanks go to my wife, Amy. She was a constant source of motivation and validation in the course of developing this book and, in the 15 years we've been together, has done at least one proofread of everything I've written.

Bill Zietzke was around at the very beginning of the process. It was a conversation I had with him while we were both contracting at an insurance company in Bellevue, Washington, that got this whole thing started.

Beau Bender helped discover the mechanism I prescribe for controlling the coupling between databases and their clients. For that, I am grateful.

My good friend and mentor, Scott L. Bain, is also deserving of thanks. It was he who first pushed me to get published and it was his influence that helped make it happen. He has also played an instrumental role in developing this technique by contributing valuable questions, criticisms, and observations along the way.

Alan Shalloway has also been a friend and mentor to me throughout the majority of my career. He helped me decide that my first idea—teaching everything to everyone—was not the right one. I am certain that, without his very constructive criticism, you would be reading a completely different book, probably written by a completely different author.

Both Alan and Scott played pivotal roles in my recent development as a professional software developer. Each nurtured the skills he already saw and supplied me with skills that were missing in a format that circumvented the considerable defenses that protect me from new things and ideas.

Of equal, and possibly greater, value was their advice on how to deal with people. At the time of this writing, I'm not exactly a beloved consensus builder, but I am a lot better at persuasion than I was before I met Scott and Alan. Without that guidance, without showing me how important it is to share what we know in an accessible format, I probably wouldn't even have cared to write a book in the first place.

Some of my recently acquired friends and colleagues have served as guinea pigs, reading early versions of various chapters of the book for me. This allowed me to acquire feedback soon enough to act and helped me decide to put this book through its second transformation. Without feedback from Seth McCarthy and Michael Gordon Brown, I would have tried to release a much larger book about "agile" database development instead of the focused, technical book you are reading now.

It goes without saying that my parents are in part responsible because, without them, there would be no me. However, my father played a special role in my development as a young programmer. Without his influence, I would probably be something useless, like a mathematician or a Wall Street analyst.

About the Author

Max Guernsey is currently a Managing Member at Hexagon Software LLC. He has 15 years of experience as a professional software developer. For nearly half that time, he has been blogging, writing, and delivering lectures on the topic of agile and test-driven database development.

For much of Max's professional career, he has been a consultant, advising a variety of software companies in many different industries using multiple programming and database technologies. In most of these engagements, he spent months or even years helping teams implement cutting-edge techniques such as test-driven development, object-oriented design, acceptance-test-driven development, and agile planning.

Max has always been a "hands-on" consultant, working with teams for long periods of time to help them build both software and skills. This series of diverse, yet deep, engagements helped him gain a unique understanding of the database-related testing and design problems that impede most agile teams. Since 2005, he has been thinking, writing, blogging, lecturing, and creating developer-facing software dedicated to resolving these issues.

Max can be reached via email at max@hexsw.com. He also posts regularly on his Twitter account (@MaxGuernseyIII) and his blog (maxg3prog.blogspot.com).

Chapter 1

Why, Who, and What

This is a book about how to effectively apply the discipline of test-driven development (TDD) to the tasks surrounding delivery of database functionality. It is a book for people who want to know how to apply the discipline of test-driven development to database programming. To get to *how,* though, one first needs to examine why, who, and what.

Why

When I started writing this book, the working title was *Agile Database Development: From Requirements to Delivery.* The fact that its name and scope has changed a couple times seems quite fitting.

Due to both feedback and revelation, this book has undergone several radical metamorphoses, first starting out as a book that was mostly about process with a little bit of technique thrown in, transforming into a book about how the differences in TDD influence the process of agile database development, and finally shedding the team-level process stuff altogether to become what it is today.

Why did I change the direction of the book a couple times? Primarily because almost all the process-management stuff we developers have learned about agile software development is universal to any domain; typically it's even applicable to hardware design. Much of what I was writing felt like it was doomed to be ineffective, either duplicating something someone else wrote or preaching to the converted. My advice to those of you seeking counsel on how to do agile development when building a database is this: Learn how to do agile software development and then do it for a database.

Of course, if you do that, you will discover that you need to learn how to do TDD while developing databases. The discipline of test-driven development is absolutely and, I believe, non-controversially critical to the success of any agile development endeavor. You need a suite of executable specifications that tell you whether or not a change you made was safe. Without that, you cannot make agility work.

That's where things get tricky: Test-driven development is one thing that differs quite a bit between traditional object-oriented development and database development. That is, although the principles of TDD apply everywhere, the corresponding practices developed for building application and middle-tier logic don't always translate over to the database world perfectly.

That said, you can still make use of test-driven development even if your organization isn't ready to embrace agile software development just yet.

Agility Progressively Invades Domains Every Day

A great tide in civilization governs how humans do things. When that tide goes out, we centralize, establish command and control structures, and attempt to find efficiencies in large batches and long queues. When the water starts to come back in, we break down those structures, start to drive control down into the hands of "common" folk, and attempt to find efficiencies in the quick decisions that get made by people closest to the problem.

The tide is coming back in and will probably continue to ebb that direction for the lifespan of anyone alive at the time of this writing.

For you and me, it doesn't matter whether the tide is right or wrong any more than a man standing on the beach should care whether or not it is right that the water is coming up on shore. The wave is coming and you had better be ready whether you like it or not. Developers have to get better at developing in smaller increments and delivering value more quickly if for no other reason than that society is no longer willing to tolerate long waits for the things it wants.

Some believe that databases are an exception—a special case that can ignore the ubiquitous drive to change more frequently and in response to actual needs. There's no nice way to put it: Those people are wrong. The database is no exception. Sure, database developers might be able to hold the world at bay for a little longer than other domains of product development, but you can't stop the tide. Over the next few years or decades, the pressure to make changes quickly will become overwhelming and, frankly, those who resist it will end up being relegated to less critical roles than the ones to which they have grown accustomed.

Agility Cannot Work Without TDD

There's just one problem with trying to get a quick turnaround: Change is a dangerous thing. If you have something that is delivering value then changing it inherently jeopardizes continued delivery of that value. If your product stops delivering value, you start to lose good will with your customers. If that erosion is allowed to continue for long enough, you start to lose the customers themselves.

With the exception of hedge-fund operatives holding proxies for borrowed shares they've already sold, and similar sorts of folks, nobody wants to lose customers. So a mechanism has to be put in place that defends value even when changes are made very quickly. Such a mechanism allows us to change things quickly.

That mechanism is test-driven development. Test-driven development provides numerous advantages but, in the context of this book, its primary advantage is substantial and meaningful coverage of a software component by automated tests. Having tests in place gives you immediate feedback when you break something and prevents you from releasing something in a broken state, both of which are indispensable.

In addition to those most critical benefits of test-driven development, numerous other benefits are touted by many as the "primary" benefits of TDD, including things such as enhanced analysis or dramatic reduction in overbuild. I don't want to downplay those things. They are very important and I cover them, but they don't let you go fast—they help you go a little faster.

TDD in the Database World Is a Challenge

The reason this book exists is that TDD is very hard to do with databases, especially in a way that enables you to quickly develop, vet, and release changes.

This difficulty largely stems from the way developers build databases in the first place. In many organizations, databases are monuments. Specific database instances are very important, and the importance of these instances overshadows the importance of design itself.

I've seen many cases in which people think exclusively about database design in terms of these all-important instances. That is, they think about the design of "the" development database, "the" test database, and "the" production database, and their primary concern is how to propagate changes from one to another. That kind of thinking must be turned inside out for database design to adopt test-driven development.

I'll explain how to do that throughout the rest of the book.

Who

Before I get to what the true nature of the problem is and how to fix it, I want to cover just a little bit about whom this book targets. I don't want to preclude anyone who might get value from it, but I think you need some prerequisite skills to make use of this book.

You still need this book, though, so go ahead and buy it now and you can just hang on to it while you pick up those other skills.

TDD and OOP

To utilize the techniques in this book, you need to be someone who understands the benefits of test-driven development and object-oriented programming. You don't need to be an expert but you do need to know what the benefit to you of having implemented these things will be. Here are some assertions that should make sense to you:

- TDD enables you to develop quickly by keeping you on the right track.

- OOP enables you to develop quickly by keeping unrelated things encapsulated and thus separate from each other.

If those sound right to you, then you're good on the knowledge front.

Applications and Databases

The next thing you need is some idea of how applications talk to databases and some understanding of how databases work. Not having the latter seems nearly impossible—why would you have even looked at this book otherwise? The former is ever so slightly more likely to be an issue. If you have never written a line of application code, you'll need to pick up a C#, Java, C++, Ruby, or JavaScript book and teach yourself just enough to start writing some basic algorithms and defining some basic interfaces.

What

So what is the real problem? What's really in the way of implementing test-driven development for databases? Fundamentally, it is that databases—individual servers and database instances—are the execution platform for persistence solutions. A single database is more like a process containing the JVM and a particular session of an application than it is like the design that was used to produce a set of application binaries that would ultimately be loaded into any particular session.

Developers need to shift away from that practice and move toward building designs for databases that are not tied to any particular instances.

Databases Are Objects

Databases are objects. They are long-lived objects, from an object-oriented programmer's perspective, but they are objects nonetheless. The way many people treat databases, these days, is akin to ancient times when computer programmers truly programmed *computers*, rather than writing programs that would *run on computers* like they do now.

With a few legacy exceptions, that way of developing application code has gone the way of the dodo for very good reasons. The most obvious reason is that the complexity of modern environments demands the ability to add or remove hardware at will. Another good reason is because many applications have to run on diverse hardware or in environments that are physically separated from the programmers doing the development.

TDD Works on Classes, Not Objects

The biggest impediment to TDD in the database world lives in the very nature of testing, though. Tests inherently operate on objects. When a person runs a manual test, he interfaces with a large number of objects—an instance of the application he is using along with instances of numerous business logic objects that make decisions based on their input and/or that produce results.

Other industries don't do testing that way. Companies that produce absolutely critical things that last a long time, such as artificial replacements for damaged hip joints, test every single instance that comes off the line. Companies that make things that don't last or are not likely to result in serious personal injury upon failure, such as pencils, create a close approximation of testing every single object they make by testing a statistically significant portion of their product.

Why is it that software developers can get away with testing just a few instances of what they make?

What makes the way testing is done in the software industry possible is the fact that two objects of the same class behave the same way. You can use a class to produce any number of objects that all have the exact same behavior.

This property, unique to what software developers do, allows any one instance of a class to serve as a prototype for every other instance of that class. This means that testing just one object tells something about the class of objects itself which, in turn, tells us something about the set of all objects that ever have been and ever will be made by that class.

However, what if developers didn't have that? What if every instance of a class were assembled by hand or by an unreliable process on a different computer? In that case, testing one object wouldn't tell you very much about another. You would have to test a statistically representative subset of the systems you build, and the number you would need to test would correspond with the amount of risk you could accept.

That's the position developers are in with regard to the database world. Very rarely does one develop a design and have an easy way to introduce changes to that design into new or existing database instances. More often, you manually reconcile design changes with all the various important instances of a type of database. This is the equivalent of manually modifying and checking the assembly code (or perhaps some very primitive source code) on each computer you want to update, then recompiling the binaries on that computer.

When you do things that way, you need to create a close approximation of testing every production instance you make. However, in the software industry, tests are typically abusive to the things they test. You cannot subject live data to the kind of danger posed by a test. Some database instances, especially production databases, simply cannot be tested.

We Need Classes of Databases

If you need to know something about a database but aren't allowed to test that database, then you need to find a way to know that database will work by testing a proxy. As I've already stated, the mechanism that allows us to do that in the application development world is the class.

So the foundation of test-driven database development is to build classes of databases rather than particular database instances. The class you define is responsible for building and updating test instances. After you've gotten enough feedback from test instances to validate a change to a class, then it is responsible for updating production databases in exactly the same way that it updated the test instances.

In this way, you can be sure that your test instances are good prototypes for the production instances against which you don't want to run any tests. You'll see throughout the course of this book that the same process allows you to vet not only what a revision to a database will do but how it will be introduced. This gives you complete confidence that, by the time you want to roll a database change out to any production environment, it will "just work"—the same way that you don't really consider the possibility that a constructor for an object might not work.

Summary

At the time of this writing, lean and agile software development are taking over the world, but database development remains a bottleneck in the process. To unblock whole organizations, developers have to figure out how to get databases to be able to change quickly.

Yet you cannot do so at the expense of confidence in your changes—databases are too important to allow for additional risk. That's where TDD comes in. It enables you to make frequent, rapid changes, with less risk than the slowest, most careful changes made without it.

You cannot simply apply the techniques you've already learned for "regular" software development without modification, though. You have to take into account the different forces present in the database world and that's exactly what I intend to help you do in the following chapters.

The next chapter goes through the steps required to establish a class of databases.

Chapter 2

Establishing a Class of Databases

The first thing you need to do to start test-driving your databases is to start defining classes of databases and stop worrying so much about particular database instances. When you're done with the book, you will probably start pulling away from allowing any manual changes to any meaningful database instance. To help you get to that point, this chapter digs a little bit deeper into what a class is and how it helps, and also delves into how the forces in database development differ from application development.

After reconciling the nature of a class with the new forces seen in database development, this chapter lays out the requirements for a class of databases and then shows you a how to implement one. Giving you the requirements separate from the implementation will, I hope, enable you to more easily adapt the output of this chapter to your environment.

The Class's Role in TDD

A class's primary role in test-driven development is to provide a mechanism by which numerous objects with identical behavior can be created. This is of paramount importance because the way you test software is by checking the behavior of a single object and using that to predict the behavior of all other instances from the same class.

When you don't have a class, testing only tells you something about a particular object. When you do, testing tells you something about how that object will be made and, therefore, how all others will be made.

A Reliable Instantiation Process

One of the things that really raises the hackles on the back of my neck is when people say "I wrote an object that does X." No, you didn't—you wrote a class of objects that does X. If you absolutely must shorten it, and I admit I often do in verbal conversations, then you wrote a class that does X.

However, as with many things, you can glean a nugget of wisdom from this pet peeve of mine. People say they wrote objects because the line between a class and an object is so thoroughly blurred for them by now. Having a class typically means you can get an object. Being able to get an object typically means you have a class.

If I write a class of objects in C#, instantiation is not something I even consider. Inherent in having developed the class is the fact that it will give me as many objects as I ask for with complete reliability. They will all be made, they will all work, and they will all work exactly the same way as every other instance of that class.

Tests Check Objects

That classes produce objects safely and consistently is such a fundamental fact that developers take it completely for granted. Sure, when I'm teaching an application developer to do test-driven development, I might have him write a few tests for his constructor, but I only have him test the behavior he wants to add to the constructor, never that the object being created gets created properly.

In small part that's because I don't think such things should be tested any more than that you should test that a method call is a method call. However, I cannot really claim that principle is the main reason I don't teach people to do that.

The real reason I don't teach people to test that constructors construct is because it doesn't even occur to me that a chance exists they might not. Of course, such a chance exists but it's somewhere in the vicinity of the chance that this book will turn into a weasel while you are reading it. So I don't bother thinking about it.

It is so ingrained in me that I had to force myself to think about it another way for the purpose of writing this book and explaining the concepts herein. When I'm doing test-driven development for an object-oriented system, I actually think in terms of relationships between classes. My test class tests my production class, my production class uses a service class, and so on.

Yet that's not how it really works, is it? When I write a test class for a production class, the test class really doesn't test the production class. Instead, the test class produces a test object with a bunch of tests in it. The tests in the test object then get instances of my production class and ask them to do things, performing analyses and reporting on the results.

I can typically run the same test hundreds of times in a row and see the exact same results despite the fact that each run uses completely new test and production objects. This repeatability is what allows me to be sure that, in a deployed environment, my production objects will function properly. In fact, that predictability allows me to think in terms of the relationships between classes and not the objects they create.

Classes in Object-Oriented Programming Languages

Why did the class of objects come to the application development world so much sooner than the class of database? For one thing, there were forces necessitating classes in the application development world that aren't as strong in the database world. I won't get into those just now. For another, building a reliable way to create objects in an application session is a lot easier than it is for database instances.

Making Classes Is Easy: Just Make New Objects

Classes in the OOP world really just have two responsibilities: make new objects and destroy discarded ones. Destruction doesn't really matter for the purposes of this book. However, creation definitely does.

When a class of objects in a language such as C#, Java, or Ruby is asked to make a new object, what it starts with is an empty block of memory. That memory's content is absolutely irrelevant, so the class blithely overwrites it with the stuff required to make the new object. In some cases, that's as simple as adding a pointer to a virtual method table, zeroing out the remainder of the bytes, and delegating to the constructor for further initialization instructions. In others, it's as complex as building structured data that point to all kinds of metadata, methods, and what-have-you.

In no case, however, is it so complex that some simple mathematical rules cannot be used to translate between a developer's expression of design and the precise set of steps needed to create an instance of a type.

One Path: Destroy If Necessary

You might do a number of things with a class of objects. A lot of them have to do with design. For instance, you might develop a class from scratch using the test-first technique. You might use existing tests to rewrite a class. You might alter your suite of tests for a class to change its behavior.

Some of the things you need to do with a class have to do with deployment, the two main categories of which are building a new object and updating an existing one. Those two things sound different and thinking of them differently makes sense because programmers might have to handle each case separately, but from the compiler's perspective, they are really just one thing.

The key to why creating classes in an application development environment is so easy lies in my description of the starting condition. An OOP class is handed a block of bytes that it doesn't have to care about at all. It is free to just zero them all out. In some platforms, the bytes are guaranteed to start as all zeroes.

This kind of class of object only ever has to build new instances. If you need to upgrade old instances, what do you do? Usually, you store their content somewhere else, destroy the old objects by shutting down the application, update the class by updating the binaries in which it lives, start the upgraded application, and create new objects by pulling the old state that you stored in some kind of persistent, simplified format.

Classes of Databases

Notwithstanding the fact that, at least half the time, databases are the "somewhere else" you store an object's content while it is not being used, applying this model to database development is just not practical. The closest thing I can think of would be migrating data from an old database to its newly created successor every time you want to update behavior. I suppose that, for many databases, this might still be faster than what a lot of people do right now, but because I know a way to do things that supports a faster-still development process, I'm going to disregard that as an option.

Two Paths: Create or Change

In a lot of environments, there are two paths for an instance of a "type" of database to be created. One path is for a database to be created fresh from nothing. This often happens in test or development environments. Another path is for a database to be repeatedly updated with increments of behavior as its design evolves over time. That tends to happen in production environments.

This is often best illustrated by application development teams. I was on one team that had a script that represented "the database" that was shared by some nefarious mechanism such as email or a shared folder on the network. When a developer messes up his database, he drops everything and runs this script.

As people come up with design changes that make sense, they add them to "the script." Sometimes a lazy developer might regenerate "the script" from an instance he has manipulated through some GUI.

This worked alright within the development team. However, the scripts the development team wrote and tested against were never used in production. Instead, they would submit their new design to a database expert who would create a new instance and run a diff tool to figure out what changed. Of course, the output of that tool could never be trusted so the database expert just used it as guidance when writing a new script that applied the update. He would then manually back up the production databases, apply the changes, and verify that everything was working.

In the half-dozen times that we released during my engagement with that company, this worked flawlessly once. Having the backup protected us from real catastrophes. The fact that all the users had gone home for the weekend defended against significant interruptions in service. Staying until nine-thirty or later on a Friday night sure made me mad, though.

The root of the problem is that developers were trying to treat their "class" of databases like it was a typical, OOP class—something that would only be created or destroyed. They didn't worry about the modification case; that was someone else's job.

Yet every single important database in the world is created once and modified many times.

The Hard Part: Unifying the Two Paths

This duplicity in the database world is what makes defining a class of databases a difficult task: How do you build a class for something that might be created from scratch in one case and might be built in numerous iterations, each separated by computationally vast periods of time, in another?

The "two paths" problem can't really be solved. The only reasonable solution is to eliminate it altogether. This means programmers have to find one path of instantiation that can both produce new instances and update existing instances of a database class.

Real Database Growth

Finding that path might be challenging for you or you might immediately see the solution. When it is difficult to find a solution, I find it often helps to look at what is really happening. In this case, examining how real production databases are built and grow is helpful.

After all the boring stuff such as creating an empty database instance, the first thing that happens is that a series of DDL statements are run to imbue in a database all the behavior it should initially have. Often, the same SQL script used by the development team is executed against a database to make this happen.

Eventually, the decision is made that a database's design needs to change in some way. Some kind of work occurs to validate the change, build surrounding features and infrastructure, and make sure everything works together. Then a change is applied to the production database to get from one design to another.

After a while, the process is repeated and another transformation is applied to get the database to its next version and so on.

A clear pattern is emerging: Production databases are typically transitioned from each released version to its successor, then to the next, then to the next. One obvious question that comes to mind is, "Can we possibly get around that?"

I think the answer is "no." Almost by definition, a long-lived database's design is going to have to change periodically.

How About Making Every Database Build Like Production Databases?

So if you can't change the way that production databases are built, consider the alternative: building every database that way. What's wrong with that? I'm sure someone will come up with something but for most of us, the answer is "Building every database exactly the way that we absolutely must build our production databases makes a hell of a lot of sense."

The rule is simple enough:

1. Treat an empty, initialized database instance as version zero.

2. To get a new database, build a script to transition from version zero to one.

3. To upgrade a database, build a script from version N to $N+1$.

4. When building a database, run all the scripts from its current version up to the target version in order.

So, to build a new database of version three, you would execute the version one script, followed by the version two script, followed by the version three script. To upgrade a version one database to version three, you would execute the version two script followed by the version three script.

All DBs Would Follow the Exact Same Path

The point is that you can get from any one version to any of its successors by executing all the intervening scripts in order. No extra work is required to figure out how to get from version five to version seven; you already know how to do it by knowing how to get from version five to six and six to seven.

Doing this, alone, is an enormous step toward being able to properly test-drive the development of a database.

Incremental Build

So how would you interface with such a mechanism, then? The best way would be to document each change made to a database as a separate version and have a good way of ordering those changes (like version numbers). As long as a database identifies which changes have already been made, you can then build a generalized mechanism to apply the correct changes in the correct order.

Document Each Database Change

Start with just one change script. As long as it hasn't been applied to an important database, feel free to keep changing it as your intent and/or requirements change. At this point, it is really just a plan for what you are going to do in the near future.

However, after you commit a change to a database, stop working on it forever. A transition committed to production ceases to be the blueprints for a future change and instead becomes documentation of what happened in the past. Essentially, it is now an historical record.

After a change has been committed to history, create a new document for the next change. Continue working on that until it is committed in an irreversible way, then stop working on it and create another document.

Documenting the order in which each step was executed is also important. This can be as simple as assigning a version number to each document (version one is the thing that was used to create an initial database, version two was used to add some more structures, and so on), or as complex as calling out which transition precedes which. It could also be something completely different, like adding a date stamp to a committed version that identifies exactly when it was first committed to production.

Identify Current Version

Your database build mechanism must be able to identify which changes have been applied to a given database instance. This is important so that you can avoid reapplying changes already applied in the past. This is one of the easier parts to figure out how to do. I typically just have a table in a database that identifies what version scripts were applied and when.

Apply Changes in Order as Needed

After you have these pieces in place, you can build a mechanism that applies the right changes at the right time. In the simplest cases where just a linear progression of versions exists, each with exactly one predecessor and at most one successor, you can write this mechanism very inexpensively. I have some pseudocode that shows how such a mechanism might work that I'll present a little later. There is also an example implementation in the companion code for this book, which shouldn't be too difficult to translate to your platform of choice. Go to http://maxthe3rd.com/test-driven-database-development/code. aspx to download the code.

Implementation

Now that I've described the way you might primitively describe and instantiate a class of databases, I give you some ways to implement one. I start with the general requirements, and then I give you a pseudocode implementation you could translate into any platform.

Requirements

Let's examine exactly what the requirements for a good database class instantiation mechanism would be. Knowing them enables you to write your own mechanism or adapt one of the ones suggested in this book to your circumstances, if they deviate significantly from what I anticipate.

I have identified four requirements. I have also found words that each start with a "C" to describe each one so that I can call them "The Four Cs." I hope that catches on.

The Four Cs are as follows. A database class instantiation mechanism must be *Complete* in that it executes all changes required for a particular version. It also must be *Correct* in that it never applies the same change twice. Such a mechanism must be *Consistent* by applying changes in the same order every single time it is asked to apply them. Finally, it has to be *Controllable* in the sense that you must be able to specify a target version to which you want a particular database built.

Pseudocode Database Instantiation Mechanism

The algorithm to update a database reliably and in a repeatable manner is surprisingly simple. At least, after years of refining it, I am always surprised by its simplicity when compared to the monstrosity I started with:

```
UpgradeDatabase(<db>, <design>, <target version>)
  <current version> = current version of <db>
  <required versions> =
    versions from <design> after <current version> and up through
➥<target version>
  sort <required versions> in ascending order
  for each <version> in <required versions>
    execute transition for <version> against <db>
    update current version of <db> to version number of <version>
```

I'll leave the implementation details to you, but I typically express the database design in terms of XML documents and store the already-applied versions in a table. The "current" version of a database can then be inferred by selecting the most recent row from that table.

Pseudocode Input

The input for the previous algorithm could be an XML file or a bunch of different text files. It could really be any format as long as each version is identified, can be properly ordered, and declares the steps required to instantiate a database instance.

For the purposes of the book, I give you some simple XML containing the script to build and/or upgrade a little database:

```
<database>
  <version id="1">CREATE TABLE FOO(A I NT)</version>
  <version id="3">CREATE TABLE BAR(C CHAR(30))</version>
  <version id="2">ALTER TABLE FOO ADD B NVARCHAR(20)</version>
</database>
```

As you can see, this XML document contains all the information required to order, identify, and execute the statements required to build or update a database to any particular version.

Summary

When tests are run, they check the behavior of a particular object. What makes that useful is that a reliable instantiation process exists, ensuring all objects of a particular class are the same. That linkage means that if you test one object of a class, you have tested them all and, thus, it is as if you tested the class itself.

This is the first place where database development really differs from traditional object-oriented development. A class constructor for in-memory objects can just annihilate whatever was previously sitting in the memory it has allocated and follow a single, simple path to building a working object.

Yet, when building a database, respecting what was already there is often necessary. So, it can appear that whatever makes a database has to be able to follow two paths: one for upgrade and one for building a new database. That's how a lot of development environments work today, but it makes having a true class of databases difficult and, therefore, hard to test-drive development of a database.

The solution is to force every database of a particular class to follow the exact same build path. Eliminate the distinction between building a new database and upgrading an existing one. Instead, just define the steps required to get from one version to the next, treating an empty database as the very first step, and execute the necessary steps to get from one version to another.

Knowing that you have to build a database that way makes me want to express database designs in similar terms: as a series of deltas that accumulate to produce a database of the most recent version. After a database is defined in those terms, ensuring that each transition is applied once, and only once, and in the correct order is easy.

Making that little change to how a database's design is defined and writing that small amount of automation—or using the accompanying code for this book as a starting point—lays a foundation, a reliable class of databases, upon which you can build test-driven database development.

The accompanying code for this book can be found on my website at:

http://maxthe3rd.com/test-driven-database-development/code.aspx

Chapter 3

A Little TDD

This chapter gives you a crash course in test-driven development (TDD) in case you are not familiar with the discipline.

A staple of the TDD process is the test-first technique. Many people who are new to test-driven development actually confuse it with the test-first technique, but they are not the same thing. Test-first is one tool in the TDD toolbelt, and a very important one at that, but there is a lot more to TDD.

The chapter then covers a test's proper role in your organization. Tests are best thought of as executable specifications. That is, they not only test something but they also document what that thing should do or how it should look.

One very powerful benefit of cyclically defining and satisfying executable specifications is that it forces your design to emerge incrementally. Each new test you write demands that you revisit and, if necessary, revise your design.

Following that discussion, I cover what you actually want to specify and, probably at least as important, what you do not want to specify. In a nutshell, the rule is "specify behaviors only." Deciding what a database's behavior should be can be a little difficult, and I cover that topic in Chapters 6, "Defining Behaviors," and 7, "Building for Maintainability." This chapter deals with the behaviors inherent in tables.

Finally, an important piece of test-driven development is to drive behaviors into a database from outside, not the other way around. Again, you can find a lot more advice on how a database should actually be structured later in the book. This chapter deals only with traditional design concepts.

The Test-First Technique

If I were in an elevator, traveling to the top of a building with a software developer I would never see again who had never heard of TDD or the test-first technique, I would try to teach him the test-first technique. I would choose that because it is so easy to teach and it is so easy to get people to try. Also, if done blindly, it creates problems that will force someone to teach himself test-driven development.

The technique is simple, and the following is often enough to teach it:

1. Write a test.

2. See it fail.

3. Make it pass.

4. Repeat.

There's nothing more to test-first. There's a lot more to test-driven development, but test-first really is that simple.

Write the Test

The first step in the technique is to write your test. If you've never done this before it might be a little bit uncomfortable at first. You might be thinking "How do I know what to test if there's nothing there?" That's a pretty normal feeling that I want you to ball up really tightly and shove down into your gut while you do this a few times. Later you will discover that the best way to determine what should be tested is to write the test for it, but convincing you of that is hard; you'll have to convince yourself by way of experience.

Anyway, start out by writing a test. Let's say that I want a database that can store messages sent between users identified by email addresses. The first thing I would do is write a test that requires that ability to be there in order to pass. The test is going to need to create a database of the current version, connect to it, and insert a record. This test is shown in the following listing as one would write it using NUnit and .NET:

```
[TestFixture]
public class TestFirst {
  private Instantiator instantiator;
  private IDbConnection connection;

  [SetUp]
  public void EstablishConnectionAndRecycleDatabase() {
    instantiator = Instantiator.GetInstance(
      DatabaseDescriptor.LoadFromFile("TestFirstDatabase.xml"));
    connection = DatabaseProvisioning.CreateFreshDatabaseAndConnect();
  }
```

```
[TearDown]
public void CloseConnection() {
  connection.Close();
}

[Test]
public void TestTables() {
  instantiator.UpgradeToLatestVersion(connection);
  connection.ExecuteSql("
    INSERT INTO USERS VALUES(1, 'foo@bar.com')");
  connection.ExecuteSql(
    @"INSERT INTO MESSAGES " +
    "VALUES(1, 'Hey!', 'Just checking in to see how it''s going.')");
}
}
```

That code, as is, won't compile because I delegate to a little bit of infrastructure that has to be written. One such tool is the DatabaseProvisioning class, which is responsible for creating, tearing down, and connecting to test databases. This class is shown in the following example code, assuming I wanted to test against a SQL Server database:

```
public class DatabaseProvisioning {
  public static IDbConnection CreateFreshDatabaseAndConnect() {
    var connection = new SqlConnection(@"Data Source=.\sqlexpress;" +
      "Initial Catalog=master;Integrated Security=True");
    connection.Open();
    connection.ExecuteSql("ALTER DATABASE TDDD_Examples SET " +
      "SINGLE_USER WITH ROLLBACK IMMEDIATE");
    connection.ExecuteSql("DROP DATABASE TDDD_Examples");
    connection.ExecuteSql("CREATE DATABASE TDDD_Examples");
    connection.ExecuteSql("USE TDDD_Examples");

    return connection;
  }
}
```

The other piece of infrastructure (following) is a small extension class that makes executing SQL statements—something I'm going to be doing a lot in this book—a little easier. For those of you who aren't C# programmers, what this does is make it look like there is an ExecuteSql method for all instances of IDbConnection.

```
public static class CommandUtilities {
  public static void ExecuteSql(
    this IDbConnection connection, string toExecute) {
    using (var command = connection.CreateCommand()) {
      command.CommandText = toExecute;
```

```
        command.ExecuteNonQuery();
    }
  }
}
```

The next step is to see a failure.

Stub Out Enough to See a Failure

I like my failures to be interesting. It's not strictly required, but there's not a really good reason to avoid it, so assume that making a failure meaningful is implied in "see the test fail." The main reason you want to see a test fail is because you want to know that it isn't giving you a false positive. A test that can't fail for a good reason is about as useful as a test that cannot fail for any reason.

The test I have would fail because there is no database to make, which isn't a very interesting reason to fail. So let's create a database class and make it so that the database gets created.

```
<Database>
  <Version Number="1">
  </Version>
</Database>
```

With that change in place, my test would fail for an interesting reason: The table into which I was trying to insert doesn't exist. That's a meaningful enough failure for me.

See the Test Pass

Now that a test is giving me a worthwhile failure, it's time to make it pass. I do that by changing the class of databases to create the required table. If I had committed the most recent version of the database class to production, I would create a new version to preserve the integrity of my database class. As it stands, because this new database class hasn't ever been deployed in an irreversible way, I'll just update the most recent version to do what I want it to do.

```
<Database>
  <Version Number="1">
    <Script>
      <![CDATA[
CREATE TABLE Users(ID INT PRIMARY KEY, Email NVARCHAR(4000));

CREATE TABLE Messages(
  UserID INT FOREIGN KEY REFERENCES Users(ID),
  Title NVARCHAR(256),
  Body TEXT);
```

```
]]>
    </Script>
  </Version>
</Database>
```

That update causes my database class to create the message table in version 1. When I rerun my test, the database gets rebuilt with the appropriate structures required to make the test pass. Now I'm done with a test-first programming cycle.

Repeat

After the cycle is complete, there is an opportunity to start another cycle or to do some other things, such as refactoring. I'm going to go through one cycle just to show you how a design can emerge incrementally. After thinking about the design I created, I decided I don't like it. I don't want the email addresses to be duplicated.

How should I handle that? I'll start by adding a test.

```
[Test]
public void UsersCannotBeDuplicated() {
  instantiator.UpgradeToLatestVersion(connection);
  connection.ExecuteSql(
    @"INSERT INTO Users(Email) VALUES('foo@bar.com')");
  try {
    connection.ExecuteSql(
      @"INSERT INTO Users(Email) VALUES('foo@bar.com')");
  } catch {
    return;
  }

  Assert.Fail("Multiple copies of same email were allowed");
}
```

After I get that compiling, I'll watch it fail. It will fail because I can have as many records with a well-known email address as I want. That's an interesting failure, so I can go on to the next step: adding the constraint to the new version of my database.

```
<Database>
  <Version Number="1">
    <Script>
      <![CDATA[
CREATE TABLE Users(ID INT PRIMARY KEY, Email NVARCHAR(4000));

ALTER TABLE Users ADD CONSTRAINT OnlyOneEmail UNIQUE (Email);

CREATE TABLE Messages(
  UserID INT FOREIGN KEY REFERENCES Users(ID),
```

```
    Title NVARCHAR(256),
    Body TEXT);
]]>
      </Script>
    </Version>
  </Database>
```

Recompiling and rerunning my test shows me that it passes. Had that new behavior caused another test to fail, I would update that test to work with the new design constraint, rerun my tests, and see everything pass. After I've done that, I decide I'm done with this phase of updating my database class's design and move on to other activities.

Tests as Specifications

Another important thing to understand about test-driven development is this simple fact: Tests are specifications. A lot of people make the argument that tests aren't really tests, but are specifications. Others argue that they aren't really specifications, but are tests as the name implies.

My position is that both sides of that argument are half right. Tests are specifications. Tests are also tests. The two are not contradictory or even complementary; they are synonymous. What really distinguishes an automated test from other kinds of specifications and other kinds of tests is that it is the automation itself.

"Tests Aren't Tests, They Are Specifications"

A large group of people exists who frequently tell new developers that tests aren't really tests, or at least that they don't start off that way. Tests are specifications and the fact that they also do some testing is just a side effect.

You can get into all kinds of mental gymnastics to justify this argument, and a lot of them have to do with definitions of the words *test* and *specification*. The best one I've heard is that tests cannot be tests without something to test, so a test is a specification until it passes; then it "falls" into the role of a test later in its life.

In my opinion, terminological correctness is just a device working in service of another motivation. That motivation is that when people think of tests as specifications, they write better tests. Another motivation is to circumvent any preconceived notions a student might have attached to the word *test*. Both are noble.

The "shock and awe" school of andragogy pulls stunts like this all the time. "To teach, I must first dislodge my student from his mental resting place," teachers say. "Otherwise, hysteresis will drag him back to where he started," they add.

Consider the following code:

```
[Test]
public void BadSpecification() {
  var processor = new Processor();
  Assert.That(processor.Process(-2), Is.EqualTo(-1));
  Assert.That(processor.Process(-1), Is.EqualTo(0));
  Assert.That(processor.Process(0), Is.EqualTo(1));
  Assert.That(processor.Process(5), Is.EqualTo(216));
  Assert.That(processor.Process(25), Is.EqualTo(17576));
}
```

The people in this camp would argue that this test might be succeeding as a test but failing as a specification and, because being a specification is what a test should really do, it is a poorly written test. By contrast, they would argue that the following test is vastly superior because a human reading it could easily understand the rule:

```
[Test]
public void GoodSpecification() {
  var anyInput = 4;

  var processedResult = new Processor().Process(anyInput);

  Assert.That(
    processedResult,
    Is.EqualTo((anyInput + 1)*(anyInput + 1) * (anyInput + 1)));
}
```

Let's hear from the other side of the argument.

"Tests Aren't Specifications, They Are Tests"

When I first heard someone say that tests aren't really tests, my knee jerked and I reacted quite badly. I can't imagine how badly I would have reacted if I didn't consider that person a friend, but we probably wouldn't have become friends if that was his first impression of me.

Some people, when they hear something that they believe to be wrong, immediately throw what they already think they know at the problem to see whether it goes away—and that's exactly what I did. "No way," I thought. "Tests aren't specifications. They are obviously tests. That's why we call them tests. That's why we see them fail."

The old me would have looked at the test with the formula and said it was a bad test because making it pass without really implementing the right rule was

easy. Old me also would have said the test with many examples and no explana-
tion of what the rule is was a good test because it forced my production code to
do what it really should do.

Tests Are Executable Specifications

The problem was that I was doing exactly what my teacher didn't want. I was
clinging to a preconceived notion and not hearing what he was trying to tell me.
It was a reaction to something I knew was not right but it was still holding me
back.

Each camp is half right.

The kinds of tests you write in test-driven development are not distinct
because they are specifications. Nor are they distinct because they are tests. Programmers have been creating both of those artifacts for, literally, generations.
The interesting new bit about TDD is that it produces *executable specifications*.

The process produces specifications that, by definition, must be precise enough
to be run frequently by a machine and, consequently, are forced to always stay
up to date. That's what makes TDD so powerful and that is why, when you
have a suite of tests that hasn't been run for any significant amount of time, an
enormous amount of work typically has to be done to make it useful.

Keep in mind that a test is a specification and a test also provides guidance on
how to make better tests. If each side of the argument said that one of the two
tests I showed earlier was better than the other and each side is half right, then
what's the right answer in the contest between those tests?

The right answer is, "Both of those tests have good things about them but
neither is the better test." Instead of choosing one, make a test that clearly specifies the rule but also cannot easily be cheated. One option is to randomly select
a number for the test that uses a formula.

```
private int AnyInteger() {
  return new Random().Next(0, 1000);
}

[Test]
public void GoodSpecification() {
  var anyInput = AnyInteger();

  var processedResult = new Processor().Process(anyInput);

  Assert.That(
    processedResult,
    Is.EqualTo((anyInput + 1)*(anyInput + 1) * (anyInput + 1)));
}
```

Another option is to factor the formula test out into a method and then execute that method with several concrete values.

```
private void RunSpecification(int anyInput) {
  var processedResult = new Processor().Process(anyInput);

  Assert.That(
    processedResult,
    Is.EqualTo((anyInput + 1) * (anyInput + 1) * (anyInput + 1)));
}

[Test]
public void GoodSpecificationWithExamples() {
  RunSpecification(-2);
  RunSpecification(-1);
  RunSpecification(0);
  RunSpecification(1);
  RunSpecification(5);
  RunSpecification(25);
}
```

I tend toward the former option and, when I'm doing middle-tier development, I don't much care which option a person chooses because they are both alright and they are both better than the two earlier options offered by thinking of tests exclusively as tests or as specifications.

Incremental Design

A side-effect of test-driven development is that it enables you to work in an incremental fashion regardless of the kind of process you use to regulate work in your organization (for example, Scrum or Waterfall).

Every time you write a test, you extend the body of specifications defining what your software should do a little bit. To make that test pass, you have to change your product's behavior or design slightly. Before you can start working on the next tiny piece of your product, you have to make all your tests pass.

As a result, test-driven development has the effect of focusing work, driving you to extend your software a little bit at a time, while keeping all the existing features working. In short: It imposes a little bit of agility on your process regardless of organizational constraints.

> ### Advantages of TDD
>
> Numerous other benefits and aspects of test-driven development exist that aren't covered in this book. They are valuable and important for you to learn, but outside the scope of this book. Numerous resources already explore those advantages and, if you are interested, you should probably use them to research the topic on your own.

Building Good Specifications

You could specify many different kinds of things with tests in any given software development endeavor. You could specify structures, public interfaces or private constructs, or what's in a class. In database terms, you could specify tables, views, and stored procedures.

A test should specify behavior, but should not specify structure. The more behavior-focused a test is, the better off you will be because structures tend to change a lot more quickly than behaviors. This is true even in the database world where, frankly, the pace of change is nigh unto glacial. If you object to my use of the word *quickly*, you can think of it this way: Structures change a lot less slowly than behaviors in a database design.

However, tests have to couple to something in order to invoke the behaviors they define. In fact, many structure decisions are involved in making a test pass. The key is to drive those design decisions into a class of databases from the outside, not the other way around.

Specify Behavior, Not Structure

The odds that you are not a software developer are extremely low. My suspicion is that many of the readers of this book are accomplished computer programmers who also do database work and want to learn how to do what they already know how to do in a database domain. You might also be someone who works only or primarily on databases.

The chance also exists that you are an extraterrestrial archeologist sifting through the intellectual ruins of a species long-since turned to dust. If so, I hope I just sent a shiver up whatever your equivalent of a spine is. Also: Hello, and sorry we didn't survive long enough for our paths to cross—unless you exterminated us, in which case I'm sorry our paths crossed and I hope you caught some horrible disease from us in the process.

Database programmers and application programmers are both still programmers. Both groups are responsible for writing software, which itself is an act of prescribing behaviors and relationships. In the case of object-oriented programming, what those things mean is pretty clear. At least, it is pretty clear now; it might not have been decades ago.

In the case of database development, it's a little less intuitive what the behaviors being defined are. People often want to think of databases as collections of tables and relationships. The good thing about that is the focus on a database's primary responsibility: storing stuff. Yet, it's still a structure-oriented way of considering design.

A table is a bundle of related features tied to a kind of data. The two basic behaviors a table supports are data manipulation and data querying. Other structures carry with them other behaviors and certain platforms offer extra behaviors with various structures.

Those are what you should specify in tests. Don't specify that there is a table. Specify that you can store and retrieve data of an interesting sort. Don't specify that there is a view; specify that you can perform useful searches across bodies of data. That decision might seem meaningless now, but as the book proceeds it will become more and more valuable to you.

Drive Design In from Without, Not the Other Way Around

In the procedural days, entities were just data—purely passive things subject to the whims of whatever function might have access to them. With the advent of object-oriented design, they became reactive things that told the world what they could do and then waited for instructions. Modern development practices make classes of objects into servants, told what they should be able to do by tests and then told to do it by other objects and, ultimately, by people.

When you write a test, you want it to specify the behaviors that live in a class of databases, but it's going to have to talk to something to do that. An implication of specifying a behavior is that you must also specify the minimal amount of public interface required to invoke that behavior. The key to discovering that is to learn it from writing tests first.

Let's consider a problem. Imagine I need to write an application that keeps a database of streets and cross references them with other intersecting streets. I could drive the requirements from tests, specifying behaviors and required interface, or I could define my design inside out—starting with capabilities, then building an interface around it. I'll try the latter first.

Defining the Design Inside Out

Well, the obvious thing I need is a table in which to store streets. So let's start there (see Figure 3.1).

Figure 3.1 *Simple design*

Of course, streets exist in cities, so I need a cities table. Maybe later I'll need a states table, too, but for now, I can live without it. Let's add a cities table with a state column so I can track which street I am dealing with (see Figure 3.2).

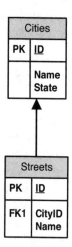

Figure 3.2 *Streets segregated by city*

Some streets span many cities, such as highways and interstate freeways. So I need to account for those, too (see Figure 3.3).

Now there's the fact that I need to track the intersections, so let's add that. It seems like it should be a cross-reference table with the address on each street at which the intersection takes place. Because streets sometimes cross in multiple places, I need a primary key that is distinct from the foreign keys on that table so I can support multiple links, as shown in Figure 3.4.

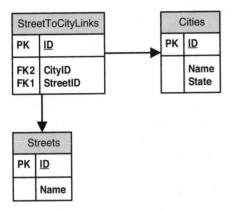

Figure 3.3 *A street going through multiple cities*

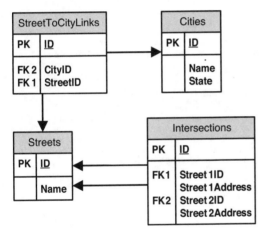

Figure 3.4 *Streets organized by city and cross-referenced by intersection*

From there, I can start hypothesizing how the data might be used, adding views and stored procedures to support those needs. Then, I could write tests for all the behaviors I developed. Eventually, I'll think I have enough to start writing an application.

Of course, I won't.

For one thing, there is a distinct database for every city supported by the application. So, every application is encumbered by adding noise structures. The Cities and StreetToCityLinks tables are completely unnecessary as are the constraints surrounding them.

Also, the application doesn't care where two streets connect, only that they connect. So, the Street1Address and Street2Address fields of the Intersections table serve no purpose but to waste the time of everyone who touches them or reads about them.

Defining the Design Outside In

What if I try going the other direction? Suppose I want to start at the outside and work my way inward. In that event, by the time I'm defining a database design, I probably would have written the user interface and application logic already.

Having done those things would provide me with context and understanding as to what was really needed. If I work exclusively with the database, then someone else would provide the context for me and I would have a very clear idea of what the requirements are.

Either way, that understanding would be something that could be translated into tests as in the following:

```
[Test]
public void CreateAndFindStreet() {
  connection.ExecuteSql("INSERT INTO Streets VALUES(5, 'Fun St.')");

    var id = connection.ExecuteScalar(
      "SELECT ID FROM Streets WHERE NAME LIKE '%Fun%'");

    Assert.That(id, Is.EqualTo(5));
}
```

That test would drive me to build a database class as follows:

```
<Database>
  <Version Number="1">
    <Script>
      <![CDATA[
CREATE TABLE Streets(ID INT PRIMARY KEY, NAME NVARCHAR(4000))
    </Script>
  </Version>
</Database>
```

Knowing that I also needed the capability to find related streets, I might write another test as follows:

```
[Test]
public void CreateConnectedStreetsAndFindFewestIntersectionsConnected()
{
  connection.ExecuteSql("INSERT INTO Streets VALUES(1, 'A St.')");
  connection.ExecuteSql("INSERT INTO Streets VALUES(2, 'B Dr.')");
  connection.ExecuteSql("INSERT INTO Streets VALUES(3, 'C Ave.')");
  connection.ExecuteSql("INSERT INTO Streets VALUES(4, 'D Ln.')");
  connection.ExecuteSql("INSERT INTO Streets VALUES(5, 'E Blvd.')");
```

```
connection.ExecuteSql("INSERT INTO Intersections VALUES(1)");
connection.ExecuteSql("INSERT INTO IntersectionStreets VALUES(1, 1)");
connection.ExecuteSql("INSERT INTO IntersectionStreets VALUES(1, 2)");

connection.ExecuteSql("INSERT INTO Intersections VALUES(2)");
connection.ExecuteSql("INSERT INTO IntersectionStreets VALUES(2, 1)");
connection.ExecuteSql("INSERT INTO IntersectionStreets VALUES(2, 3)");

connection.ExecuteSql("INSERT INTO Intersections VALUES(3)");
connection.ExecuteSql("INSERT INTO IntersectionStreets VALUES(3, 3)");
connection.ExecuteSql("INSERT INTO IntersectionStreets VALUES(3, 4)");
var result = connection.ExecuteScalar(
  "SELECT Depth FROM Connections() WHERE StartID = 2 AND EndID = 4");

Assert.That(result, Is.EqualTo(3));
}
```

That test would drive me to develop the design in the next snippet:

```
<Database>
  <Version Number="1">
    <Script>
      <![CDATA[
CREATE TABLE Streets(ID INT PRIMARY KEY, NAME NVARCHAR(4000))
CREATE TABLE Intersections([ID] INT PRIMARY KEY)
CREATE TABLE IntersectionStreets(
  [IntersectionID] INT FOREIGN KEY REFERENCES Intersections(ID),
  [StreetID] INT FOREIGN KEY REFERENCES Streets(ID))
  ]]>
    </Script>
    <Script>
      <![CDATA[
CREATE VIEW ImmediateConnections AS
SELECT s.StreetID AS StartID, e.StreetID AS EndID
FROM IntersectionStreets AS s
INNER JOIN IntersectionStreets AS e
ON s.IntersectionID = e.IntersectionID and s.StreetID <> e.StreetID
      ]]>
    </Script>
    <Script>
      <![CDATA[
CREATE FUNCTION Connections
  (
  )
RETURNS @Result TABLE (Depth INT, StartID INT, EndID INT)
AS
BEGIN
  DECLARE @Temp TABLE (StartID INT, EndID INT)
  DECLARE @Depth INT
  SET @Depth = 0
```

```
  INSERT INTO @Temp SELECT ID AS StartID, ID AS EndID FROM Streets;

  WHILE EXISTS (SELECT TOP 1 * FROM @Temp)
  BEGIN
    INSERT INTO @Result SELECT @Depth, StartID, EndID FROM @Temp;
    DELETE @Temp;

    INSERT INTO @Temp SELECT r.StartID, ic.EndID FROM @Result AS r
      INNER JOIN ImmediateConnections AS ic ON r.EndID = ic.StartID

    DELETE @Temp FROM @Temp AS tc INNER JOIN @Result AS r
      ON tc.StartID = r.StartID AND tc.EndID = r.EndID

    SET @Depth = @Depth + 1
  END;
RETURN
END
    ]]>
    </Script>
  </Version>
</Database>
```

Note how narrow and focused the interface for the database that was designed outside-in is compared to the one that was designed inside-out. Yet, in certain areas such as the recursive view, the behavior is much deeper than with the inside-out design. The two side-effects of driving design into a system rather than designing a system and making clients find a way to use it are that you write something that can actually be used, and you spend more of your time developing worthwhile functionality.

Summary

A distinction exists between test-first programming and test-driven development. The former is an easy practice to convey whereas the latter is a hard discipline to learn. Test-first is, however, a stepping stone that helps you get to test-driven development.

TDD is more than just getting good specifications in place that happen to be tests. It is also more than just getting good tests in place that happen to be specifications. It is about building executable specifications. That is, it is about creating documents that are both tests and specifications to such a degree of quality that you don't need any other documents to do either of those jobs.

Test-driven development has a lot more to it, but this chapter should give you the context you need to get started. Throughout the remainder of the book, remember these things: Try to specify behaviors in tests before implementing them, and grow your designs inward from the point at which a test couples to what it tests.

The next step is to put in place structures that allow you to change your designs with great confidence, especially with regard to the safety of production data.

Chapter 4

Safely Changing Design

I've frequently alluded to the fact that you should only design what you need for now because later you will safely be able to change your design. I thank you for keeping an open mind about that until this chapter, in which I cover how to actually make the right things happen.

Of course, I have to define "safe," as you can never truly be 100% risk free. The cop-out definition would be "without introducing any more risk than the process you have now over any given period of time." I think for the vast majority of people reading this book, I can hit that mark, but I want to set the bar a little higher.

For this process to work, you have to be able to change your data structures even though some inherent risk exists in so doing. There are a couple of mitigations available for the threat inherent in changing data structures. The obvious one is to back up production databases before a deployment and roll them back if anything goes wrong. Always do that.

Another technique that can protect you from the threat of mischanging a table is called *transition testing*. I wrote about it in 2009, and I'll write about it some more in this chapter. Basically, transition tests validate how a database changes rather than what it does.

Since I first wrote about transition testing, I've expanded the idea of transition testing to the point where it can safely validate changes to production databases as well as test databases. When you pair a transition test run against a production database with backing up before a deployment and restoring if a failure occurs, you get an extremely powerful combination: immediate validation that your changes were not injurious and immediate remediation if it turns out they were.

What Is Safe?

I'm going to say that "safe" means "so close to 100% risk free that you can treat it as such" with the caveat that, should the unthinkable happen, you find a way to ensure that class of catastrophe never happens again. Regardless, I'm pretty sure that, if this process fails to prevent a catastrophe, you won't care about getting your database back online and working. You'll have bigger problems like finding food, clean water, other survivors, and a place on your continent where green things can still grow in the ground.

Different design-changing activities carry different levels of risk. For instance, in the majority of circumstances, changing public interface is a lower-risk activity. You run a slight risk of interrupting service and possibly even losing some new data or giving an application some bad answers, if the risk expresses in a subtle-enough way. Even so, an error in the way you change a public interface is likely to be quickly identified and fixed at very little cost.

At least relatively speaking, that's true. When you compare the cost of things going wrong because a database's public interface changed in an uncontrolled or unpredicted manner to the cost of losing knowledge as a result of flubbing a table alteration, it's a drop in the bucket. Loss of meaningful data is absolutely unacceptable and it is totally preventable.

You must do everything in your power to avoid losing knowledge as a result of a design change, and it turns out it is within your power to all-but-eradicate that risk. You learn how to do that in the course of this chapter.

You also have to do whatever you can to avoid violating the contract between a database and its clients. Fortunately, this is also something over which you actually have a great deal of control, and Chapter 5, "Enforcing Interface," covers how to do it.

Breaking a Contract Is a Little Bad

Every time a database's public interface changes, no matter how much research you do in advance, a small chance always exists that you will cause some client application to stop working. Imagine, for instance, that you have a very successful database with numerous clients. Auditing those clients to find every point at which they touch your database becomes an odious task.

As the applications and the clients grow, auditing will simply become too big a task to do every time you want to change design.

Two typical responses to this are to stop changing the existing public interface for a database, or stop doing a thorough job of finding all the places all applications touch a database.

Both of these responses have negative outcomes. Classes, be they classes of database or classes of middle-tier objects, have to change. Their requirements will change and their public interfaces will need to change to reflect the changes in their requirements. Some people would tell you otherwise but they are either ivory-tower academics who've never done any real software work or escaped mental patients. I suppose the possibility exists that they could be both.

Locking down the public interface of a thing creates a rift between what that thing claims it can do and what it must be able to do. Interactions with it will become increasingly cumbersome. This is as true of databases as it is of everything else in the universe: very nearly certain.

Alternatively, not doing the work required to find where changes will cause problems is a roll of the dice, except that most dice games have some limited potential for you to win something. In "let's see whether this change worked," your best possible outcome is that you don't lose anything.

I defer solution of this problem to Chapter 5 to focus on the more pressing task of protecting a database from losing valuable knowledge in the transition from one version of design to another.

Losing Data Will Probably Get You Fired

For those of you who don't know about thedailywtf.com, it's a site where you can find some of the dumbest IT mistakes ever made. On that site, you will find the following story which is entitled "Production Promote."

Excerpt from thedailywtf.com:

"John, it's about time I showed you how to do a production install," Dave said.

John had only been at the job for a few weeks, and was still learning the ins-and-outs of their shop. It was a small team, with the stereotypical alpha-geek at the top, people like Dave in the middle, and John at the bottom. They lived to support a complex pile of applications that all existed to extend or manage their flagship application.

Said flagship was a .NET web app with hundreds of external corporate customers that considered it "mission critical." It was still in .NET 1.1, but the upgrade was coming soon. It was still running on SQL Server 2000, but again, the upgrade was coming soon. That the flagship was a little rickety didn't matter; the application was a "big deal," and that was what the business cared about.

"So, you know the Enterprise Manager," Dave said as he pulled the application up and logged into the test database. "I'm going to export a CREATE script for all of the stored procedures off the test DB." With that done, he explained the next steps as he executed them: log onto production, navigate down the tree to where the stored procedures were, delete that entire branch of objects without mercy, and run the script to recreate them.

While they waited for the delete step to complete, John asked, "Does it usually take this long?"

"No, not usually," Dave admitted. He frowned at the screen and waited a few minutes longer before adding, "I hope it isn't hung... I always worry about just killing something like this. I'm afraid I'll lose data in the database." The task finally completed, and Dave ran the script to create the procedures.

It failed. The procedures, it seemed, already existed. Dave expanded the branch and confirmed that they were still there. "Then what did I delete?" he wondered.

A frantic call from the user support reps answered that question: the tables. Dave had selected the wrong branch and deleted gigabytes of customer-generated data. Stunned by the immensity of his screw up, Dave stared at the screen, like it was the oncoming headlamps of a semi. "Should... should we start restoring from back-up?" John asked.

"Backup?" Dave said the word, but it held no immediate meaning. "Backup? Backup!" The semi sailed by, and Dave relaxed. The day was saved! They could restore from backup! Dave started hunting down the most recent backup so that they could get the restore underway ASAP.

Unfortunately for Dave, the most recent backup was months old. The backup maintenance task, also Dave's responsibility, had fallen out of the scheduler, and no one had ever confirmed that it was running. The next day, John helped Dave's replacement, Phil, reverse engineer as much data as they could off of other servers and databases. It took weeks to complete. The company lost hundreds of thou-sands of dollars from the downtime alone, breached several contracts, lost several major customers, and a significant chunk of their reputation.

It wasn't all a loss. John learned a valuable lesson about how not to do a produc-tion install.

I'm not saying that a botched deployment resulting in a rollback and some more work will get you fired. However, if you permanently destroy any substan-tial quantity of important data, then you are definitely toast, and you'll probably end up being referenced on that website.

Not Changing Design Is Also Dangerous

All the risks associated with changing existing table schemas might lead you to believe that the right course of action is to never change structures that contain knowledge. The problem with that is that you have to predict the right design upfront, which is impossible.

If you commit to preserving an existing design, you doom yourself to have every problem be a little harder to solve than the last. Each new feature adds some inherent complexity to your database, but the amount of complexity that gets added varies with how the feature is implemented. If bolted onto the side of your database, the complexity will be much higher than if neatly integrated into it.

Take the design in Figure 4.1, which is the backend for an ice cream shop application.

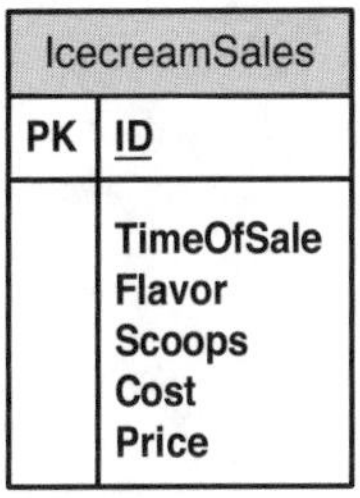

IcecreamSales	
PK	ID
	TimeOfSale
	Flavor
	Scoops
	Cost
	Price

Figure 4.1 *A trivial database design:* IcecreamSales

The class for that database would look like what follows:

```
<Database>
  <Version Number="1">
    <Script>
      <![CDATA[
CREATE TABLE IcecreamSales(
  ID INT IDENTITY(1, 1) PRIMARY KEY,
  TimeOfSale DATETIME NOT NULL,
  Flavor NVARCHAR(100) NOT NULL,
  Scoops INT NOT NULL,
  Cost NUMERIC(12, 2) NOT NULL,
  Price NUMERIC(12, 2) NOT NULL);
    ]]>
    </Script>
  </Version>
</Database>
```

For whatever reason, the designers of this database did not foresee people wanting to purchase multiple items in a single transaction. Let's say you are extending the database to support a new feature that allows people to buy multiple items in a single transaction. You could go about it a number of ways, but the cleanest is to refactor your database so that transactions and line items are in separate tables (see Figure 4.2).

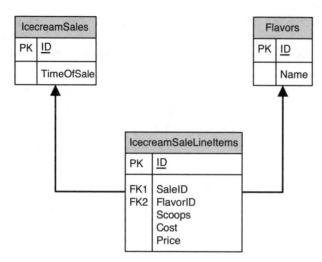

Figure 4.2 *A more sophisticated design*

This would be accomplished as follows:

```
<Database>
  <Version Number="1">
    <Script>
      <![CDATA[
CREATE TABLE IcecreamSales(
  ID INT IDENTITY(1, 1) PRIMARY KEY,
  TimeOfSale DATETIME NOT NULL,
  Flavor NVARCHAR(100) NOT NULL,
  Scoops INT NOT NULL,
  Cost NUMERIC(12, 2) NOT NULL,
  Price NUMERIC(12, 2) NOT NULL);
      ]]>
    </Script>
  </Version>
  <Version Number="2">
    <Script>
      <![CDATA[
CREATE TABLE Flavors(
  ID INT IDENTITY(1, 1) PRIMARY KEY,
  Name NVARCHAR(100) NOT NULL);

CREATE TABLE IcecreamSaleLineItems(
  ID INT IDENTITY(1, 1) PRIMARY KEY,
  SaleId INT NOT NULL FOREIGN KEY REFERENCES IcecreamSales(ID),
  FlavorId INT NOT NULL FOREIGN KEY REFERENCES Flavors(ID),
  Scoops INT NOT NULL,
  Cost NUMERIC(12, 2) NOT NULL,
  Price NUMERIC(12, 2) NOT NULL)
```

```
INSERT INTO Flavors(Name)
  SELECT DISTINCT Flavor FROM IcecreamSales

INSERT INTO IcecreamSaleLineItems
  (SaleId, FlavorId, Scoops, Cost, Price)
  SELECT s.ID, f.ID, s.Scoops, s.Cost, s.Price FROM
    IcecreamSales s INNER JOIN Flavors f ON s.Flavor = f.Name

ALTER TABLE IcecreamSales DROP COLUMN Flavor
ALTER TABLE IcecreamSales DROP COLUMN Scoops
ALTER TABLE IcecreamSales DROP COLUMN Cost
ALTER TABLE IcecreamSales DROP COLUMN Price
      ]]>
    </Script>
  </Version>
</Database>
```

That carries some risk of data loss with it if done wrong, so let's consider some of the other options. You could also try duplicating the item-related stuff in a table to support the maximum number of items you anticipate in a transaction. Aside from being a horrible design decision, it creates an unnecessary limitation, so ignore that option. Another choice might be to create a true transaction row that links to the old transaction rows, which are really line items with a little bit of transaction stuff in them (see Figure 4.3).

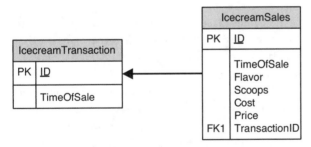

Figure 4.3 *An alternative design leaving old interfaces untouched*

Now you are left with the problem of what to do with the extra columns on the table that stores line items. Do you duplicate the transaction data into them? That is unnecessary extra complexity. Maybe you leave them null, but that would create complexity in how any clients that couple to that column behave.

The more you resist making the right design choices, the harder your job will become and the more likely someone will be to start abusing the design, putting the cleanliness of your database at risk.

Solution: Transition Testing

You are left with another little puzzle: You can't change a database unsafely and cannot safely leave a design unchanged. Obviously the thing to do is to find a way to change data structures safely but how can you do that when such changes carry inherent risk? The answer to that question is the answer to almost every variant of the "How do we mitigate risk?" question in the software development industry: rigorous automated testing.

In this section, I introduce you to a technique called *transition testing*. Transition tests specify how a database is transformed from one version to another. In a nutshell, you build a test database up to one version, fill it with data, advance it to another version, and then check that the initial data were properly transformed.

Test-Driving Instantiation

Construction in the object-oriented world is an easy problem. Flatten a bunch of bytes so that they are all zeroes, imbue structure upon them, delegate to custom initialization code, and you're done. Construction of a database is a much harder problem. You have pre-existing data, clients that need to be upgraded to take advantage of any new interface—all kinds of interesting factors for which you must account.

You have this handy little class of databases that will force every database to march along the same path. You can easily use it to create test databases that were built exactly as production databases. Future production databases will be built exactly as the test databases created before release.

This puts you in a position to fastidiously test the transformations that occur within a database as it moves from one version to the next. A body of unit tests forms a complete specification for how a class behaves. In much the same way, a body of transition tests forms a complete specification for how a database is transformed through each of its versions, including any version you intend to deploy in the near future.

Transition Testing Creation

Some would argue that writing transition tests for the very first version of a database is pointless because, by definition, no data is in jeopardy for this version. It's true, but transition testing version one builds a foundation of specification that helps keep your database class stable as it grows.

The real reason, however, is the same as why I never walk out of a bad movie or why I test trivial adapter classes: I hate to have something be incomplete.

The tiny gap in specification that formed several versions later, when the design changed significantly, would drive me crazy.

You can decide for yourself later whether testing version one is worth it, but for now assume it is so you can get an idea of how this process works.

Your class of database should already allow you to choose the version of a database class to which you want to build. If it doesn't have that feature, it should be pretty cheap to add.

```
[TestFixture]
public class SimpleTransitionTesting
{
  private IDbConnection connection;
  private Instantiator instantiator;

  [SetUp]
  public void SetUp()
  {
    connection = DatabaseProvisioning.CreateFreshDatabaseAndConnect();
    instantiator = Instantiator
      .GetInstance(DatabaseDescriptor.LoadFromFile("RecordStore.xml"));
  }

  private void AssertColumnDetails(
    StructureDescription table,
    string name,
    string type,
    int width = -1)
  {
    var column = table.GetColumn(name);
    Assert.That(column.Exists);
    Assert.That(column.DataType, Is.EqualTo(type));

    if (width >= 0)
    {
      Assert.That(column.Width, Is.EqualTo(width));
    }
  }

  [Test]
  public void RecordsTableExistsInVersion1()
  {
    instantiator.UpgradeToSpecificVersion(connection, 1);
    var desc = connection.GetStructureDescription("Users");
    Assert.That(description.Exists);
    AssertColumnDetails(desc, "ID", "int");
    AssertColumnDetails(desc, "DisplayName", "nvarchar", 100);
    AssertColumnDetails(desc, "Email", "nvarchar", 100);
    AssertColumnDetails(desc, "PasswordHash", "char", 64);
  }
}
```

Never mind exactly how you get a descriptor for an object in the database. In SQL Server, I use `sp_help` and parse the results. In another platform, you would use another mechanism. Those kinds of details are outside the scope of this book.

The previous test fails to compile, so I'll put a database class in place in order to see my test fail.

```
<Database>
  <Version Number="1">
  </Version>
</Database>
```

After I have a failing test, it's safe to add the required structures.

```
<Database>
  <Version Number="1">
    <Script>
      <![CDATA[
CREATE TABLE Users(
  ID INT,
  DisplayName NVARCHAR(100),
  Email NVARCHAR(100),
  PasswordHash CHAR(64))
      ]]>
    </Script>
  </Version>
</Database>
```

Adding those structures causes my test to pass. In any decent database design, you're going to want something a little more structured than that. For instance, I want ID to be a primary key. I also want it to be a SQL Server IDENTITY field. To that end, I specify those details in a revised version of the previously shown test.

```
[Test]
public void RecordsTableExistsInVersion1()
{
  instantiator.UpgradeToSpecificVersion(connection, 1);
  var desc = connection.GetStructureDescription("Users");
  Assert.That(desc.Exists);
  AssertColumnDetails(desc, "ID", "int");
  AssertColumnDetails(desc, "DisplayName", "nvarchar", 100);
  AssertColumnDetails(desc, "Email", "nvarchar", 100);
  AssertColumnDetails(desc, "PasswordHash", "char", 64);

  var constraint = desc.GetConstraint("UsersPrimaryKey");
  Assert.That(constraint.Exists);
```

```
Assert.That(constraint.Description,
  Is.EqualTo("PRIMARY KEY (clustered)"));
Assert.That(constraint.Keys, Is.EquivalentTo(new[] { "ID" }));

Assert.That(desc.GetIdentity("ID").Exists);
}
```

Because no `UsersPrimaryKey` primary key and no `ID` identity exist, that test would fail allowing me to update my database class file as follows (changes are in **bold**):

```
<Database>
  <Version Number="1">
    <Script>
      <![CDATA[
CREATE TABLE Users(
  ID INT IDENTITY(1, 1),
  DisplayName NVARCHAR(100),
  Email NVARCHAR(100),
  PasswordHash CHAR(64))

ALTER TABLE Users ADD CONSTRAINT UsersPrimaryKey
  PRIMARY KEY CLUSTERED (Id)
    ]]>
    </Script>
  </Version>
</Database>
```

Questioning why I am coupling these tests to private implementation details of a database when I just spent a whole chapter arguing that you shouldn't do that would be reasonable. I wrestled with it for a long time, myself.

The reason it is okay to test internal structure is that transition tests don't test your database. They test your database class itself. That is, they aren't testing that the database does what it should do; that's the job of a unit test. Instead, they are testing that your database forms the way it should.

Transition Testing Addition

One could also argue that additive changes don't require transition testing. I would make the same counterargument, and its underpinnings would be the same neuroses. You can make the call later, but for now let's follow the process a little further.

Imagine that version 1 of the database class shown previously has been deployed and one of its instances is happily collecting knowledge from users. Now it's time to extend the schema to support some more variation—let's say allowing users to specify a list of interests.

It is useful to me to know that a transition doesn't hurt existing data even when it is unreasonable to assume that it might, so I'll start by writing a transition test that shows my user data are kept safe. Because it is expected that this behavior is already implemented, I'm going to use a technique called *pinning*. When pinning behavior, you write a test that breaks because its assertions are wrong.

```
[Test]
public void RecordsPersistedInVersion2()
{
  var getRecords = "SELECT * FROM Users ORDER BY ID ASC";
  var addRecordSqlFormat =
@"INSERT INTO Users(DisplayName, Email, PasswordHash)
  VALUES('{0}', '{1}', '{2}')";

  instantiator.UpgradeToSpecificVersion(connection, 1);
  connection.ExecuteSql(string.Format(addRecordSqlFormat,
    "MaryJU", "mary.j.user@users.org", "abcdefg"));
  connection.ExecuteSql(string.Format(addRecordSqlFormat,
    "JQPub123", "john.q@public.net", "hijklmn"));
  connection.ExecuteSql(string.Format(addRecordSqlFormat,
    "JackTrades", "jack.all@trades.com", "zzzzz"));

  instantiator.UpgradeToSpecificVersion(connection, 2);

  Assertions.AssertRowsAreEqual(
    new IDictionary<string, object>[0],
    connection.ExecuteQuery(getRecords));
}
```

It will fail because no transition exists for version 2, so I'll add an empty version 2.

```
<Database>
  <Version Number="1">
    <Script>
      <![CDATA[
CREATE TABLE Users(
  ID INT IDENTITY(1, 1),
  DisplayName NVARCHAR(100),
  Email NVARCHAR(100),
  PasswordHash CHAR(64))

ALTER TABLE Users ADD CONSTRAINT UsersPrimaryKey
  PRIMARY KEY CLUSTERED (Id)
      ]]>
    </Script>
  </Version>
  <Version Number="2">
  </Version>
</Database>
```

Now my test is failing because it expected no data from the query but it got some. So I'll change the expected data to match what I actually have. Pinning is a pretty safe way of developing a test that specifies some software should keep doing what it did.

```
[Test]
public void RecordsPersistedInVersion2()
{
  var getRecords = "SELECT * FROM Users ORDER BY ID ASC";
  var addRecordSqlFormat =
@"INSERT INTO Users(DisplayName, Email, PasswordHash)
  VALUES('{0}', '{1}', '{2}')";

  instantiator.UpgradeToSpecificVersion(connection, 1);
  connection.ExecuteSql(string.Format(addRecordSqlFormat,
    "MaryJU", "mary.j.user@users.org", "abcdefg"));
  connection.ExecuteSql(string.Format(addRecordSqlFormat,
    "JQPub123", "john.q@public.net", "hijklmn"));
  connection.ExecuteSql(string.Format(addRecordSqlFormat,
    "JackTrades", "jack.all@trades.com", "zzzzz"));
  var originalData = connection.ExecuteQuery(getRecords);

  instantiator.UpgradeToSpecificVersion(connection, 2);

  Assertions.AssertRowsAreEqual(
    originalData,
    connection.ExecuteQuery(getRecords));
}
```

With the identity transformation for the knowledge stored in the existing table protected by a test, I can safely start working on the new kinds of knowledge I want my class of database to store. There again, I start by writing a test.

```
[Test]
public void InterestsTableExistsInVersion2()
{
  instantiator.UpgradeToSpecificVersion(connection, 2);
  var desc = connection.GetStructureDescription("Interests");
  Assert.That(desc.Exists);
  AssertColumnDetails(desc, "ID", "int");
  AssertColumnDetails(desc, "UserID", "int");
  AssertColumnDetails(desc, "Description", "nvarchar", 128);
  AssertPrimaryKeyDetails(desc, "InterestsPrimaryKey", "ID");
  Assert.That(desc.GetIdentity("ID").Exists);
}
```

After I see it fail, I add a table to make it pass.

```
<Version Number="2">
  <Script>
    <![CDATA[
CREATE TABLE Interests(
```

```
ID INT IDENTITY(1, 1),
UserID INT,
Description NVARCHAR(128))

ALTER TABLE Interests ADD CONSTRAINT
  InterestsPrimaryKey PRIMARY KEY CLUSTERED (ID)
     ]]>
    </Script>
  </Version>
```

Having the interests table is not quite enough. I also need a relationship between it and the users table, so I write a test for that.

```
[Test]
public void InterestsTableHasAForeignKeyConstraintToUsers()
{
    instantiator.UpgradeToSpecificVersion(connection, 2);

    var desc = connection.GetStructureDescription("Interests");
    Assume.That(desc.Exists);
    var constraint = desc.GetConstraint("InterestsUsersForeignKey");
    Assert.That(constraint.Exists);
    Assert.That(constraint.Description, Is.EqualTo("FOREIGN KEY"));
    Assert.That(constraint.ReferencedTable, Is.EqualTo("Users"));
    Assert.That(constraint.Keys, Is.EquivalentTo(new[] { "UserID" }));
    Assert.That(
       constraint.ReferencedKeys, Is.EquivalentTo(new[] { "ID" }));
}
```

Note again how I set up the test to check that the relationship exists, not that the relationship works as I want it to. Remember: The database involved here is not the object under test—it is the output of what is being tested, which is the class of databases that I am developing. Hopefully, I also have a suite of unit tests that specify how that relationship should work.

The previous test's failure signals to me that I should also change my version 2 upgrade script to add the specified relationship (changes in **bold**).

```
<Version Number="2">
  <Script>
    <![CDATA[
CREATE TABLE Interests(
  ID INT IDENTITY(1, 1),
  UserID INT,
  Description NVARCHAR(128))

ALTER TABLE Interests ADD CONSTRAINT
  InterestsPrimaryKey PRIMARY KEY CLUSTERED (ID)

ALTER TABLE Interests ADD CONSTRAINT
  InterestsUsersForeignKey FOREIGN KEY (UserID)
  REFERENCES Users(ID)
```

```
]]>
  </Script>
</Version>
```

> ### *Simplified Construction Logic*
>
> I hope you've noticed a lack of IF EXISTS and CREATE OR REPLACE type structures in my creation scripts.
>
> A consequence of building databases using a class comprised of linear upgrade steps is that there is never a reasonable question as to whether or not a structure exists. It either existed as a result of upgrading to the previous version or it didn't.
>
> Of course, this cannot be relied upon if you allow *any* manual intervention in the formation of production databases. Rather than making your database create scripts and transition tests more complex to account for such variation, do whatever you can to prevent it from creeping into your process.

After recompiling and rerunning my tests, I see they all pass. I now have an extremely high degree of confidence that a database can safely proceed from version 0 to version 1 and on to version 2. Of course, because all of my changes were additive, that's not saying much.

Transition Testing Metamorphosis

So let's take a look at the big enchilada: changing an existing data structure. Imagine that version 2 has been deployed to production and users have flooded my database with indications of their interest. Marketing is hot to trot about the ability to perform analyses involving users with shared interests.

One option is to write a service that helps you find a bunch of users based on a particular interest. That has limited applicability, might end up being slow, and also doesn't jive very well with my goal of writing a book about this stuff. So, instead, the development team decides to factor interests out as their own entities and allow users to associate with those entities.

My job is to transfer all the distinct, title-cased interests into their own table with identities, and then create a many-to-many mapping between users and interests. Let's assume I've gotten the business of protecting data I want left untouched out of the way and I want to write a test that specifies the appropriate transformation.

The first test I write specifies that no duplicate interests are permitted.

```csharp
[Test]
public void OnlyDistinctInterestsArePreserved()
{
  instantiator.UpgradeToSpecificVersion(connection, 2);
  var addUserSqlFormat =
@"INSERT INTO Users(DisplayName, Email, PasswordHash)
  VALUES('{0}', '{1}', '{2}');
  SELECT @@Identity";
  var user1ID =
    connection.ExecuteScalar(string.Format(addUserSqlFormat,
      "User1", "u1@users.com", "aaa"));
  var user2ID =
    connection.ExecuteScalar(string.Format(addUserSqlFormat,
      "User2", "u2@users.com", "aaa"));
  var addInterestsSqlFormat =
@"INSERT INTO Interests(UserID, Description)
  VALUES({0}, '{1}')";
  connection.ExecuteSql(string.Format(addInterestsSqlFormat,
    user1ID, "Unique 1"));
  connection.ExecuteSql(string.Format(addInterestsSqlFormat,
    user1ID, "Non-unique"));
  connection.ExecuteSql(string.Format(addInterestsSqlFormat,
    user1ID, "Unique 2"));
  connection.ExecuteSql(string.Format(addInterestsSqlFormat,
    user1ID, "Non-unique"));

  instantiator.UpgradeToSpecificVersion(connection, 3);

  var interestDescriptions = connection
    .ExecuteQuery("SELECT Description FROM Interests")
    .Select(r => r["Description"])
    .ToArray();
  Assert.That(
    interestDescriptions,
    Is.EquivalentTo(new[] { "Unique 1", "Unique 2", "Non-unique" }));
}
```

Admittedly, it's a touch ugly when squeezed into the pages of a book. I apologize for that. Probably a bigger problem for people who aren't familiar with .NET is the following:

```csharp
var interestDescriptions = connection
  .ExecuteQuery("SELECT Description FROM Interests")
  .Select(r => r["Description"])
  .ToArray();
```

That line, in a nutshell, says "execute this query and turn the results for a particular column into an array."

Anyway, the preceding test fails but it drives me to write transition logic that blasts all the duplicate interest entries (following), which is clearly not the right thing:

```
<Version Number="3">
  <Script>
    <![CDATA[
CREATE TABLE ##Dummy(
  ID INT,
  Description NVARCHAR(128));

INSERT INTO ##Dummy
  SELECT MIN(UserID), Description
  FROM Interests
  GROUP BY Description

TRUNCATE TABLE Interests

INSERT INTO Interests(UserID, Description)
  SELECT * FROM ##Dummy
    ]]>
  </Script>
</Version>
```

I intentionally created this error to make a point. One of the key values of transition testing is that it forces you to make your worst mistakes in a test environment, where they are non-fatal.

I need another test that specifies all the knowledge in my database survives the change.

```
[Test]
public void AllUserInterestAssociationsArePreserved()
{
  instantiator.UpgradeToSpecificVersion(connection, 2);
  var addUserSqlFormat =
@"INSERT INTO Users(DisplayName, Email, PasswordHash)
VALUES('{0}', '{1}', '{2}');
SELECT @@Identity";
  var user1ID =
    connection.ExecuteScalar(string.Format(addUserSqlFormat,
      "User1", "u1@users.com", "aaa"));
  var user2ID =
    connection.ExecuteScalar(string.Format(addUserSqlFormat,
      "User2", "u2@users.com", "aaa"));
  var addInterestsSqlFormat =
@"INSERT INTO Interests(UserID, Description)
VALUES({0}, '{1}')";
  connection.ExecuteSql(string.Format(addInterestsSqlFormat,
    user1ID, "Unique 1"));
```

```
connection.ExecuteSql(string.Format(addInterestsSqlFormat,
    user1ID, "Non-unique"));
connection.ExecuteSql(string.Format(addInterestsSqlFormat,
    user1ID, "Unique 2"));
connection.ExecuteSql(string.Format(addInterestsSqlFormat,
    user1ID, "Non-unique"));

var originalData = connection.ExecuteQuery(
@"SELECT u.ID, i.Description FROM Users u INNER JOIN Interests i ON
u.ID = i.UserID
ORDER BY u.ID, i.Description");

instantiator.UpgradeToSpecificVersion(connection, 3);

var newData = connection.ExecuteQuery(
@"SELECT u.ID, i.Description FROM Users u INNER JOIN UserInterests
➥ui ON
u.ID = ui.UserID INNER JOIN Interests i on ui.InterestID = i.ID
ORDER BY u.ID, i.Description");

Assertions.AssertRowsAreEqual(originalData, newData);
}
```

That test drives me to build the right transition logic.

```
<Version Number="3">
  <Script>
    <![CDATA[
EXEC sp_rename 'Interests', 'UserInterests', 'Object'

CREATE TABLE Interests(
  ID INT IDENTITY(1, 1) PRIMARY KEY,
  Description NVARCHAR(128))

INSERT INTO Interests(Description)
  SELECT Distinct(Description) FROM UserInterests

ALTER TABLE UserInterests ADD InterestID INT

UPDATE UserInterests SET InterestID = Interests.ID
  FROM Interests INNER JOIN UserInterests
  ON Interests.Description = UserInterests.Description

ALTER TABLE UserInterests DROP COLUMN Description
    ]]>
  </Script>
</Version>
```

That causes my transition tests to all pass and I know that the knowledge in a database is going to be transformed from its version 2 shape to its version 3 shape. To ensure my data structures are built correctly, I am inclined to go a little further and develop a test that ensures a relationship is formed between the UserInterests table and the Interests table.

```
[Test]
public void UserInterestsTableHasAForeignKeyConstraintToInterests()
{
  instantiator.UpgradeToSpecificVersion(connection, 3);

  var desc = connection.GetStructureDescription("UserInterests");
  Assume.That(desc.Exists);
  var constraint = desc.GetConstraint
➡("UserInterestsToInterestsForeignKey");
  Assert.That(constraint.Exists);
  Assert.That(constraint.Description, Is.EqualTo("FOREIGN KEY"));
  Assert.That(constraint.ReferencedTable, Is.EqualTo("Interests"));
  Assert.That(constraint.Keys, Is.EquivalentTo(new[]
➡{ "InterestID" }));
  Assert.That(constraint.ReferencedKeys, Is.EquivalentTo(new[]
➡{ "ID" }));
}
```

When that fails, my response is to create the required relationship with the following code.

```
<Version Number="3">
  <Script>
    <![CDATA[
EXEC sp_rename 'Interests', 'UserInterests', 'Object'

CREATE TABLE Interests(
  ID INT IDENTITY(1, 1) PRIMARY KEY,
  Description NVARCHAR(128))

INSERT INTO Interests(Description)
  SELECT Distinct(Description) FROM UserInterests

ALTER TABLE UserInterests ADD InterestID INT

UPDATE UserInterests SET InterestID = Interests.ID
  FROM Interests INNER JOIN UserInterests
  ON Interests.Description = UserInterests.Description

ALTER .TABLE UserInterests DROP COLUMN Description

ALTER TABLE UserInterests ADD CONSTRAINT
  UserInterestsToInterestsForeignKey FOREIGN KEY (InterestID)
  REFERENCES Interests(ID)
    ]]>
  </Script>
</Version>
```

Because of my already-confessed weakness for completeness, I would probably go so far as to specify that the UserInterests table still had its relationship with Users and that the Interests table no longer had direct any relationship with Users. If I renamed structures like the original relationship so that it better matched the current design of my database class, I would also specify that with transition tests.

Why Not Use the Public Interface?

You still might not be convinced that you should be writing transition tests that are focused on the private details of a database's structure. You might be thinking, "I like the idea of protecting my data with transition tests, but I don't feel like testing the creation of relationships or ID columns," for instance.

That's okay. The critical thing to do is to preserve the knowledge in a database. The implementation details are, I think, important and valuable but will not break your back if you don't specify them in transition tests.

Transition Safeguards

That said, I would point out that you can use another form of testing that can deliver a lot of value and that should usually be pointed at your database's public interface in addition to unit testing. I call this kind of testing *transition safeguards*.

The distinction between transition tests and transition safeguards is that transition tests specify how a database changes whereas transition safeguards specify that, when a database changes, its knowledge is preserved. Another distinction between tests and safeguards is that tests are run in a particular test environment while safeguards should be able to be run against any environment.

Whereas transition tests should prevent you from deploying a bad version of a database, transition safeguards should cause a deployment with some unforeseen consequence to fail, trigger a rollback, and prevent any application upgrades from being deployed against a bad database.

Building knowledge-protecting transition tests that leverage existing safeguards is possible, thereby preventing some duplication. However, if you really want the kind of detailed specification that a transition test offers, you still need to write transition tests that specify the structural changes you intend to apply to a database.

Read/Read Transition Tests

Fundamentally, transition safeguards are transition tests that are read-only. Because a transition test is typically operating against a newly created database of a certain version, it must write data to a database to ensure that knowledge is preserved in the course of a refactor.

A transition safeguard, however, does most of its work in a production database, where data should already exist. Therefore, it can take samples of knowledge from before and after a transition and ensure that they line up.

Let's look at adding a safeguard to the class of databases I developed in the previous section. I start with the safeguard for the transition from version 1 to version 2.

```xml
  <Version Number="1">
    <Script><!-- SNIPPED: Same as before --></Script>
    <Script>
      <![CDATA[
CREATE PROCEDURE GetUserData @id INT
AS
BEGIN
  SELECT DisplayName, Email, PasswordHash FROM Users
    WHERE ID = @id
END;
      ]]>
    </Script>
    <Safeguards>
      <Add Name="UsersData">
        <SetUp>
          <![CDATA[
CREATE TABLE ##Users_IDs(UserID INT)
INSERT INTO ##Users_IDs SELECT TOP 3 ID FROM Users
          ]]>
        </SetUp>
        <Sample>
          <![CDATA[
DECLARE IDCursor CURSOR FOR
  SELECT UserID FROM ##Users_IDs
OPEN IDCursor

DECLARE @id INT
FETCH NEXT FROM IDCursor INTO @id

WHILE @@FETCH_STATUS = 0
BEGIN
  EXEC GetUserData @id
  FETCH NEXT FROM IDCursor INTO @id
END

CLOSE IDCursor
DEALLOCATE IDCursor
          ]]>
        </Sample>
        <TearDown>
          <![CDATA[
DROP TABLE ##Users_IDs
          ]]>
```

```
          </TearDown>
        </Add>
      </Safeguards>
    </Version>
```

Notice that I added a public interface stored procedure (GetUserData). Safeguards measure the protection of knowledge by extracting information from a real database. Therefore, they are going to be most resilient to things such as design changes when they are clients to your database's public interface. So I added some public interface to which my safeguard could couple.

You should also notice that I added some XML to my database class document with a safeguard in it. The safeguard is broken up into three parts. The first part (setup) randomly selects a few users to measure and tracks their identities in a temporary table.

The next part is what I call *sampling*. It is a query to be run by a database class before and after each transition to a version after the one in which the safeguard is defined. This sampler query iterates over the list of selected users and executes the stored procedure to get their data.

After each transition, the database class then takes another measurement using the same sampling query. It then checks the two snapshots to make sure they are exactly equal. If they are, the database class continues. If not, it aborts the upgrade and reports an error.

Regardless of whether or not the safeguard passes, the script in the teardown block will be run after a transition. This allows you to keep your database and your session clean so that a transition can be run again and again.

Now look at the transition from version 2 to version 3.

```
<Version Number="2">
    <Script><!-- SNIPPED: Same as before --></Script>
    <Script>
      <![CDATA[
CREATE PROCEDURE GetUserInterests @UserID INT
AS
BEGIN
  SELECT Description
    FROM Interests i
    INNER JOIN Users u ON i.UserID = u.ID
    WHERE u.ID = @UserID
END
      ]]>
    </Script>
    <Safeguards>
      <Add Name="UsersAndInterests">
        <Sample>
          <![CDATA[
DECLARE IDCursor CURSOR FOR
  SELECT UserID FROM ##Users_IDs
OPEN IDCursor
```

```
DECLARE @id INT
FETCH NEXT FROM IDCursor INTO @id

WHILE @@FETCH_STATUS = 0
BEGIN
  EXEC GetUserInterests @id
  FETCH NEXT FROM IDCursor INTO @id
END

CLOSE IDCursor
DEALLOCATE IDCursor
        ]]>
      </Sample>
    </Add>
  </Safeguards>
</Version>
```

I didn't add a safeguard for the users table because the safeguard rule hasn't changed and, in the database build mechanism associated with this book, safeguards are inherited from version to version. I highly recommend you add a similar feature to the infrastructure for your class of databases. Managing safeguards without something like that is going to be a nightmare for you.

I did add a new safeguard that ensures the relationships between users and interests is preserved across the transition from version 2 to version 3. It does this by fetching the interests for each randomly selected user and returning a table expressing those relationships in queries before and after. The database class will then compare the results and raise a red flag if anything is wrong.

Safeguards and Tests Overlap

Note that, if I had this safeguard while I was developing my transition, I would not have needed to write an extra transition test to prevent myself from maliciously deleting "unnecessary" relationships. The safeguard would have prevented my first transition test from passing.

To keep things fast, I prefer to validate a random sampling of the knowledge in a database. If you are working with life-critical systems and you can afford the additional upgrade time, you probably will want a larger sample, something in the vicinity of 100 percent of your data. For the vast majority of situations, a small sample is good enough.

Run by the Class of Databases on Every Upgrade

Whether you use the language I've created, find something else, or "roll your own" tool, you should set things up so that relevant safeguards are run on every transition that occurs for every database in a class. The only exception should be if your public interface has changed and a safeguard rule is no longer relevant.

This might seem like overkill to you but, remember, it should be fast; it should cost you very little to do; and even the biggest, most complex databases will typically only have one safeguard run at a time.

Backup and Rollback on Fail

Safeguards are useful because they provide one last screen of defense against something having gone wrong. However, they only tell you whether something went wrong. They don't correct errors that have occurred. After all, how could they? By their nature, they only fail when something happened that was unexpected!

Your job is to make sure that your process includes good standard practices such as taking backups before performing dangerous surgery on your database. If you do that, then safeguards, coupled with transition tests, can work together to prevent damage from occurring and to give you recourse when it does.

If a safeguard raises a red flag, you should restore your most recent backup, back out any application upgrades that have occurred since you started a deployment, and avoid any other application upgrades.

Making Transition Tests Leverage Transition Safeguards

Although I wouldn't want to give up transition tests, I also wouldn't want you to have to develop two identical bodies of test-like things. In the case of protecting the knowledge in your database, a transition test can be as simple as making sure that a database at a certain version is populated with the appropriate amount of knowledge and relying on your safeguards to tell you when transition logic corrupts data.

Here is an example of a transition test that leverages a transition safeguard for data about users.

```
[Test]
public void UsersDataArePreserved()
{
  var addRecordSqlFormat =
@"INSERT INTO Users(DisplayName, Email, PasswordHash)
VALUES('{0}', '{1}', '{2}')";
  instantiator.UpgradeToSpecificVersion(connection, 1);
  connection.ExecuteSql(string.Format(addRecordSqlFormat,
```

```
    "MaryJU", "mary.j.user@users.org", "abcdefg"));
connection.ExecuteSql(string.Format(addRecordSqlFormat,
    "JQPub123", "john.q@public.net", "hijklmn"));
connection.ExecuteSql(string.Format(addRecordSqlFormat,
    "JackTrades", "jack.all@trades.com", "zzzzz"));
connection.ExecuteSql(string.Format(addRecordSqlFormat,
    "TomTom", "tom@tom.com", "qqqq"));
connection.ExecuteSql(string.Format(addRecordSqlFormat,
    "JJBinks", "ruined@franchise.com", "1234"));
connection.ExecuteSql(string.Format(addRecordSqlFormat,
    "CandyManX3", "keep.lights@on.com", "jgalpqmn"));

instantiator.UpgradeToLatestVersion(connection);
}
```

There's something interesting about this example that I want to make sure you notice. That is that this test keeps working for you every time you add a new version. It is dandy to be able to whip out a test for the identity transformation in a flash, but what's even better is to not have to write a new test for the identity transformation every time you add a version.

More to the point: That's really what you want to specify with a transition test about knowledge anyway. You don't want to have to keep saying, "and still don't destroy that vital data." You want to say, "these facts should remain accessible forever."

That said, I still think having the lower-level transition tests that specify precise structural changes is useful, but to each his own. At the time of this writing, my preference is to use transition safeguards to protect knowledge and transition tests to specify everything else.

Summary

The big risk associated with changing databases' designs is loss of knowledge. Most people think of losing knowledge in a cataclysmic way, by messing up some transition logic and somehow damaging content. The other way knowledge loss can occur is by not changing a design and allowing applications to "shove" data into a database where it wouldn't naturally fit.

Changing design frequently is necessary to avoid the database being a bottleneck as well as to spare it the slow corrosion of hacky data practices. Yet you need to make those rapid changes in a very safe way. Fortunately, by breaking database builds down into a sequence of deltas, each one representing the transition to another version, you give yourself the tools you need to do just that.

Transition tests let you plan and specify exactly what changes you intend to make against a database without touching a production database. They enable you to model these changes and their consequences with such precision that you have almost no chance of creating a breaking change. Transition safeguards allow you to put in place a screen of checks that protects every database within a class from knowledge loss.

The two put together, paired with a good back-out process for botched deployments not only all but eliminate the risk of data corruption as a result of a design change but, if you have a good failure-handling process, you can also avoid significant interruption in service.

Having that basic safety net in place allows you to start thinking about another class of problems: How do you help developers avoid misuse of your database? The next chapter, "Enforcing Interface," tackles that issue.

Chapter 5

Enforcing Interface

An important part of doing test-driven development is defining the right interface. I've been drumming for a while now on the fact that a database is really an object and that it has a class. One of the properties of a class is that it tends to have a fairly strong interface.

In compiled languages, the validity of most coupling is enforced at compile-time. In dynamic languages, it's validated shortly before you access part of an object. In databases, though, coupling isn't validated until a command is transmitted to a database. This makes testing objects that talk to the database harder because mocking a database robs you of the feedback you get when coupling to it.

A way exists to give clients coupling to a database the same kind of feedback they would get from any other object in their platform. In this chapter, I show you how to make a breaking change in your database design cause a compile-time error in compiled clients to your database. For dynamic clients, if their mocking tool is smart enough, they will get a run-time error while running their tests.

After you apply what's in this chapter, your worst-case coupling scenario will be that you forget to update the thing that embodies your interface definition, causing your unit and transition tests to fail and reminding you that you need to do that. Your best-case scenario will be that you cannot even compile your tests or your class of databases if there is fundamentally invalid coupling.

The solution involves decoupling database client code from the names of the objects in your public interface. It also includes a mechanism for coupling various clients to the right versions of your public design so as to minimize duplication and arbitrary maintenance tasks.

63

Interface Strength

You don't just want a good interface. You want a strong interface, too. Whatever kind of feedback the developers using your database are accustomed to with "normal" objects is the kind of feedback your class of databases should be providing to them. In addition to accelerating the development process of anything that has to do with a database, it entices developers to use the interface structures you have built.

The languages with the strongest coupling mechanisms warn a developer of fundamentally wrong coupling while they are trying to turn source code into programs. In fact, these days, the compiler is always running and I actually get feedback in my IDE as I'm typing. Weaker languages wait a little longer but in all cases, the platform prevents inherently wrong operations from even attempting to execute.

Databases do not provide that protection. Most of the time, when a client couples to a database, it's pretty much just sending "any old string" to the database, expecting the server to do all parsing and validation. Notwithstanding something along the lines of bouncing a radio signal off of Mars, that's about the slowest feedback loop you can have.

The root of the problem is duplication. It is commonplace for the symbols involved in a database's public interface to be duplicated all over the place. Typically, at best they are duplicated across each database client, the database class, and every database instance. Kudos if you're doing better than that.

Stronger Coupling Languages

A nice strong language such as C# will stop me from even making a program or class library that is fundamentally invalid. Take, for instance, the relationship between the following two classes:

```
public class A
{
  public void Use(B b)
  {
    b.DoSomething();
  }
}

public class B
{
  public void DoSomething()
  {
  }
}
```

Class A uses class B's DoSomething method. What happens if I change class A so that it doesn't conform to the contract it has with class B as follows?

```
public class A
{
  public void Use(B b)
  {
    b.DoAThing();
  }
}
```

The compiler will report an error and will not produce a binary. That's kind of interesting, but there's an even more interesting case. Imagine that class B is maintained by a different group and that group has decided that DoSomething should actually be called UpdateReportData.

The group goes through the various processes for notifying client developers that they are going to change the name of the method and nobody complains, so they decide to make the change.

```
public class A
{
  public void Use(B b)
  {
    b.DoSomething();
  }
}

public class B
{
  public void UpdateReportData()
  {
  }
}
```

However, I was on vacation while all this happened so I wasn't able to update class A in time. The next time someone tries to compile my application, he gets an error message and there is no build output. A developer is immediately notified of the problem and can quickly fix it.

Weaker Coupling Languages

In a language with less-strong coupling tools, a very similar interaction occurs. A mocking tool can be used to produce an object with an interface just like a real object. When someone breaks the contract between two classes, there is the potential that a unit test will fail and notify him of the problem.

Even if the unit tests do not fully protect against miscoupling, usually a body of integration tests (tests that test how groups of objects work together) can give some form of feedback before a set of changes that do not reconcile are deployed to production or even to a realistic test environment.

The Common Thread

Test-driven development brings a common theme to both stronger and weaker coupled languages: stopping broken code from getting to a fully deployed environment so that problems can be quickly found and corrected. That's not to say that code with bugs never goes out to a test environment or even out the door to customers. It does say that code which can easily be determined by a machine to have no chance of working is typically caught before it reaches an environment in which a human might find it.

The amount of time it takes to find a problem varies. The mechanism by which notification of a problem is delivered to developers varies. The basic defense against obviously wrong coupling is always there, though.

Coupling to Database Classes

Thus far, I've only talked about building a class of databases without consideration for how a client actually deals with a database instance. In most environments, applications connect to databases in ways that are extremely primitive when compared to how they couple to, say, another object in their process.

In fact, the way objects in a middle-tier application connect to web services, objects in other processes, or even objects on other machines is substantially more advanced than the manner in which they talk to database instances.

Every place I've worked or consulted, the means by which I was warned that my application code was not properly using a structure in a database was either for me to look at a database and see how I should interface with it or for my application to connect to a database with an updated schema and fail. The former option is extremely flakey and the latter is extremely slow.

The Problem Is Duplication

The core of the problem is that a bunch of design information is duplicated, for all intents and purposes, everywhere anyone can think to duplicate it. Now I don't much care about symbols being duplicated between various database instances any more than I care about function names being duplicated across all the instances of a JavaScript class or zeroes and ones being duplicated throughout all those pesky memory chips all over the world.

I don't care about those because they are derivatives of the classes that made them. I do care about duplication that I have to maintain, though. If someone changes the public interface for a database, I don't want to wait until the string representing the name of a table I duplicated into my application fails to produce a proper SQL statement. When I finally learn of the problem, I don't want to correct it by making sure my copy of that string is up to date.

I want a compiler error because I am compiling-in the definition of a database's interface maintained by someone else. In dynamic languages, I want a runtime error in my unit tests because my code is automatically updated with those symbols.

Client-Object-Like Enforcement

The absolute ideal would be to have proxy objects in every required client language that made a data object look like "just another object." This object would hide even the connection with the database it proxies and expose all the stored procedures as methods. That can be done, but implementing it is out of the scope of this book.

There is a close approximation that you can implement with very little cost. It involves creating libraries of classes that serve as repositories of symbols that can be used by other classes that want to talk to a database. By driving all database coupling through these classes, you can completely hide all the names you use for your public interface from all your clients while, at the same time, causing them to fail quickly when they incorrectly couple to a class of databases.

Creating Demand for a `DatabaseDesign` Class

The first client to any given unit of public interface should always be a unit test. It's no different for coupling classes. Assume that you have written the following unit test, which demands a database with a particular schema:

```
[TestFixture]
public class DemandingDesignEncapsulationTests
{
  private IDbConnection connection;

  [SetUp]
  public void SetUp()
  {
    connection = DatabaseProvisioning.CreateFreshDatabaseAndConnect();
    var instantiator = Instantiator
      .GetInstance(DatabaseDescriptor.LoadFromFile("TrivialDB.xml"));
    instantiator.UpgradeToLatestVersion(connection);
  }
```

```
[Test]
public void PutAndGet()
{
   var id = connection.ExecuteScalar(
@"INSERT INTO SimpleTable(Name) VALUES('Candy')
SELECT @@Identity;");

   var value = connection.ExecuteScalar(
@"SELECT Name FROM SimpleTable WHERE ID = " + id);

   Assert.That(value, Is.EqualTo("Candy"));
 }
}
```

For now, to keep things simple, assume you only have to deal with a .NET client. To start enforcing coupling to your class of databases, you'll want to concentrate references to any given symbol into a single place.

The simplest implementation is nothing more than a repository of constants whose names represent the logical names of various structures and whose values are their physical names in the database.

Start by retooling the unit test so that its coupling is also routed through a coupling class:

```
[Test]
public void PutAndGetUsingDatabaseDesign()
{
  var simpleTable = new DatabaseDesign.SimpleTable();
  var id = connection.ExecuteScalar(string.Format(
    "INSERT INTO {0}({1}) VALUES('Candy'); SELECT @@Identity",
    simpleTable, simpleTable.Name));

   var value = connection.ExecuteScalar(string.Format(
    "SELECT {1} FROM {0} WHERE ID = {2}",
    simpleTable, simpleTable.Name, id));

   Assert.That(value, Is.EqualTo("Candy"));
 }
```

Because that doesn't compile, you will need to create a DatabaseDesign class with all of those symbols (discussed next). They don't need good values, yet. They just need to exist.

Specifying the DatabaseDesign Class

The next step is to get the DatabaseDesign class to have the right values. Because all the symbols are handily exposed as constants, you can write simple tests specifying the value of each. Just using constants ends up being a little hard, so go a little further and specify a lightweight object model representing the structure of your database class:

```
[Test]
public void DatabaseDesignSpecification()
{
  var simpleTable = new DatabaseDesign.SimpleTable();

  Assert.That(simpleTable.ToString(), Is.EqualTo("SimpleTable"));
  Assert.That(simpleTable.ID.ToString(), Is.EqualTo("ID"));
  Assert.That(simpleTable.Name.ToString(), Is.EqualTo("Name"));
}
```

Those failing tests would lead you to develop something like the following class:

```
public class DatabaseDesign
{
  public class SimpleTable
  {
    public override string ToString()
    {
      return "SimpleTable";
    }

    public IDColumn ID { get { return new IDColumn(); } }

    public class IDColumn
    {
      public override string ToString()
      {
        return "ID";
      }
    }

    public NameColumn Name { get { return new NameColumn(); } }

    public class NameColumn
    {
      public override string ToString()
      {
        return "Name";
      }
    }
  }
}
```

Seeing the tests pass would let you know that the public interface for your database design was properly specified and could be used in clients. This means that you can see your unit test fail as you expect and proceed with the rest of the test-driven development process.

Getting Rid of Duplication with Multiple Client Platforms

There are all-Java shops. There are all-Ruby shops. There are all-.NET and all-C++ shops. A good portion of database classes are only ever connected to by clients running on one particular platform. Then again, there are shops that have client applications in C++, Java, Ruby, and .NET. So there are a fair number of software development environments where a database design must support a variety of clients.

Stay with me even if you aren't in that boat because, for one thing, you might one day be and, for another, what you learn in this subsection is directly applicable to the next.

Let's say that you need to support access from C++ and from Ruby. One option would be to duplicate the coupling class for a database into each of those languages and to duplicate the tests as well.

Another option would be to keep one suite of tests and find some way to interoperate between those tests and both client languages so that the duplication only exists in your implementations of the coupling class.

An even simpler and far more sustainable solution is available that completely eliminates the duplication. Create an intermediate format, and then write a single tool that translates from that intermediate format into each of the target languages. Let's look at what the intermediate format might be:

```
<Interface>
  <Element Id="SimpleTable" Value="SimpleTable">
    <Element Id="ID" Value="ID"/>
    <Element Id="Name" Value="Name" />
  </Element>
</Interface>
```

I'm not going to bother showing you what the tool would look like that translates such a format into a simple class with constants in it. That's the dreaded "exercise for the reader." The companion code contains an example of how to implement all the suggestions in this chapter. Suffice it to say that some very simple rules can translate from that XML into the previous C++ and Ruby coupling classes.

If you can trust that all the generated classes are equivalent in their respective languages, then how many of them do you really need to test to be sure you're exposing the right interface to your clients? If you've properly tested the tool that creates the classes in each language, you will only need to test the output in the language of your choosing to validate the intermediate design specification.

What Happens When Coupling Goes Bad?

Let's take a moment to look at what you've developed so far. Now you have a single document that can be used to define a database's public interface. That document can be used to generate a symbol table in any language it supports. The values of all the symbols in said table are test driven and covered by your unit tests. That symbol table can be used to compile any SQL statement in any supported client language.

What happens if a Java client tries to use a symbol that doesn't exist? It gets a compiler error: Sorry, `DatabaseDesign.SimpleTable.FunkyColumn` doesn't exist.

What happens if a JavaScript client tries to use a symbol that doesn't exist? It gets a unit test failure: Sorry, the object `'SimpleTable'` doesn't have a member `'FunkyColumn'`.

Every developer who behaves himself gets this feedback. Honestly, what reasonably senior developer wouldn't use your coupling class to get that kind of feedback? Because everyone wants to behave, you can project design changes far and wide without people's consent while having as minimal an impact on them as their chosen development environment will permit.

The practice of enforcing your database's interface can be taken further and you'll be glad you did if you do.

Eliminating Duplication Between Database Build and Client Code

It seems like you're just a hop and skip away from concentrating all the symbols for a database design into a single document. A tool already exists that allows you to eliminate duplication between all of your unit tests and client applications. Let's find a way to avoid duplicating those symbols into your class of databases.

There's an easy solution. Imagine you've already written the tool that walks through your intermediate interface document and produces a coupling class for each client language you support. Now consider the following interface specification and database class XML files and see whether you can deduce how to eradicate all duplication:

```
<!-- Interface definition -->
<Interface>
  <Element Id="SimpleTable" Value="SimpleTable">
    <Element Id="ID" Value="ID"/>
    <Element Id="Name" Value="Name" />
  </Element>
</Interface>
```

```
<!-- Database class definition -->
<Database>
  <Version Number="1">
    <Script>
      <![CDATA[
CREATE TABLE SimpleTable(
  ID INT IDENTITY(1, 1),
  Name NVARCHAR(50))
      ]]>
    </Script>
  </Version>
</Database>
```

Did you see it?

The way I suggest doing it is to have the same tool that generates your various coupling classes also take your database build scripts as an input, scan them for references to symbols, and replace them with the physical names of the appropriate structure.

You have to change how you specify a database class a little first, though:

```
<Database>
  <Version Number="1">
    <Script>
      <![CDATA[
CREATE TABLE $SimpleTable(
  $SimpleTable.ID INT IDENTITY(1, 1),
  $SimpleTable.Name NVARCHAR(50))
      ]]>
    </Script>
  </Version>
</Database>
```

That database class file can easily be scanned for references to the symbols defined in the previous interface definition XML file. Your little code-generator tool could then spit out a ready-to-execute database class XML.

If your input database class file references a symbol that doesn't exist, what happens? That's right: You get a compiler error and cannot update any of your public interface files until you correct the problem.

Decoupling Implementation from Design

A nice side-effect that you've probably already noticed is that you completely hide any physical structure names from everyone who uses your coupling class. This means that you can work within whatever naming constraints you might have while leaving all application development efforts unburdened by those same constraints.

Do you have a mandatory prefix before all stored procedures? What about a limit to the number of characters that can be in a table's name? How about a rule that names have underbars between their words? Those all become private concerns of a database design.

Let's take the arbitrary prefix case because it is extremely common. For the sake of argument, let's say you work at an organization where all tables have to have the prefix tbl_, all integer columns have to have the prefix int_, and all character columns have to have the prefix chr_. This means a lot of noise exists in any code that talks to a database, but with the interface encapsulated and decoupled from physical names, it doesn't have to be that way.

Consider the following interface definition:

```
<Interface>
  <Element Id="SimpleTable" Value="tbl_SimpleTable">
    <Element Id="ID" Value="int_ID"/>
    <Element Id="Name" Value="chr_Name" />
  </Element>
</Interface>
```

As long as your code generators use the Id attribute to determine what the name of a variable should be and the Value attribute to determine what the physical name of a structure is, you're in great shape: Neither your database class code nor any client code would have to change in response to these symbol names. Better yet, nowhere is your code littered with those silly prefixes except in the interface file and in actual generated database instances.

Because of this, in regard to the actual physical names assigned to a structure in a database, you can do whatever you want or have to do and no reasonable person should have grounds for complaint.

Sticking Point: Change

There's just one little problem: change.

All the clients to a particular database class should use your coupling class to compile all the SQL they execute. That means your transition tests should be doing this, too. This makes change very problematic. For instance, if you were to get rid of a column from one table and move it to another table, then the interface elements upon which your old transition tests depended would no longer be present, and you would have to find a way to make them work.

The whole point of this process is to allow you to create databases that can change easily and swiftly. Yet, if you change your public design in any interesting way your strong interface falls apart.

The good thing about what I covered in the previous section is that it allows you to document design in a concentrated and concise way, eliminating duplication. The bad thing is that the design document that you've been using so far only documents the current design, essentially moving the problem a lot of development environments have with creation scripts into the area of interface definition.

The solution is to document each version of design separately and generate coupling classes for each version. Naturally, you don't want to redefine the public interface for your entire database with each version you release, so you need a technique for specifying just what changed.

After you've done this, you can couple all of your transition tests to the appropriate coupling class and couple new code to the latest coupling class. Thus, design can progress but transition tests get "left behind," permanently coupled to the version of the design that they specified.

Designs Change Over Time

Consider the following design:

```
<Interface>
  <Element Id="GetModels" />
</Interface>
```

Now imagine that you have the following database class:

```
<Database>
  <Version Number="1">
    <Script>
      <![CDATA[
CREATE TABLE Models(
  ID INT IDENTITY(1, 1),
  Name NVARCHAR(40),
  Size INT)
      ]]>
    </Script>
    <Script>
      <![CDATA[
CREATE PROCEDURE $GetModels
AS
  SELECT ID FROM Models
      ]]>
    </Script>
    <Safeguards>
      <Add Name="ModelIdentities">
        <Sample>EXEC $GetModels</Sample>
      </Add>
    </Safeguards>
  </Version>
</Database>
```

The safeguard in the preceding example might work well for as long as the applicable public interface elements exist. What if the public interface changes?

Let's say that the `GetModels` method name needs to change to `GetModelIdentities` for some reason or other.

Of course, you want to update the `ModelIdentities` safeguard, but you certainly wouldn't want to take it out of the previous versions. For one thing, they might be the foundation of your transition tests for those versions. Also, why should you give up a safeguard for such a dumb reason?

Document All Versions of Design

The way to get around this is for each version to have its own design. I like to keep my specification of the design elements for a given version of a database class with the input for that version. For example, I might rewrite the previous database class as follows:

```
<Database>
  <Version Number="1">
    <Interface>
      <Element Id="GetModels" />
    </Interface>
    <Script>
      <![CDATA[
CREATE TABLE Models(
  ID INT IDENTITY(1, 1),
  Name NVARCHAR(40),
  Size INT)
      ]]>
    </Script>
    <Script>
      <![CDATA[
CREATE PROCEDURE $GetModels
AS
  SELECT ID FROM Models
      ]]>
    </Script>
    <Safeguards>
      <Add Name="ModelIdentities">
        <Sample>EXEC $GetModels</Sample>
      </Add>
    </Safeguards>
  </Version>
</Database>
```

The tool that compiles that into an executable set of database construction scripts can just as easily walk through the design XML when it's embedded in a version element as it would in a separate document. I would also change the way I specified the interface to more represent the transition from one design to another with each version. For instance, I would change it so that I could add or remove design elements as needed with each version.

```
<Database>
  <Version Number="1">
    <Interface>
      <Add Id="GetModels" />
    </Interface>
    <Script><!-- Snipped; same as before --></Script>
    <Safeguards>
      <Add Name="ModelIdentities">
        <Sample>EXEC $GetModels</Sample>
      </Add>
    </Safeguards>
  </Version>
</Database>
```

Having that "delta from the last version" syntax in place gives me the capability to add a new version with my new proposed design.

```
<Version Number="2">
  <Interface>
    <Remove Id="GetModels" />
    <Add Id="GetModelIdentities" />
  </Interface>
  <Script>
    <![CDATA[
sp_rename '$old.GetModels', '$GetModelIdentities'
    ]]>
  </Script>
  <Safeguards>
    <Change Name="ModelIdentities">
      <Sample>EXEC $GetModelIdentities</Sample>
    </Change>
  </Safeguards>
</Version>
```

Note how I dropped the invalid design element in version 2 and added a new one in its place. This enables me to express how my design changed rather than what its final state should be as of version 2. I also modified my safeguard to support the new design. This allows the safeguard to straddle the two designs by having its "before" script coupled to the version 1 design and its "after" script coupled to the version 2 design.

The generated coupling classes can be derived from this script easily. The C# output might look something like the following:

```
public class Models
{
  public class v1
  {
    public _GetModels GetModels
    {
      get { return new _GetModels(); }
    }
```

```
   public class _GetModels
   {
     public override string ToString()
     {
       return "GetModels";
     }
   }
}

public class v2
{
  public _GetModelIdentities GetModelIdentities
  {
    get { return new _GetModelIdentities(); }
  }

  public class _GetModelIdentities
  {
    public override string ToString()
    {
      return "GetModelIdentities";
    }
  }
}
}
```

Of course, if maintaining such a thing by hand, you would want to take measures to minimize duplication. I highly recommend that you don't go down that road as it is costly and error-prone. A discussion of how to minimize the costliness and fragility of hand-rolling a coupling class is outside the scope of the book.

However you choose to implement such a thing, having coupling classes in place enables you to solve this same problem in client code. Simply couple each class to the appropriate version and you're good to go.

Couple to the Correct Version of the Design

Transition tests, for instance, are inherently version-specific things. The transition tests for the upgrade from version 1 to version 2 should always be coupled to version 1 and version 2—"always" as in "forever" as in "the sun should burn out before that coupling changes because 'when that coupling changes' should be 'never.'"

Having version-specific coupling classes enables you to do this. As an example, the transition tests from version 1 to version 2 should look something like the following:

```
[Test]
public void GetModelsBecomesGetModelIdentitiesInV2()
{
  var oldDesign = new Models.v1();
  var newDesign = new Models.v2();

  instantiator.UpgradeToSpecificVersion(connection, 1);

  Assert.That(
    connection.GetStructureDescription(oldDesign.GetModels).Exists,
    Is.True);

  instantiator.UpgradeToSpecificVersion(connection, 2);

  Assert.That(
    connection.GetStructureDescription(oldDesign.GetModels).Exists,
    Is.False);
  Assert.That(
    connection.GetStructureDescription(
      newDesign.GetModelIdentities).Exists,
    Is.True);
}
```

No matter what happens to future designs, that transition test will always exist and always be right without being a party to any duplication. That's pretty neat, right? It still gets a little better.

Sticking Point: Coupling

The rub would appear to be that the bulk of your code needs to couple to whatever the current version is, and the definition of "current" is constantly changing. Imagine having to update five database proxy classes to use version five of your database interface class instead of version four. If that doesn't make your skin crawl, imagine 25.

If that doesn't make you itch even a little, then quit your job, go back to school, and become a therapist for repeat offenders in prison or something like that because your superhuman patience is wasted on our industry.

Seriously, though. You don't want to make 1,000, 20, or even 5 changes every time you change what the current version is. You probably want to change two things: a test, and the definition of what is "current."

Various Clients Couple to Various Versions

Transition tests and transition safeguards each need to couple to at most two versions of a database design, forever and always. In an environment with many and varied deployments, a tool that connects with two databases and translates data between them might need the capability to couple to every supported historical version. End-user applications typically need to couple to the latest deployed version.

More fundamentally, there are often several different clients to any given class of databases and they each could potentially have their own rules for what version of that class they need to connect with.

Having to Change Everything All the Time Is Duplication, Too

The most pressing expression of this problem exists in applications that update frequently and need to always be coupled to the latest version of a database design, which also updates frequently. Listing 5.1 shows a class that connects to the latest version of a bookstore database.

Listing 5.1   BookstoreDatabase *Consumers (C#)*

```
public class BookContainer
{
  private IDbConnection connection;

  public BookContainer(IDbConnection connection)
  {
    this.connection = connection;
  }

  public object AddBook(
    string isbn,
    string title,
    string summary,
    string description,
    double priceUSD)
  {
    var procedure = new BookStoreDatabase.v9().AddBook;
    return connection.ExecuteStoredProcedureScalar(
      procedure,
      new Dictionary<string, object>
      {
        {procedure.ISBN, isbn},
        {procedure.Title, title},
        {procedure.Summary, summary},
        {procedure.Description, description},
        {procedure.PriceUSD, priceUSD},
      });
  }

  public BookData GetBook(object bookID)
  {
    var procedure = new BookStoreDatabase.v9().GetBookByIdentity;
```

```
  var results = connection.ExecuteStoredProcedure(
    procedure,
    new Dictionary<string, object> { { procedure.Identity, bookID } });

  var row = results.First();
  var result = new BookData();

  result.Identity = row[procedure.ResultSet.Identity];
  result.ISBN = (string)row[procedure.ResultSet.ISBN];
  result.Title = (string)row[procedure.ResultSet.Title];
  result.Summary = (string)row[procedure.ResultSet.Summary];
  result.Description = (string)row[procedure.ResultSet. Description];
  result.PriceUSD = Convert.ToDouble(row[procedure.ResultSet.
➥ PriceUSD]);

  return result;
}

public object AddBookReview(object bookID, string title, string body)
{
  var procedure = new BookStoreDatabase.v9().AddReviewToBook;
  return connection.ExecuteStoredProcedureScalar(
    procedure,
    new Dictionary<string, object>
    {
      {procedure.BookIdentity, bookID},
      {procedure.Title, title},
      {procedure.Body, body},
    });
}

public IEnumerable<BookReviewData> GetBookReviews(object bookID)
{
  var procedure = new BookStoreDatabase.v9().GetReviewsForBook;
  var rows = connection.ExecuteStoredProcedure(
    procedure,
    new Dictionary<string, object>
    {
      {procedure.BookIdentity, bookID}
    });

  foreach (var row in rows)
  {
    yield return new BookReviewData
    {
      Identity = row[procedure.ResultSet.ReviewIdentity],
      Title = (string)row[procedure.ResultSet.Title],
      Body = (string)row[procedure.ResultSet.Body],
      UpVotes = Convert.ToInt32(row[procedure.ResultSet.UpVotes]),
      DownVotes = Convert.ToInt32(row[procedure.ResultSet.DownVotes]),
```

```
      Flags = Convert.ToInt32(row[procedure.ResultSet.Flags]),
    };
  }
}

public void AddReviewFeedback(
  object reviewIdentity, ReviewFeedbackType reviewFeedbackType)
{
  var procedure = new BookStoreDatabase.v9().AddResponseToBookReview;
  connection.ExecuteStoredProcedure(
    procedure,
    new Dictionary<string, object>
    {
      {procedure.ReviewIdentity, reviewIdentity},
      {procedure.VoteType, ConvertFeedbackTypeToChar(
➥ reviewFeedbackType)},
    });
}

private string ConvertFeedbackTypeToChar(ReviewFeedbackType type)
{
  switch (type)
  {
    case ReviewFeedbackType.Upvote:
      return "U";
    case ReviewFeedbackType.Downvote:
      return "D";
    case ReviewFeedbackType.Flag:
      return "F";
  }

  throw new InvalidOperationException("Unknown: " + type);
}

public IEnumerable<object> FindBookByKeywordInTitle(string keywords)
{
  var procedure = new BookStoreDatabase.v9().FindBooksByKeywords;

  return connection.ExecuteStoredProcedure(
    procedure,
    new Dictionary<string, object>
    {
      { procedure.Keywords, ProcessKeywords(keywords) },
      { procedure.SearchTitle, 1 },
      { procedure.SearchSummary, 0 },
      { procedure.SearchDescription, 0 },
      { procedure.SearchReviews, 0 },
    }).Select(d => d[procedure.ResultSet.BookIdentity]);
}

public IEnumerable<object> FindBookByKeywordInAnyBookProperty(
  string keywords)
```

```
    {
       var procedure = new BookStoreDatabase.v9().FindBooksByKeywords;

       return connection.ExecuteStoredProcedure(
         procedure,
         new Dictionary<string, object>
         {
            { procedure.Keywords, ProcessKeywords(keywords) },
            { procedure.SearchTitle, 1 },
            { procedure.SearchSummary, 1 },
            { procedure.SearchDescription, 1 },
            { procedure.SearchReviews, 0 },
         }).Select(d => d[procedure.ResultSet.BookIdentity]);
    }

    public IEnumerable<object> FindBookByKeywordAnywhere(string keywords)
    {
       var procedure = new BookStoreDatabase.v9().FindBooksByKeywords;

       return connection.ExecuteStoredProcedure(
         procedure,
         new Dictionary<string, object>
         {
            { procedure.Keywords, ProcessKeywords(keywords) },
            { procedure.SearchTitle, 1 },
            { procedure.SearchSummary, 1 },
            { procedure.SearchDescription, 1 },
            { procedure.SearchReviews, 1 },
         }).Select(d => d[procedure.ResultSet.BookIdentity]);
    }

    private string ProcessKeywords(string keywords)
    {
       return string.Join(" AND ", keywords.Split(' '));
    }
}
```

Now suppose you want to add a version 10 to the bookstore database and that none of those changes affect the design from the perspective of the previous code. What has to be done with it? You would have to go in and change every single point of coupling to reference BookstoreDatabase.v10.

Besides the obvious reason why that is bad, tedium, there is the problem that all duplication has: *Shalloway's Law,*[1] which says that whenever there are multiple places to make a change, at least one was missed. Imagine that law strikes when updating BookContainer and you miss one point of coupling:

---

[1]http://www.netobjectives.com/blogs/shalloway's-law-and-shalloway's-principle

```
public IEnumerable<object> FindBookByKeywordInTitle(string keywords)
{
  var procedure = new BookStoreDatabase.v9().FindBooksByKeywords;

  return connection.ExecuteStoredProcedure(
    procedure,
    new Dictionary<string, object>
    {
      { procedure.Keywords, ProcessKeywords(keywords) },
      { procedure.SearchTitle, 1 },
      { procedure.SearchSummary, 0 },
      { procedure.SearchDescription, 0 },
      { procedure.SearchReviews, 0 },
    }).Select(d => d[procedure.ResultSet.BookIdentity]);
}
```

Furthermore, let's stipulate the corporate policy about how to name stored procedures has changed. Now, every procedure name needs to be formatted as follows: PrimaryEntityName_ActionDescription.

Dutifully, you change the underlying database design with a new version that changes the logical names of every column to comply. This causes a number of clients, including the example code you are working with now, to fail to compile. The person given the task of complying with the new database interface rightly doesn't want to do the task and delegates it to a global find-and-replace operation, missing the coupling to version 9.

It's not the end of the world. Test coverage will tell you that a problem exists when it happens. Decent tests will even give you hints as to what the problem is. Nevertheless, why wait for test feedback against a live database when you can have the compiler tell you about problems like this before you even check in a change? This kind of situation is both common and preventable in our industry.

Introducing the Lens Concept

Consider the following graphical representation of a database's design (see Figure 5.1).

Each of those version-specific coupling classes is like a lens in that it shapes what clients see in a database design. When a client is looking at a database through its version 1 lens, it sees one design (see Figure 5.2).

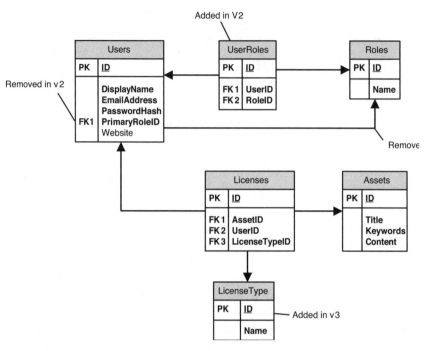

Figure 5.1 *All versions of a design tangled together*

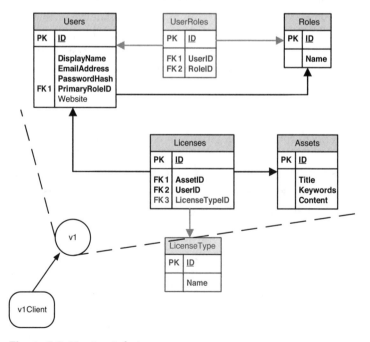

Figure 5.2 *Version 1 design*

When a client looks through its lens for version 2, it sees yet another (see Figure 5.3).

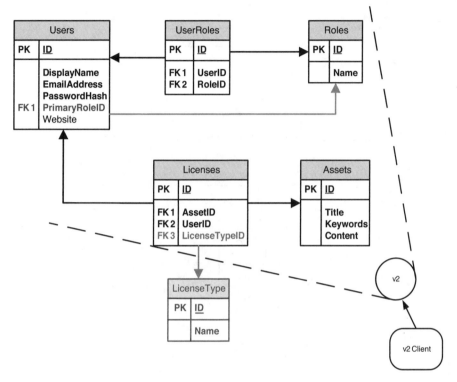

Figure 5.3 *Version 2 view of the assets database class*

Version 3's lens yields yet another view (see Figure 5.4).

It's already been established that all client code should view a database's design through one of these "lenses."

Virtual Lenses

It is true that databases have an actual, inarguable list of transformations they go through. That list is concrete and can only accept additions, never subtractions. For each of those versions, there should definitely be a coupling class that allows a client to access public structures of a database.

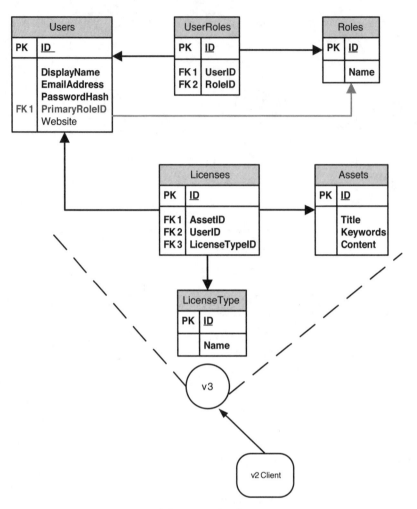

Figure 5.4 *Version 3 view of the assets database*

Suppose I work in an organization with a division in a foreign country. I maintain an application that is used both in the United States and in that country. Primary application development is happening where I live and changes roll out every month.

However, each release has to be localized before it can be deployed in the foreign environment and the overworked team responsible for that takes about three months to finish the job. As a result, database changes lag by approximately one quarter of a year in that part of the world.

To make matters worse, a two-way synchronization problem has to be addressed for some parts of the database, and those parts do occasionally change, at least once per quarter. This means that a special tool has to be written that connects to my deployed database in the U.S. and the foreign one to copy relevant data back and forth. Figure 5.5 depicts this scenario.

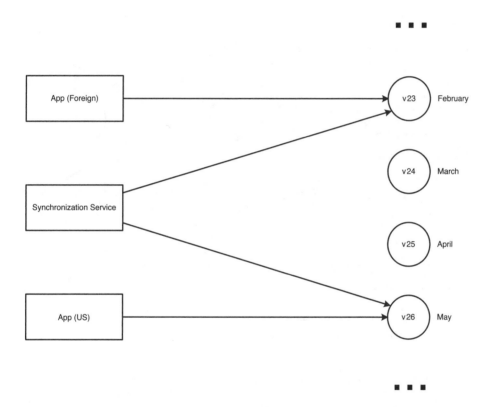

Figure 5.5 *A deployment problem compounds already-complex coupling issues*

This means that my updating problem is doubled. Every time I roll out a new version, I have to point all of my client code at it. Every time the foreign integration team rolls out a version, they have to update the synchronization tool to deal with their new design. That's a hideous process.

However, there's nothing to say that a database design might not also have one or more *virtual* versions. A virtual version is as simple as an alias for another version. To solve the problem I just mentioned, we could install a virtual version that allows my synchronization tool to couple to whatever the foreign deploy-ment version is, as shown in Figure 5.6.

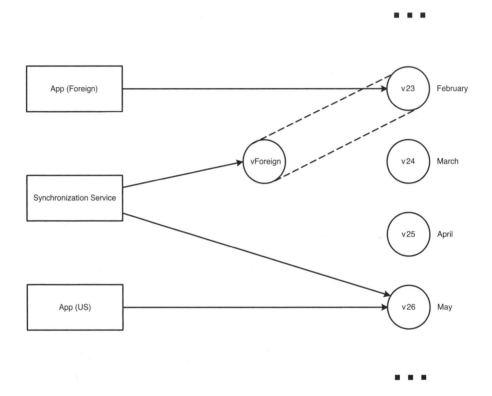

Figure 5.6 *Encapsulating reference to old version for synchronization tool*

Having done that, the foreign development team's job becomes much sim-pler: update the definition of the vForeign virtual version to point to the new version they are getting ready to roll out, and then follow the compiler errors and test failures.

In terms of how you might implement this in your class of databases, you might try something like the following:

```
<Database>
  <Lenses>
    <Map Name="Foreign" ToVersion="23" />
  </Lenses>
```

```
<!-- ... -->
<Version Number="23"><!-- SNIP --></Version>
<Version Number="24"><!-- SNIP --></Version>
<Version Number="25"><!-- SNIP --></Version>
<Version Number="26"><!-- SNIP --></Version>
<!-- ... -->
</Database>
```

Your tool that generates coupling classes can handle that input in whatever manner makes sense for you. It could generate a vForeign class with all the same contents as the version it aliases. In certain languages, it could make a vForeign class that inherits from the aliased version. However you want to deal with it is probably fine as long as it addresses the forces in your development environment.

The "Current" Lens

I'm going to suggest a great candidate for a virtual version that is almost universally useful right now: the "current version" lens. Although it is true that you need to maintain the capability to connect with all supported database versions, it is also true that the vast majority of client code only really cares what the current design actually is. For those clients, the past is interesting only in that it is the means by which you got to the present.

If you take the lagging foreign deployment problem and apply the vCurrent virtual version (see Figure 5.7), then seeing what this buys you is fairly easy.

As I add new versions, I simply point the current lens at the newest version and follow my compiler and test feedback. As the foreign deployment team adds support for versions, they update the vForeign lens and follow the feedback. The addition of a vCurrent lens also enables me to route most of my client coupling through it (see Figure 5.8).

This means that my entire application marches forward whenever I update the vCurrent lens to point to a new version. All the components yell and scream whenever their coupling is no longer valid, and I can keep everything in order as I'm making my changes rather than having consequences trickle in for weeks after a change.

The "New" Lens

A number of people have told me that they believed "The universe was set up to work." Another way to say it, one that corroborates better with my fatalism and agnosticism, is "We define what works as a consequence of how the universe is."

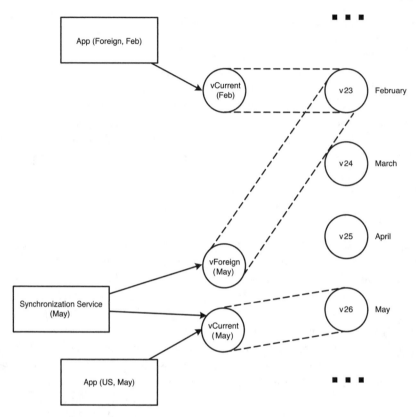

Figure 5.7 *Applications released in February use virtual lenses from that time, as with those deployed in May*

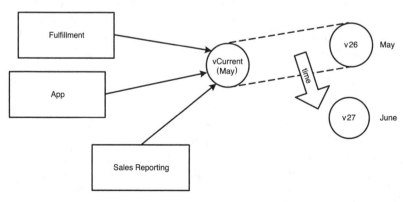

Figure 5.8 *Most clients coupled through* vCurrent *lens, automatically coupling to the latest version*

Any way you slice it, the fundamental observation is the same: When you do things the "right" way, you feel blessed and, when you are doing things "wrong," you feel like a martyr. This is, I think, a great opportunity to listen to the feedback created by the test-driven database development process.

The version-oriented manner in which a database design must be developed is a little more work than client application development in one way but, in another, it is far less work. When changing the design of a "normal" object that lives in a middle tier or user interface application, you often create disruptions—the things dealing with that interface stop working or stop compiling.

Sure, a few people claim you can always avoid this, but I don't really believe them. I've been doing this for what feels like a long time. It is accepted by most that I am very good at it. I have never found a way to always work without creating the occasional disruptive shockwave. I've found ways to take the entire burden on myself and I've found ways to limit the extent of the shockwaves so that they take no more than an hour to remedy, but no way to completely eliminate them.

When developing a database design, however, you have exactly that opportunity because old and new designs not only can, but must, coexist. Consider the design in Figure 5.9.

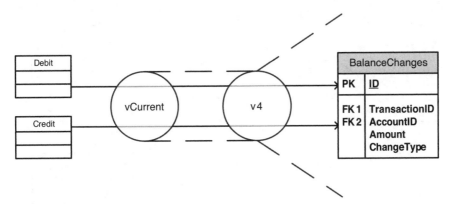

Figure 5.9 *Two classes coupled to current version of a database*

If changing the design of an application object, I would need to reconcile those changes with both clients. However, through the magic of virtual versions, I can avoid this pain and deal with them one at a time. All I have to do is create a vNew virtual version.

Whenever I start working on a new version of my database design, I point the vNew version at it. As clients require new capabilities, I couple them to the vNew version and use them to drive the various features I want into the newest version of my database design. This can be done without any consideration for classes coupled to the current version because that still points to the version out in production (see Figure 5.10).

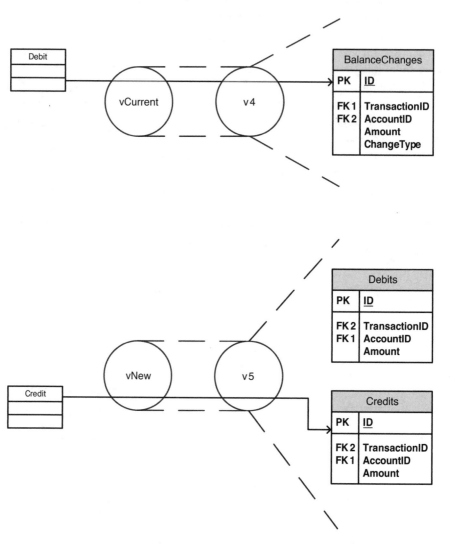

Figure 5.10 *One class coupled to new version, one to current*

I can repeat this process with another client, switching that client over to using the vNew virtual version. After I'm satisfied that I've reconciled all my changes, I can change my current version to point to the newest version, point everything that was in progress back at the current lens, and delete the vNew lens.

If I happen to have missed something, that second step will force me to find it and deal with it. Thus, it is very important that you never roll out a new version of your database with a transient virtual version like one that indicates work in progress. I like to add a test to my test suite that ensures there is no vNew lens. This test typically runs only in continuous integration or when explicitly selected by a developer. That prevents any installers or database deployment artifacts from being generated while open work is in progress and also embarrasses someone who checks in an incomplete change that he easily could have finished.

You might argue that with only two clients, who cares if you have to deal with them all at once? If you're in that boat, I actually agree with you. I wouldn't bother with this technique if the number of client classes is few. However, in a healthy, valuable application, having a small number of database client classes is usually not the case.

Summary

Making the definition of your database's interface a principal component of a database class and using lightweight automation to generate the artifacts you need gives you a lot of power. For one thing, it allows you to concentrate the technical details of a database into a single document, somewhat shielding from them the decisions you make about your logical design.

More importantly, it allows you to project design changes into applications with the same force that any other class author would have. For strong-coupling languages such as C#, C++, Java, and Go, you can prevent bad programs from even being produced. For the weaker languages, you can cause unit tests to fail before they ever connect to the database, with an error that is about as clear as you can get.

That's a simple problem to solve, though. The complexity comes from doing it in such a way as to embrace the many-versioned nature of a database class without introducing duplication into design specifications and without forcing clients to undergo needless changes just to support a new version.

Part of the solution is to express design in an incremental way, associating design changes with their corresponding database versions. The other part is to create logical versions that are merely pointers to physical versions and "float" as designs change. In this way, things that couple to logical versions are forced to update as soon as a breaking change is introduced.

Putting a mechanism like this in place gives you the tools you need to do test-driven development against a database. In the next chapter, you start exploring what TDD means in the database context by defining the primary thing that a test should specify: a behavior.

Chapter 6

Defining Behaviors

One of the things that some people find tricky about test-driving a database design is getting their head around what its behavior actually is. A lot of people tend to think of a database as a thing that is acted upon, rather than a thing that acts. Frankly, much of the time in which someone actually thinks about how a database should behave, they are giving it the wrong behaviors, like adding business rules to a database.

Databases are actually containers for knowledge. They absorb information, store it as knowledge, and then later emit information based upon requests for the knowledge they hold. The ways that a database translates between knowledge and information are its behaviors. Even when you define something seemingly passive, such as a table, you are really telling a database instance that you want a whole slew of storage and retrieval behaviors.

One of the major benefits of test-driven development is that it forces you to think about how a class will interact with its clients. Your test is your first client, and it becomes the major driver for how what it tests exposes its behaviors. After you've crafted your interface, you build the capabilities required to fulfill the need you've demonstrated with your test.

This outside-in way of doing things limits the amount of overbuild present in a design. Rather than building a library of capabilities and then figuring out how to create a solution out of them, you start with a specification of what is needed, then build the capabilities required to fulfill that need.

When test-driving a class of databases, or of any object for that matter, you want every single structure in that class to be justified by a test. Not that you need to explicitly specify every detail of how a database should work in tests, but you should not be able to remove any part of your database design without causing a test to fail.

If you maintain a strong relationship between a class of databases and the tests for it, you will be able to safely change behavior or design, which is the key to a quick turnaround on new requirements.

A New Group of Problems

In previous chapters, I've already outlined and addressed a few problems. Now, it's time to move on to some more subtle issues.

Shortly, I will divide database design into three roles: knowledge, information, and behavior. This might seem like an academic distinction to make. I think it's very important in the database world because it helps us frame behavior with the kind of stuff on which it acts.

A very frequent problem among database developers is a struggle to gain control over the coupling between a database and its clients. Some policies do little to control coupling, allowing applications nearly complete access to a database's implementation details. Others impede the progress of application developers, creating adversarial relationships and inviting developers to find hacks around encapsulation.

Note that both of these problems can exist when the database developer and the application developer are the same person. Let's consider some extreme cases of encapsulating or not encapsulating database design and see where they go.

No Encapsulation

The first case to consider is no encapsulation whatsoever. Just make some tables and couple to them. It's nice because the intimate relationship between the database's design and an application's object model starts out looking very natural. Developers can use a simple mechanism to map their domain objects directly into the database.

Two factors conspire to end the honeymoon very quickly. The first is that, for a successful database, other applications will start to want access to the valuable data therein. The second is that the object model used in an application needs to vary as new requirements come into play.

The precedent of direct coupling to a source-of-record data model makes it likely that new consumers will couple directly to the data as well, creating additional resistance to change with each new client. At the same time, new requirements create a drive to change. The solution is to force the database's design to be add-only, disallowing changes to or removal of existing structures.

The result is a Frankenstein's monster of features. Every time the database has to change, you tack some more structures onto the outside of the existing design, do some work to stitch it together with what's already there, and then bend over backwards in any client that needs those structures to deal with the fact that your data model and your object model are not comparable.

Let's try to not do that.

Hide Everything

Another technique is to hide everything behind (for instance) stored procedures and then prohibit direct access to underlying tables. This is not as bad as full exposure of the database's design but it creates its own host of problems.

The main issue ends up being that you are exposing what is often called a "capabilities interface" rather than a "needs interface." That is, a database that exposes four "CRUD" (create, read, update, and delete) stored procedures for every table forces its clients to couple to its underlying table structure indirectly.

If you had a needs interface, you would never expose the four CRUD operations for a table. Instead, you would expose stored procedures and views that caused the database to do exactly what its client applications needed it to do.

This is a highly flexible kind of interface because it is so narrow. It completely hides your database's design from application logic, so changing a database's design is very easy, at least insofar as coupling is concerned. Adding support for new needs by adding new public-facing structures is easy, and continuing to support older elements of your interface is not that difficult.

From an application developer's standpoint, coupling to a needs interface is a pleasure. You ask it for exactly what you want, and it gives you exactly what you asked for. It is easy to encapsulate in a method that can be mocked out, and the logic of that method is trivial enough that you don't need to write unit tests that simulate talking to a database to ensure that the coupling was done right.

A capabilities interface, on the other hand, is a pain to talk to. You often have to provide extraneous data that is not relevant to you but is necessary on account of some implementation detail or other. You are constantly running the risk of a capability being "extended" and having to update your coupling to account for a feature some other client needs. The mapping between need and capability is non-trivial and must be tested. You get the idea.

Don't build capabilities interfaces and focus instead on needs interfaces.

Business Logic in the Database

"So you want to implement a needs interface." I like to imagine those words emanating from an old reel-to-reel film projector displaying a grainy '50s-style educational video.

A seemingly obvious choice would be to take the logic in an application and move it to the database, turning the database client into a thin wrapper for the database. Many reasons exist for why people believe this should be done, including that pernicious specter who casts a shadow over the entire industry: hypothetical performance benefits. I can think of two good reasons why you should never do this.

One reason is that the programming languages and tools that databases provide are extremely advanced with regard to solving the kinds of problems that databases are meant to solve and extremely primitive with regard to solving the kinds of problems that application logic languages are meant to solve. Solving the right problem in the right place is a big part of turning a feature around quickly and this kind of policy turns database designs into bottlenecks.

Then there's the bigger problem: This isn't really even an attempt to solve the coupling problem at all. Putting business logic in the database all but guarantees it access to any private structure it wants to touch. This creates the exact same potential for accidental coupling that existed when all of your structures are public with the possible mitigation that all the coupling lives in your database code so you have a finite amount of code to sift through to ensure any given change is safe.

Even if neither of these were true, the simple fact that it shifts most of the burden of development to database development and forces all business rules to reconcile against each other in a single place would turn a successful database into an enormous bottleneck.

Don't do this, either.

Knowledge, Information, and Behavior

You are left with a little bit of a conundrum. You want a needs interface with strong encapsulation instead of a capabilities interface or weak encapsulation, but the most obvious route to get there has some serious flaws.

It's probably time to visit the needs that a database might fulfill. A database is typically a piece of a deployed application. All the pieces together are responsible for delivering on users' needs but each individual piece is only responsible for doing its part. Answering the question, "What is a database's part?," is probably the key to the puzzle of how its interface should be shaped.

My answer to that question is that a database's job is to store and retrieve the knowledge an application or applications might accrue in the course of their use. Keep in mind that I'm talking about "source of record" databases, not all database instances. I don't really care about "secondary" databases that much because they can typically be rebuilt pretty easily.

"How does a database get its knowledge and how does it give it back when asked?" you might ask. The answer is "information." Applications inform a database of what they want stored. Later, they ask a database to inform them of something it has persisted.

This all ties in nicely with one of the basic rules of test-driven development: Tests specify behaviors. One of the struggles when test-driving a database is determining what the behaviors actually are but knowing about the distinction between knowledge and information resolves that problem. If databases communicate with information and store knowledge, then something has to translate between the two. That something is behavior and that is what you test.

Another principle of test-driven development is that your test couples to public interface. Knowing that a database communicates with information makes it easy to determine what the public interface you should use is: the units of information sent to and received from a database. Implicit in this is that your tests and your other clients should be protected from the implementation details of how a database accomplishes its task, generally the structures in which a database's knowledge resides.

Therefore, the three basic units of database design are information, knowledge, and behavior. Information is data transmitted from one entity to another that has the potential to influence any course of action taken by the recipient. Knowledge is the stuff that a database stores; not necessarily every bit it stores but the valuable, actionable data it stores. Behavior is how a database converts back and forth between the two.

Understanding databases from this perspective helps you understand what you want to specify when writing tests about them. It also drives you to build databases with public interfaces that do not necessarily map directly to any one application's object model, forcing application development to separate persistence from business logic.

Information

The fundamental mechanism used by all software to deliver value is information. It is not merely data nor is it just data minus noise. Information is data transmitted between two entities that the recipient did not already know. A good way to remember the distinction between information and "just data" is this: Any data that informs its recipient is information.

Thinking about the information that goes into and comes out of a database gives you a nice, clean mechanism for defining interfaces. Do you need to store some data? The data that you need to store are a kind of information, so build a public interface around them. Do you need to retrieve some related data? The shapes of the data that must be retrieved are another kind of information.

Making information in and information out the basis for a contract between applications and databases forces the interface of a database to represent what it should: the needs of the applications that use it. Maintaining such a contract and treating it as part of an application's design in a non-abstract way is also very easy.

Take a look at how you might define a database's external design in terms of information. Imagine that you are developing an application that stores some customer information. The first feature you want to build is the ability to store information about a new customer and retrieve that information for later use.

Of course, the application layer would have to be developed in order to collect this information from a customer and to display it later. If you expose CRUD, you might design a database that has an `insert_Customer` stored procedure.

In that environment, you wouldn't want to have the customer's address be a part of the customer table, so you would create an `Addresses` table and an `insert_Address` stored procedure, forcing application developers to first call `insert_Address`, then take some kind of identity object and pass that into `insert_Customer`. This design is shown in Figure 6.1.

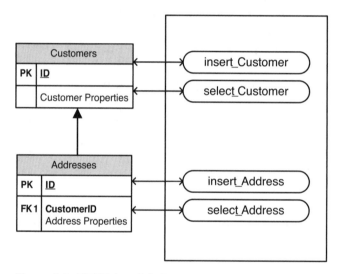

Figure 6.1 *CRUD-based design*

When developing an information-oriented interface, however, you would take a different approach. You would ask yourself, "What kinds of information will the application feed the database?" With only one use case, the answer is pretty simple: The most natural bundle of information for an application to add to a database would be all the customer account data complete with their addresses (see Figure 6.2).

Getting the information out is equally simple: You would only ever want to query a customer record by identity and display all of its data including address. Because you are not coupling directly to the internal design of a class of databases, you can safely constrain your database's search behavior to support only the requirements of today: finding a customer by account-number-password-hash pair and returning all of a customer's data, including a primary address (see Figure 6.3).

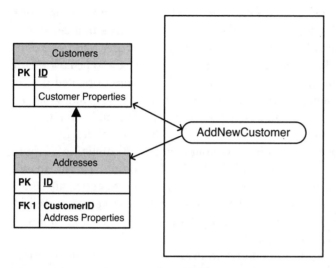

Figure 6.2 *An information-based design for adding customers with addresses*

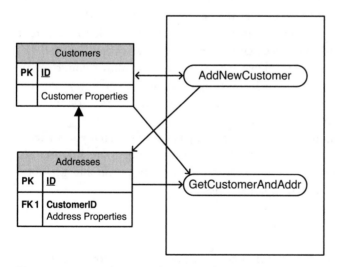

Figure 6.3 *Extending an information-based interface to support reads*

You'll see how this fits into test-driven development in the next section.

Knowledge

Knowledge is the other side of the equation. It is the carefully tended body of facts stored in a database. Its value lies in its ability to be turned back into information upon request. Hence, all the data that can be used to create information are knowledge and all other data are either noise or implementation details.

The basic unit of knowledge-storage is the table. Tables are collection points for facts. If they are publicly available, they also are interface and behavior—the database equivalent of a public member variable in an object-oriented design. When kept private, though, tables really can be treated as passive things that are acted upon by the rest of your database's design—just storage and nothing more.

Later in the book, you will learn a way to keep the internal design you use to store knowledge clean and minimal without giving up its ability to adapt to new requirements. For now, though, it's probably okay to think of a database's internal design in more traditional terms wherein you tend to anticipate future kinds of variation. In fact, it serves the purpose of this chapter quite well by helping you see the distinction between a database's knowledge layer of design and its information layer of design.

In traditional thinking, you would try to break out the various data entities that a database is modeling, storing each kind in its own table and creating relationships between the rows in each table. In the previous example, regardless of the interface you chose, you would probably treat addresses and customers as distinct entities and break them into at least two tables. Depending on the amount of forecasting, you might create an intervening table that creates a many-to-many relationship between customers and addresses (see Figure 6.4).

Separating public interface from private implementation allows you to organize data in any way you want. For instance, you could even go crazy and start out with all of your data being stuck in a so-called "triple-store" (essentially a database within a database; see Figure 6.5).

Regardless of what implementation decision you chose—even if you switched from one to another—the client would never know and, more importantly, would never care as long as the information it wants to put in and get out is supported within reasonable time constraints.

Behavior

If a database were a design sandwich, knowledge and information would be the bread and behavior would be the contents in between. Behavior is what translates information into knowledge or translates knowledge into information.

If your internal design closely mirrors your information in and out, then behavior might be as simple as delegating to the various CRUD behaviors intrinsic to the structures in which your knowledge is stored.

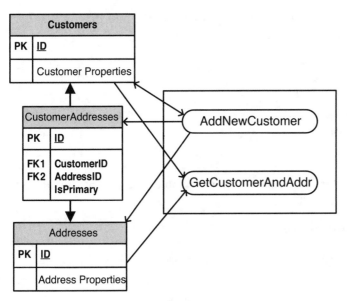

Figure 6.4 *Customers and addresses with a many-to-many relationship built in up front*

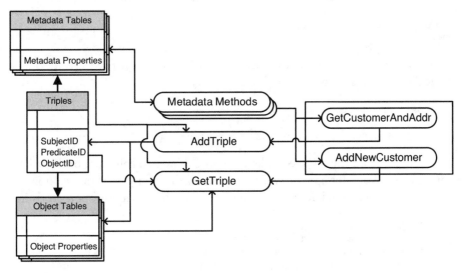

Figure 6.5 *Storing customers and addresses in a triple store*

Following is a table definition that is shaped like the information that goes into and comes out of a primitive database design:

```
CREATE TABLE Customers(
   ID INT IDENTITY(1, 1),
   FirstName NVARCHAR(20) NOT NULL,
   LastName NVARCHAR(20) NOT NULL,
   Address1 NVARCHAR(100) NOT NULL,
   Address2 NVARCHAR(100),
   City NVARCHAR(24),
   State CHAR(2));
```

The stored procedure to create a customer would insert its parameters into the Customers table as follows:

```
CREATE PROCEDURE AddCustomer
   @firstName NVARCHAR(20),
   @lastName NVARCHAR(20),
   @address1 NVARCHAR(100),
   @address2 NVARCHAR(100),
   @city NVARCHAR(24),
   @state CHAR(2)
AS
BEGIN
   INSERT INTO
      Customers(FirstName, LastName, Address1, Address2, City, State)
      VALUES(@firstName, @lastName, @address1, @address2, @city, @state)

   SELECT @@Identity AS ID
END
```

Your GetCustomer stored procedure would just pull a row directly out of your database as follows:

```
CREATE PROCEDURE GetCustomer @id INT
AS
   SELECT * FROM Customers WHERE ID = @id
```

If things are a little more complex, you might have to roll more of the behavior on your own. Suppose you wanted to start with a many-to-many relationship between customers and addresses despite the fact that no application needs it.

```
CREATE TABLE Customers(
   ID INT IDENTITY(1, 1) PRIMARY KEY,
   FirstName NVARCHAR(20) NOT NULL,
   LastName NVARCHAR(20) NOT NULL);

CREATE TABLE Addresses(
   ID INT IDENTITY(1, 1) PRIMARY KEY,
   Address1 NVARCHAR(100) NOT NULL,
   Address2 NVARCHAR(100),
```

```
   City NVARCHAR(24),
   State CHAR(2));

CREATE TABLE CustomerAddresses(
   ID INT IDENTITY(1, 1) PRIMARY KEY,
   CustomerID INT NOT NULL
      FOREIGN KEY REFERENCES Customers(ID),
   AddressID INT NOT NULL
      FOREIGN KEY REFERENCES Addresses(ID));
```

The stored procedure that inserts the information that comes in from an application would then have to be a little bit more clever that with the simpler design.

```
CREATE PROCEDURE AddCustomer
    @firstName NVARCHAR(20),
    @lastName NVARCHAR(20),
    @address1 NVARCHAR(100),
    @address2 NVARCHAR(100),
    @city NVARCHAR(24),
    @state CHAR(2)
AS
BEGIN
  DECLARE @customerID INT
  DECLARE @addressID INT

  INSERT INTO Customers(FirstName, LastName)
    VALUES(@firstName, @lastName);

  SET @customerID = @@Identity;

  INSERT INTO Addresses(Address1, Address2, City, State)
    VALUES(@address1, @address2, @city, @state);

  SET @addressID = @@Identity

  INSERT INTO CustomerAddresses(CustomerID, AddressID)
    VALUES(@customerID, @addressID)

  SELECT @customerID
END
```

As would your getter procedure.

```
CREATE PROCEDURE GetCustomer @id INT
AS
SELECT
    c.ID, c.FirstName, c.LastName,
    a.Address1, a.Address2, a.City AS City, a.State AS State
    FROM Customers c
  INNER JOIN CustomerAddresses ca ON c.ID = ca.CustomerID
  INNER JOIN Addresses a ON ca.AddressID = a.ID
  WHERE c.ID = @id
```

Either way, behavior of persisting information as knowledge and then later retrieving that knowledge as information is what your tests specify.

Outside-In Development

Now that you know the three layers of database design and how tests relate to each, it's time to start test-driving database design. Most of the time in a test-driven development environment, you employ a technique called "test-first." The test-first technique goes as follows:

1. Write a test.

2. See it fail.

3. Make it pass.

4. Repeat.

An implication of this process is that you sometimes write tests against things that don't exist. It makes some people uncomfortable at first but this is actually a good thing: You are driving design into what you are building from its first client rather than adding a capability, then figuring out how to use it.

Defining the Test

The first step is to define the tests. All test examples will be delivered in .NET with NUnit, but you should be able to translate them into whatever your preferred platform demands.

I would start by adding a little bit of infrastructure to your database unit tests. Databases are expensive to create, so put in place something that ensures a database is only created once per test session. I'll leave that as an exercise for you.

Next, write a test that specifies an interesting behavior for the use case of storing a customer with an address. Because you cannot couple your tests to anything but public interface, the only way to really test any behavior is to put some information in and then get it back out of a database instance. In fact, one might argue that without both a write and a read side, no behavior exists at all.

In any case, the test for that behavior might look something like the following example:

```csharp
[Test]
public void AddAndGetCustomer()
{
  var userName = "FooBar";
  var pwHash = "###$$$%%%";
  var address1 = "123 Street Dr.";
  var address2 = (string)null;
  var city = "Citysville";
  var state = "AR";

  connection.ExecuteStoredProcedure(
    design.AddCustomer,
    new Dictionary<string, object>
    {
      { design.AddCustomer.UserName, userName },
      { design.AddCustomer.PasswordHash, pwHash },
      { design.AddCustomer.Address1, address1 },
      { design.AddCustomer.Address2, address2 },
      { design.AddCustomer.City, city },
      { design.AddCustomer.State, state },
    });

  var result = connection.ExecuteStoredProcedure(
    design.GetCustomer,
    new Dictionary<string, object>
    {
      { design.GetCustomer.UserName, userName },
      { design.GetCustomer.PasswordHash, pwHash },
    }).First();

  Assert.That(
    result[design.GetCustomer.ResultSet.UserName],
    Is.EqualTo(userName));
  Assert.That(
    result[design.GetCustomer.ResultSet.Address1],
    Is.EqualTo(address1));
  Assert.That(
    result[design.GetCustomer.ResultSet.Address2],
    Is.EqualTo(address2));
  Assert.That(
    result[design.GetCustomer.ResultSet.City],
    Is.EqualTo(city));
  Assert.That(
    result[design.GetCustomer.ResultSet.State],
    Is.EqualTo(state));
}
```

That test will fail to compile because there is no AddCustomer and no GetCus-tomerByAccountAndPasswordHash stored procedure in the database design.

Growing Interface

After you have a test that specifies interface and underlying behavior, it's time to
add the interface so you can see it fail properly.

```
<Database>
  <Version Number="1">
    <Interface>
      <Add Id="AddCustomer">
        <Add Id="UserName" Value="@userName" />
        <Add Id="PasswordHash" Value="@passwordHash" />
        <Add Id="Address1" Value="@address1" />
        <Add Id="Address2" Value="@address2" />
        <Add Id="City" Value="@city" />
        <Add Id="State" Value="@state" />
      </Add>
      <Add Id="GetCustomer">
        <Add Id="UserName" Value="@userName" />
        <Add Id="PasswordHash" Value="@passwordHash" />
        <Add Id="ResultSet">
          <Add Id="UserName" />
          <Add Id="Address1" />
          <Add Id="Address2" />
          <Add Id="City" />
          <Add Id="State" />
        </Add>
      </Add>
    </Interface>
    <Script>
      <![CDATA[
CREATE PROCEDURE $AddCustomer
    $AddCustomer.UserName NVARCHAR(32),
    $AddCustomer.PasswordHash CHAR(24),
    $AddCustomer.Address1 NVARCHAR(100),
    $AddCustomer.Address2 NVARCHAR(100),
    $AddCustomer.City NVARCHAR(24),
    $AddCustomer.State CHAR(2)
AS
BEGIN
  SELECT 1
END
      ]]>
    </Script>
    <Script>
      <![CDATA[
CREATE PROCEDURE $GetCustomer
  $GetCustomer.UserName NVARCHAR(32),
  $GetCustomer.PasswordHash CHAR(24)
AS
BEGIN
  SELECT 1
END
      ]]>
```

```
        </Script>
      </Version>
  </Database>
```

Recompiling and rerunning your existing test will produce a more interesting failure: The test expected a valid record to be returned but what came back was actually garbage.

Rerunning the test and seeing it fail again might seem unimportant to do, but it really is important. After all, you are going to trust this test to tell you a specified behavior has not been broken or removed for a long time. You want to know that your test fails the way you expected it to when the behavior it specifies is not there or broken.

Growing Behavior and Structures

With a test that fails in a meaningful way, going the rest of the way is permissible. I know what's in the rest of this book, which allows me to go with the simplest possible design for now, secure that I can safely transform that design into something else later on when more requirements appear, so that's what I will do.

The simplest possible design is a single table that stores all the information that comes in from a client and returns them all in a single row. I could start by defining that table and then fill in my stored procedures to talk to the table. However, I want to build my system outside in and starting with a table structure is working inside out. So, I start by filling in my stored procedures.

```
<Script>
CREATE PROCEDURE $AddCustomer
      $AddCustomer.UserName NVARCHAR(32),
      $AddCustomer.PasswordHash CHAR(24),
      $AddCustomer.Address1 NVARCHAR(100),
      $AddCustomer.Address2 NVARCHAR(100),
      $AddCustomer.City NVARCHAR(24),
      $AddCustomer.State CHAR(2)
AS
BEGIN
  INSERT INTO Customers(
    UserName,
    PasswordHash,
    Address1,
    Address2,
    City,
    State)
  VALUES(
    $AddCustomer.UserName,
    $AddCustomer.PasswordHash,
    $AddCustomer.Address1,
    $AddCustomer.Address2,
```

```
      $AddCustomer.City,
      $AddCustomer.State);
END
</Script>
<Script>
CREATE PROCEDURE $GetCustomer
  $GetCustomer.UserName NVARCHAR(32),
  $GetCustomer.PasswordHash CHAR(24)
AS
BEGIN
  SELECT
    UserName,
    Address1,
    Address2,
    City,
    State
  FROM Customers
  WHERE UserName = $GetCustomer.UserName
  AND PasswordHash = $GetCustomer.PasswordHash
END
</Script>
```

I already know my test fails for the right reasons and I know this will fail because the Customers table is missing, so no point exists in rerunning my unit test. Instead, I go on to produce the table.

```
<Script>
CREATE TABLE Customers(
  ID INT IDENTITY(1, 1) PRIMARY KEY,
  UserName NVARCHAR(32),
  PasswordHash CHAR(24),
  Address1 NVARCHAR(100),
  Address2 NVARCHAR(100),
  City NVARCHAR(24),
  State CHAR(2));
</Script>
```

Now that I think my test should pass, I can recompile and rerun my test. Seeing that it passes lets me know that this behavior is now in my database design and allows me to move on to the next behavior. If that next behavior were prohibiting customers with the same login ID, I would write a test that showed an AddCustomer failing the second time it was called with the same login ID.

This process can serve you any time you need to create new behaviors. If you want to alter a behavior, it's not much different: Change the specification for that behavior, see the test fail, alter the behavior, and see it pass.

Justification by Specification

Already, you should have some tools in your toolbelt that help you build more effective database designs that can be changed a little more safely. Being careful about building only those features that are required by your clients, specifying all of them with tests, and only exposing the minimum profile possible, enables you to have a lot more control over your database design than you would otherwise.

Work Against Present Requirements, Not Future

Only work in the context of either getting a test to fail or getting a failing test to pass. Try to avoid forecasting requirements and writing tests for features you think you will someday need. Instead, wait until an application's need to share new information with a database is imminent.

For instance, consider the following list of requirements and assume they are to be implemented in order:

- Create and review owner record

- Add Cat to owner

- Add Dog to owner

- Add Snake to owner

- Add Prescription to Animal

There is an implication of variability and commonality in the last four requirements. You might be tempted to build support for all these features at once. Don't. For one thing, building all that stuff in a batch might feel more efficient, but it's not. I cannot convince you of that in a book; you'll just have to experience it for yourself.

For another, you don't know what's going to happen. New marketing might show that dog and snake owners aren't interested in the product or might show that only dog owners are actually interested. It might even show that snake owners aren't interested, nobody wants their prescriptions tracked, cat owners want to store what wines they drink when they are watching TV with their various cats, and dog owners want to know what beer they tend to drink when they are hunting with a given dog. The point is you just cannot accurately predict the future.

The closer the time you finish building a feature is to when you discover what is truly needed, the better off you'll be. Later chapters show you techniques that will allow you to deliver so fast and with so much confidence that the safest thing to do is to wait for an application to actually expect the existence of a feature in a database and then add it.

For now, though, do whatever you consider to be the minimum amount of safe forecasting is.

Build in Increments

A requirement will almost certainly entail more than one behavior. The finer-grained your unit tests are, the more information they will give you about the health of your database design. Don't arbitrarily divide but don't arbitrarily lump things together either. Spend the time to think about how things are best broken up; no reasonable person would end up regretting it.

Imagine this requirement is what some application developer requires: Add a number of CDs to our inventory model and allow us to discover the number of a particular title on-hand. Sure, you can do that all with a single pair of methods but can you think of multiple behaviors in that requirement? I can. Following are a few:

* Given an empty database, when I query a title, then I get back zero.

* Given an empty database, when I add inventory a few times, then the sum for a title is correct.

Testing those behaviors independently will give you interesting, meaningful feedback on the suitability of your current database design to your requirements.

Limit Access to What Is Specified

Hiding the internal structures of your database from its clients is of the utmost importance. How you do that is not very important. I predict that the most popular mechanism will be to use a database's built-in security model to hide internal items from prying eyes. This might be the only good option available to some.

However, it's not the only option. You could also create a web service and then route all coupling to a database through it. You could create a library of C# or Java files that do the same hiding for you. You could do something else I haven't thought of at the time of this writing.

To settle on a mechanism, you'll need to consider many factors. Is the data publicly or privately available? How much do you trust internal consumers of a database? I imagine that your circumstances will weigh heavily on the way you do it but you definitely must do it.

In addition to hiding the private aspects of a database's design, you must also limit what you provide publicly to those elements you have tested. Hiding from everyone else anything that is not specified to work a certain way by one or more tests will give you a high degree of confidence in what you are providing and your ability to continue providing it after a change.

Summary

Agility and TDD can only work if you keep a database design open to change. What it takes to remain open to change, however, is something that people have struggled with. The oft-asked question, "How much do we encapsulate?" is not the right one to be asking. The right question is, "What do we encapsulate?"

If you believe, as I do, that knowledge, behavior, and information are the three fundamental elements of database design, then the answer is simple and clean. You expose the information needed to fulfill requirements while encapsulating behavior and knowledge.

Doing that in an aggressive way is what gives you the flexibility to support the needs of a database design's client applications. That is true for a single client and gets more prominent as client diversity increases.

Most importantly, designing to information gives you control over and understanding of what expectations clients to a database might have. Those are precious commodities for developers.

This strength of encapsulation gives a database developer complete control over how a database works. I believe this is an essential component to being able to change a database's design. After all, if everyone under the sun is coupled to your databases' implementation details, how could you ever hope to change their design? The next chapter, "Building for Maintainability," provides my view on how best to lay out the inner workings of a database to help you embrace changes in requirements later.

Chapter 7

──────

Building for Maintainability

Designing databases that can easily be maintained is important. In the application development domain, developers learned that the most maintainable things are often the things with the simplest designs that support the current requirements. That also applies in the database world as well.

Building a maintainable database depends on developing only the minimum amount of behavior required to support the current needs of the applications that use a database design. The minimum amount of behavior required is that amount that is necessary to absorb and emit the information demanded by a database's clients.

With databases, specifying only those behaviors that are actually needed is difficult, so hiding from clients any behavior that is merely an implementation detail or side effect of what they demand is important. If you don't hide such things, your clients *will* couple to them. This parallels the application-development axiom: *Encapsulate by practice, expose by exception.*

I believe I've already established that history is a far more important thing for database development than it typically is for an object-oriented design. Jealously and proactively guarding the safety of the knowledge stored in a database is imperative.

That entails some things you've learned already, such as transition testing and transition safeguarding. My belief is that not continuously maintaining the manner in which data is stored is at least as much of a threat to data integrity as changing data structures. So preserving knowledge also requires that you carefully consider and reconsider the way in which data is arranged.

Keeping designs minimal but correct is important, and there's just one little snag—the definition of what is "minimal" and what is "correct" is a moving target. Don't try to get out ahead of the target, but also don't allow yourself to lag behind. Keeping things light and correct puts you in a position to adjust your database when a new requirement makes it too light or incorrect.

115

Never Worry About the Future

Not investing any infrastructure in building toward future features is of the utmost importance. When you want to march a bunch of Roman soldiers south to crush the Samnites, infrastructure works great: You can build a road to a place because the place isn't going to move.

Product development doesn't work that way. Designing for future requirements is like building a stadium to hold a bunch of people in anticipation of a UFO sighting because that's your best guess as to where the next phenomenon will occur. People can predict the future, and they do it all the time—just not accurately. Putting your energies into things that you know you need is far better than speculating on what might happen someday.

An excellent tool for maintaining focus on what is needed now is the information transmitted between a class of databases and its clients. Information is the database parallel to the concept of an interface in an object-oriented language.

A side effect of this is that all the implementation details of all the behaviors your database has are encapsulated. Such encapsulation costs you almost nothing to implement and will pay you back frequently.

Look for Opportunities in the Now

Instead of building features that might be needed in the future but probably won't, take that energy and split it three ways. First, deliver on more requirements that are definitely needed now. Second, invest in improving the quality of your database class. Finally, invest in improving your skills as a developer in some way. The dividends from those three activities are far more likely to exceed the cost than speculation.

Consider the following scenario. You work in a larger team and you are responsible for the database design. Your team is slated to finish five user stories in the next 45 days:

- As a user, I want to log in so that I can access the system with the right privileges.

- As a customer, I want to submit a plain text search so that someone can start to find what I want.

- As a customer, I want to select a category for a submitted search so that an expert can find it.

- As a search agent, I want to find the next search in my area of expertise so that I can fulfill it.

- As a search agent, I want to recommend a link for a search so that the customer can pursue it.

Suppose for the sake of argument that you decide that building a data model for all those features at once will be more efficient than delivering them incrementally. Let's also assume no chance exists that those five stories won't be done in the prescribed 45-day window. Those are both bogus assumptions but, even if they had a grain of truth to them, an important reason still exists for only delivering on the requirement the team is building now: order.

You know for a fact that the login and logout will be done first—you have no way to do anything with the system until those parts are done. So you have an enormous incentive to get the data backing for that story done quickly. The sooner you get the data backing ready, the sooner the whole thing can be tested and put in front of a customer representative.

On the other hand, if the team has to wait for you to get the entire data model done before they can hook their software up to a realistic database, real testing efforts will be blocked until you are done. If it takes you 20 days to deliver everything, then testing is held up for 20 days. If it takes you 5 days to build one of those stories alone, testing is held up for 5 days. Which sounds better to you?

Design to Information

The application development world uses the phrase, "design to interfaces." The source of the wisdom is ancient enough that I'm not going to try and figure out who it is. As far as I'm concerned, it's one of those gifts of antiquity, like the bow and arrow. I'm pretty sure that the Gang of Four popularized it, though.

In any case, it's an extremely valuable way of designing classes of objects in middle-tier and front-end environments. It causes you to build good, narrow, clean interfaces. The primary function of these interfaces is to shape the interaction between two objects. A side effect is that they shape the very implementation details they hide in an extremely positive manner.

Consider the following code (C#):

```csharp
public int ProcessRequest(int code, int modifier, int value)
{
  var newValue = value;

  switch (code)
  {
    case 0:
      newValue *= 10;
      break;
    case 1:
      newValue /= 10;
```

```
      break;
    }

    switch (modifier)
    {
      case 0:
        newValue = (newValue * newValue) / newValue;
        break;
      case 1:
        newValue = -newValue;
        break;
      case 2:
        newValue = newValue % 1000;
        break;
    }

    return newValue;
}
```

Now compare it to this code:

```
public class RequestProcessor
{
  public int ProcessRequest(
    ValueManipulator op1, ValueManipulator op2, int value)
  {
    var newValue = op1.ManipulateValue(value);
    newValue = op2.ManipulateValue(newValue);

    return newValue;
  }
}

public abstract class ValueManipulator
{
  public abstract int ManipulateValue(int v);
}

public class TimesTen : ValueManipulator
{
  public override int ManipulateValue(int v)
  {
    return v * 10;
  }
}
// ...
```

At the very minimum, the latter is easier to draw in a meaningful way than the former, as demonstrated by Figure 7.1.

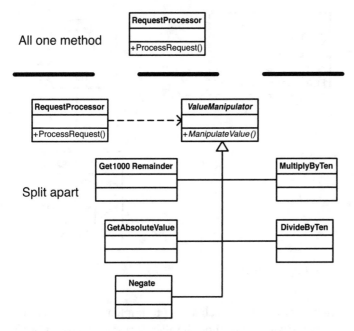

Figure 7.1 *Two different kinds of design drawn as a UML static structure diagram*

In addition, in the latter design, implementation details can be changed without affecting most of the code, as with the following code:

```
public class ScaleUp : ValueManipulator
{
  public override int ManipulateValue(int v)
  {
    return v << 3;
  }
}
```

The analog in the database world is, "design to information." That is, make the kinds of information sent and received by your database the focal point of design. Rigorously analyze and refine it so that it supports client applications but does no more, and build the backing structures' private implementation details.

I find that, at the time of this writing, stored procedures are an excellent mechanism for focusing a database's interface into discrete inputs and outputs that can easily be tested. Let's consider those five requirements for the custom search application from the last section. A very reasonable design for the knowledge containers might be something like Figure 7.2.

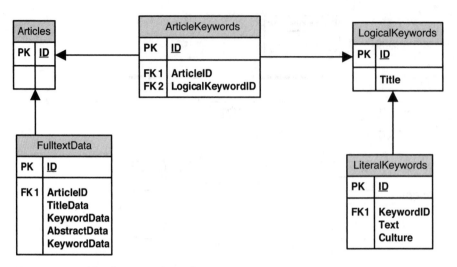

Figure 7.2 *Tables for a search application*

However, that design grants way too much access to implementation details. Clients would quickly become coupled to those implementation details and you would lose your ability to change them. If you make all the tables private and build stored procedures to support the requirements (see Figure 7.3), you can have as much flexibility as you need going forward.

That does what you want it to do without tying your hands against future changes.

One last thing I want to add is this: Don't trust people to avoid coupling on their own. It's not that people's intentions can't be trusted; typically they can. It's that you cannot trust someone to not make a mistake or do something wrong "just for now."

Instead of trusting people, use whatever built-in publicity/privacy or security features your database platform of choice provides, as shown in Figure 7.4.

Doing so forces people to connect through the public interface. Nobody worth their salt looks askance at me when I say, "Use the public interface for that class instead of poking data into one of its members." In fact, I haven't even had to tell anyone that for a long time.

Why should you accept any less encapsulation for a class of databases?

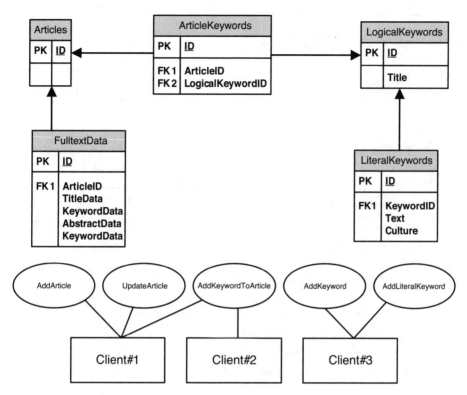

Figure 7.3 *Search application tables hidden behind stored procedures*

Translate Info and Knowledge with Behavior

This doesn't mean I'm a "stored procedure fan," mind you. I actually hate nine out of every ten stored procedures I meet because they typically add complexity to an already-complex and overexposed design. Use stored procedures and views to *expose* behaviors you have hidden rather than to *add* behaviors that don't already exist. If you are using those kinds of secondary structures to add behavior, you are probably doing something in a database that should be done in the middle tier.

Here's an example of that principle. Consider the database design in Figure 7.5.

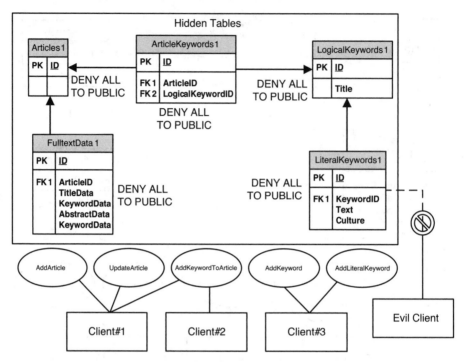

Figure 7.4 *Search applications hidden behind stored procedures with privileges denied*

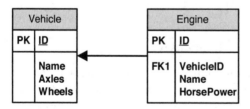

Figure 7.5 *A parent-child relationship*

If clients are coupled to those tables, then the foreign-key relationship between those two tables becomes part of the contract between your class of databases and any clients. At that point, it cannot easily be changed.

What do you do if you want to promote engines to be first-class entities that have a many-to-many relationship with vehicles? There could be any number of clients that execute something along the lines of the following SQL:

```
SELECT * FROM Vehicles v INNER JOIN Engines e on v.ID = e.VehicleID
```

Even though they never really cared about the data for that relationship, they are forced to deal with it. Now that you want to change the nature of said relationship, you're going to have to go deal with who knows how many clients and change how they get the set of engines that relate to a vehicle.

On the other hand, imagine those details were hidden behind a stored procedure, as shown in Figure 7.6.

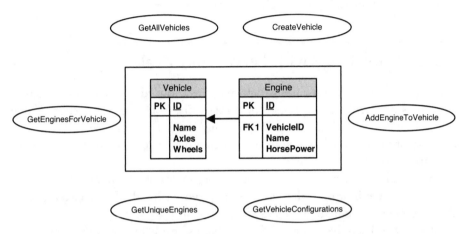

Figure 7.6 *Parent-child relationship hidden behind an information-oriented interface*

If you want to promote engines to become a kind of primary entity that is cross referenced with vehicles in that design, it's a snap. You have one place that actually touches the tables for each kind of signal sent to or by a database: a stored procedure. The new design is shown in Figure 7.7. You'll also need to add some new stored procedure to expose the additional kinds of information a database could send or receive.

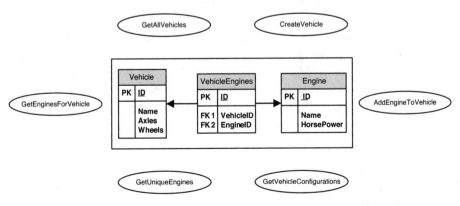

Figure 7.7 *Refactored table structures hidden behind the same stored procedures*

For instance, assume `GetVehicleConfigurations` returned the number of axles, wheels, and horsepower associated with possible `Vehicle-Engine` pairing. That stored procedure would simply need a different join than the one it had when the tables were arranged as parent and child. `AddEngineToVehicle` could be changed to favor existing engines with the same name and horsepower over creating a new one. If you did that, then you could make `GetUniqueEngines` much simpler.

Guard Knowledge with Fervor and Zeal

I've already given you some tools to protect the knowledge stored in your database. It is no accident that those tools focus on protecting knowledge in the course of a design change. My position is that the *only* way to truly protect the integrity of the knowledge in your database is to change its shape frequently to support new features as needed.

Unnatural designs invite the most pernicious threat of all into the place where your knowledge is stored: the well-meaning workaround. If you haven't seen this, you are very young, very lucky, or very blind.

The way to keep the contents of a database safest is by always storing them in the simplest design possible given the problem space. If a design is a natural expression of the shape of the knowledge going into a database, then it invites proper use.

Not Changing Is the Most Dangerous Choice

I've seen numerous cases where databases couldn't change quickly enough to avoid being a thorn in application-development's side and the response was to go around the design of the database. Structured data in text/blob fields is always a favorite and seldom appropriate.

Making a VARCHAR/CHAR column store multiple values separated by a delimiter is another thing I've actually seen done with my own eyes. My favorite, though, is when people store extra information in a packed structure because they can't get past their organization's change-management structures.

Here is an example just because it's been so long since there has been one:

```
<Database>
  <Version Number="1">
    <Script>
<![CDATA[
CREATE TABLE Cookies(
  ID INT IDENTITY(1, 1),
  Name NVARCHAR(40),
```

```
    Description NTEXT,
    Price NUMERIC(9, 2))
]]>
    </Script>
  </Version>
</Database>
```

If my application needs to store name, price, and description, then I'm likely to use that database design as intended. What if my application also stores ingredients? Maybe I'll write some code like the following:

```
private string PackDescription(Cookie cookie)
{
  var description = cookie.Description;
  description += @"
###INGREDIENTS";

  foreach (var ingredient in cookie.Ingredients)
  {
    description += Environment.NewLine + ingredient;
  }

  return description;
}

private void UnpackDescription(Cookie result, string description)
{
  var lines = description.Split(
    new[] { Environment.NewLine },
    StringSplitOptions.None);

  var index = Array.IndexOf(lines, "###INGREDIENTS");
  if (index >= 0)
  {
    result.Description = string.Join(Environment.NewLine, lines.
Take(index));
    result.Ingredients = lines.Skip(index + 1).ToArray();
  }
  else
  {
    result.Description = description;
  }
}
```

That kind of works...mostly. What if my application needs to know whether there are peanuts in a cookie? That's a life-critical fact and is too important to rely upon someone going in and editing the list of ingredients correctly. I need a separate flag for that, but there isn't a good place to put it, so I'll create another hack that packs critical warnings into the title field, as in the following code:

```
private static string PackTitle(Cookie cookie)
{
  return cookie.Title + "#WARNINGS#" + cookie.HasPeanuts;
}

private void UnpackTitle(Cookie result, string title)
{
  var divider = @"#WARNINGS#";
  var index = title.IndexOf(divider);
  if (index >= 0)
  {
    result.Title = title.Substring(0, index);
    result.HasPeanuts =
      bool.Parse(title.Substring(index + divider.Length));
  }
  else
  {
    result.Title = title;
  }
}
```

These are the deadliest threats of all. If you mess up the data in a table while performing surgery, you're probably going to notice and restore the backup you probably took prior to making any changes. If someone puts in place application logic that starts drip-feeding poorly designed data into a database, the odds are that you will not find out for months.

By the time you do figure it out, the sheer weight of the existing data will have converted a design flaw into a standard. The cost of cleaning up the mess will be huge because of the coupling between client application rules and these data structures. The cost of not cleaning up the mess will also be high as demand for access to the knowledge stuffed into the makeshift structures is likely to increase over time.

Sadly, you cannot stop people from doing these things no matter what you do.

Keep Your Design Natural

On the other hand, these kinds of design choices are typically acts of desperation in the face of almost insurmountable political barriers. So, while there is no number of sticks you can put in place to beat people away from inflicting such horrors on your database design, even the tiniest carrot will usually do the trick.

Remember, packing and unpacking structured data into a character array is a dirty thing. It embarrasses application developers to do every bit as much as it enrages data developers. If your database design is clean and amply tends to the needs of its clients, application developers won't want to do naughty things to it.

If in the previously mentioned scenario, the database design looked more like Figure 7.8, then all my code to talk to the database would produce clean data that is shaped as the design intended.

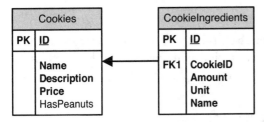

Figure 7.8 *The cookies database changes to fulfill new requirements*

This, I think, is where the impulse to overdesign a database comes from in the first place. If you can't change a database, and people will write code that corrodes its integrity over time when you don't give them a feature they want, then the only option left is to try to predict every feature that anyone might ever want and provide them all.

Deal with the Future When It Happens

I think it's becoming clear that the "you can't change a design" premise is not really true. In databases, as with application frameworks, overdesign makes changing something harder. Likewise, coupling to implementation details can make change harder. In a database, specifically, the value in existing data makes you a little skittish, too. However, if you keep your design small, encapsulate how requests are fulfilled, and use the tools I've given you to mitigate any risk posed to existing data, then you are in a position to respond to the future as it unfolds rather than try to predict it.

The way to do that might even be obvious to you at this point but, in case it's not, I'm going to state it anyway. You start by identifying what the new design should be. This usually means writing a new unit test or updating the specification for an existing behavior.

Next you'll introduce the minimal change required to make the new or changed test pass. This might require creating a new version of your database class. It will almost certainly require you to create or modify one or more transition tests and safeguards to document how the feature should actually come into existence.

Then you'll make sure all tests pass. When all of your transition tests pass, you know that your database class builds databases in a manner that does not defy what happened in the past. When all of your unit tests pass, you'll know that the latest version of your database is operating as specified. The two together let you know that what you have is safe to release.

Define New Design

Let's reconsider the design of the database that tracks cookie inventory. Imagine that design has been encapsulated as previously discussed and that the class of databases is fully encased in transition tests, as shown in Figure 7.9.

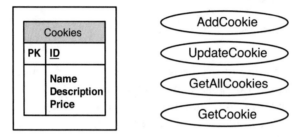

Figure 7.9 *Encapsulated design as a starting point*

Adding support for a new feature, like the ingredients list, would start with writing a test like the following:

```
[Test]
public void AddIngredientToCookieTest()
{
    var id = connection.ExecuteStoredProcedureScalar(
        design.AddCookie,
        new Dictionary<string, object>
        {
            { design.AddCookie.Name, "name" },
            { design.AddCookie.Description, "desc" },
            { design.AddCookie.Price, 1.95 },
        });

    var addSP = design.AddIngredientToCookie;
    connection.ExecuteStoredProcedure(
        addSP,
        new Dictionary<string, object>
        {
            { addSP.CookieID, id },
            { addSP.Amount, 1.34 },
            { addSP.Unit, "cup" },
            { addSP.Name, "flour" },
        });
```

```
var getSP = design.GetIngredientsForCookie;
var row = connection.ExecuteStoredProcedure(
  getSP,
  new Dictionary<string, object>
  {
    { getSP.CookieID, id },
  }).First();

Assert.That(row[getSP.Amount], Is.EqualTo(1.34));
Assert.That(row[getSP.Unit], Is.EqualTo("cup"));
Assert.That(row[getSP.Name], Is.EqualTo("flour"));
}
```

When that test fails, it does so because there is no `AddIngredientToCookie` or `GetIngredientsForCookie` stored procedure.

Introduce Minimal Changes

Because the most recent version of this database class has been released into production, I'll start by adding a new version.

```
<Version Number="2" />
```

Then I'll add a transition test that requires an `AddIngredientToCookie` method to be added.

```
[Test]
public void v2_AddIngredientToCookie()
{
  var design = new CookiesEmergentDesign.v2();
  instantiator.UpgradeToSpecificVersion(connection, design);
  var procedure = design.AddIngredientToCookie;

  var desc =
    connection.GetStructureDescription(procedure);

  Assert.That(desc.Exists);
  var parameters = desc.GetParameters();
  Assert.That(parameters.Length, Is.EqualTo(4));
  Assert.That(
    parameters[0].Name,
    Is.EqualTo((string)procedure.CookieID));
  Assert.That(
    parameters[1].Name,
    Is.EqualTo((string)procedure.Amount));
  Assert.That(
    parameters[2].Name,
    Is.EqualTo((string)procedure.Unit));
  Assert.That(
    parameters[3].Name,
    Is.EqualTo((string)procedure.Name));
}
```

This test would not compile, either, so I'll extend the interface for my database design as of version 2 to support the `AddIngredientToCookie` stored procedure.

```
<Version Number="2">
  <Interface>
    <Add Id="AddIngredientToCookie">
      <Add Id="CookieID" Value="@id" />
      <Add Id="Amount" Value="@amount" />
      <Add Id="Unit" Value="@unit" />
      <Add Id="Name" Value="@name" />
    </Add>
  </Interface>
</Version>
```

My test still fails to compile because `GetIngredientsForCookie` is not defined, so I'll repeat the process and add a transition test for that stored procedure.

```
[Test]
public void v2_GetIngredientsForCookie()
{
  var design = new CookiesEmergentDesign.v2();
  instantiator.UpgradeToSpecificVersion(connection, design);
  var procedure = design.GetIngredientsForCookie;

  var desc =
    connection.GetStructureDescription(procedure);

  Assert.That(desc.Exists);
  var parameters = desc.GetParameters();
  Assert.That(parameters.Length, Is.EqualTo(1));
  Assert.That(
    parameters[0].Name,
    Is.EqualTo((string)procedure.CookieID));
}
```

That, again, will fail to compile; a condition that is rectified by adding the following code to the interface specification:

```
<Interface>
  <Add Id="AddIngredientToCookie">
    <Add Id="CookieID" Value="@id" />
    <Add Id="Amount" Value="@amount" />
    <Add Id="Unit" Value="@unit" />
    <Add Id="Name" Value="@name" />
  </Add>
  <Add Id="GetIngredientsForCookie">
    <Add Id="CookieID" Value="@id" />
    <Add Id="Amount" />
    <Add Id="Unit" />
```

```
      <Add Id="Name" />
    </Add>
  </Interface>
```

That will compile, but the test will fail for want of the specified stored procedure in my database. When it does, I can extend my database class to contain a stubbed-out `AddIngredientToCookie` stored procedure.

```
<Script>
  <![CDATA[
CREATE PROCEDURE $AddIngredientToCookie
  $AddIngredientToCookie.CookieID INT,
  $AddIngredientToCookie.Amount NUMERIC(6, 2),
  $AddIngredientToCookie.Unit NVARCHAR(16),
  $AddIngredientToCookie.Name NVARCHAR(32)
AS
BEGIN
  SELECT 0
END
  ]]>
</Script>
```

The test still fails, though, so I'll also need to stub out the specified stored procedure. When all is said and done, the stubbed-out version will be equivalent to what follows:

```
<Script>
  <![CDATA[
CREATE PROCEDURE $GetIngredientsForCookie
  $GetIngredientsForCookie.CookieID INT
AS
  SELECT
    0 AS $GetIngredientsForCookie.Amount,
    'lbs' AS $GetIngredientsForCookie.Unit,
    'concrete' AS $GetIngredientsForCookie.Name
]]>
</Script>
```

That will get my unit test failing because the right interface exists in my database design but it has no behavior.

Get Tests Passing

The final step is to update the design to support the new feature. Doing that is not hard, either. Start by specifying how one of the stored procedures should function.

```
<Script>
  <![CDATA[
CREATE PROCEDURE $AddIngredientToCookie
```

```
  $AddIngredientToCookie.CookieID INT,
  $AddIngredientToCookie.Amount NUMERIC(6, 2),
  $AddIngredientToCookie.Unit NVARCHAR(16),
  $AddIngredientToCookie.Name NVARCHAR(32)
AS
BEGIN
  INSERT INTO CookieIngredients(CookieID, Amount, Unit, Name)
  VALUES(
    $AddIngredientToCookie.CookieID,
    $AddIngredientToCookie.Amount,
    $AddIngredientToCookie.Unit,
    $AddIngredientToCookie.Name)

  SELECT @@Identity
END
]]>
</Script>
```

That causes the database-build to not work, so the next thing to do is demand that the appropriate table be built.

```
[Test]
public void v2_CookieIngredientsTable()
{
  instantiator.UpgradeToSpecificVersion(
    connection,
    new CookiesEmergentDesign.v2());

  var desc = connection.GetStructureDescription("CookieIngredients");
  Assert.That(desc.Exists);
  Assertions.AssertColumnDetails(desc, "ID", "int");
  Assertions.AssertColumnDetails(desc, "CookieID", "int");
  Assertions.AssertColumnDetails(desc, "Amount", "numeric", 6, 2);
  Assertions.AssertColumnDetails(desc, "Unit", "nvarchar", 16);
  Assertions.AssertColumnDetails(desc, "Name", "nvarchar", 32);
  Assert.That(desc.GetIdentity("ID").Exists);
}
```

Driven by the previous test, I'll add the code to build the CookieIngredients table (following):

```
<Script>
  <![CDATA[
CREATE TABLE CookieIngredients(
  ID INT IDENTITY(1, 1),
  CookieID INT,
  Amount NUMERIC(6, 2),
  Unit NVARCHAR(16),
  Name NVARCHAR(32))
]]>
</Script>
```

At this point, all of my transition tests are passing but my unit test is still failing because the GetIngredientsForCookie stored procedure also needs to be implemented. So I'll do that.

```
<Script>
  <![CDATA[
CREATE PROCEDURE $GetIngredientsForCookie
  $GetIngredientsForCookie.CookieID INT
AS
  SELECT
    Amount AS $GetIngredientsForCookie.Amount,
    Unit AS $GetIngredientsForCookie.Unit,
    Name AS $GetIngredientsForCookie.Name
  FROM CookieIngredients
  WHERE CookieID = $GetIngredientsForCookie.CookieID
]]>
</Script>
```

Doing that causes my unit test to pass.

> **Note**
>
> Please don't get hung up on little things like my using a different naming convention than what you think is "right" or my not putting a foreign-key reference where pretty much everyone in the world would. You probably already know how to make those kinds of design decisions, so there isn't much value in my trying to "teach" them to you. As a result, a lot of the time, I'm making the conscious decision to be as concise as I can.

Stop, Think, Refactor

Now it's time to consider whether or not the internal design is good enough. The last step before moving on to the next unit test is always to take a moment to consider your design.

Immediately, the fact that the CookieIngredients table would cause the string "Sugar" to be duplicated for virtually every cookie jumps out at me. After you have passing tests, you can safely refactor so let's do that. I'll start with the transition tests. Because I haven't released this change, I can just change my transition tests and the corresponding transition.

```
[Test]
public void v2_CookieIngredientsTable()
{
  instantiator.UpgradeToSpecificVersion(connection, new
➥CookiesEmergentDesign.v2());
```

```
    var desc = connection.GetStructureDescription("CookieIngredients");
    Assert.That(desc.Exists);
    Assertions.AssertColumnDetails(desc, "CookieID", "int");
    Assertions.AssertColumnDetails(desc, "IngredientID", "int");
        Assertions.AssertColumnDetails(desc, "Amount", "numeric", 6, 2);
        Assertions.AssertColumnDetails(desc, "Unit", "nvarchar", 16);
    }

    [Test]
    public void v2_IngredientsTable()
    {
        instantiator.UpgradeToSpecificVersion(
            connection, new CookiesEmergentDesign.v2());

        var desc = connection.GetStructureDescription("Ingredients");
        Assert.That(desc.Exists);
        Assertions.AssertColumnDetails(desc, "ID", "int");
        Assertions.AssertColumnDetails(desc, "Name", "nvarchar", 32);
        Assert.That(desc.GetIdentity("ID").Exists);
    }
```

Those tests will fail, allowing me to safely change how instances of the second version of my database class are built as follows:

```
<Script>
  <![CDATA[
CREATE TABLE Ingredients(
   ID INT IDENTITY(1, 1),
   Name NVARCHAR(32))

CREATE TABLE CookieIngredients(
   CookieID INT,
   IngredientID INT,
   Amount NUMERIC(6, 2),
   Unit NVARCHAR(16))
]]>
</Script>
```

Naturally, because the table structure has changed, I would also have to update how my stored procedures are defined as well. Again, because this is all happening before I've released version 2 of my database class into the wild, I can just keep updating version 2 rather than adding new versions.

```
<Script>
  <![CDATA[
CREATE PROCEDURE $AddIngredientToCookie
  $AddIngredientToCookie.CookieID INT,
  $AddIngredientToCookie.Amount NUMERIC(6, 2),
  $AddIngredientToCookie.Unit NVARCHAR(16),
  $AddIngredientToCookie.Name NVARCHAR(32)
AS
BEGIN
```

```
DECLARE @IngredientID INT
SET @IngredientID = (
  SELECT ID
  FROM Ingredients
  WHERE Name = $AddIngredientToCookie.Name);

IF @IngredientID IS NULL
BEGIN
  INSERT INTO Ingredients(Name)
  VALUES($AddIngredientToCookie.Name)

  SET @IngredientID = @@Identity;
END

INSERT INTO CookieIngredients(CookieID, IngredientID, Amount, Unit)
VALUES(
  $AddIngredientToCookie.CookieID,
  @IngredientID,
  $AddIngredientToCookie.Amount,
  $AddIngredientToCookie.Unit)

SELECT @@Identity
END
]]>
</Script>
<Script>
  <![CDATA[
CREATE PROCEDURE $GetIngredientsForCookie
  $GetIngredientsForCookie.CookieID INT
AS
  SELECT
    ci.Amount AS $GetIngredientsForCookie.Amount,
    ci.Unit AS $GetIngredientsForCookie.Unit,
    i.Name AS $GetIngredientsForCookie.Name
  FROM CookieIngredients ci
  INNER JOIN Ingredients i
  ON i.ID = ci.IngredientID
  WHERE ci.CookieID = $GetIngredientsForCookie.CookieID
]]>
</Script>
```

I'm much more satisfied with that design. Note how it doesn't offer even one capability that wasn't demanded by an existing or impending client, yet the desire to do things with quality drove me to make a design decision that might otherwise have been the result of some speculation. For instance, under different circumstances, I might have bet on the need for a public Ingredient entity.

The client is completely unencumbered by ingredients being stored in their own table. It doesn't care at all how ingredients are stored. It only cares that they were stored and will later be available. Should I later settle on a more normalized design, or a less normalized one for that matter, my clients won't care.

This process can be repeated as many times as required to satisfy a new need. The main source of variation is the creation of a new version. You only need to do that when you are changing a database class whose most recent version has been deployed to production.

Summary

No writing of mine would be complete without a feline analogy. Cats are the world's deadliest lone predators. When they go hunting, they come back with food more often than humans. That's more often than humans with high technology, and more often than humans who hunt with bows and arrows for sustenance. Maybe a human who hunts for sustenance with high-tech equipment could compete.

Cats don't do it by planning for the future.

Sure, they probably know where the good hunting grounds are and they probably repeat tricks that have worked in the past, but those aren't the things that get their bellies full. What makes them so able to eat, and to avoid being eaten, is that every aspect of their being is optimized for quick response to changes in circumstances.

Want to run around a corner? No problem; they corner like a Formula 1 race car. Catch them off guard while they are sleeping? That's a mistake most humans make only once.

Planning for every possible contingency is impossible and it's absolutely laughable that anyone ever thought it was worth considering. Healthy entities succeed not by planning for the future but by being able to adapt to it as it unfolds.

So, in my opinion, the minimal design to support incoming and outgoing information is the best one. It meets your requirements as of the time of release, and by virtue of its simplicity, it is easier to change than virtually any other design.

Chapter 8

Error and Remediation

I would like to think that, at this point, you're pretty well armed to defend yourself against error creeping into your delivered products. Nevertheless, every tool I've given you, every tool you had before you picked up this book, and every one you will acquire in the future mitigates risk rather than eliminates it altogether. Mistakes will be made. You've probably made them in the past. You'll probably make them in the future. You've almost certainly seen them made by others in the past and will again. No process is complete without a mechanism to identify and remediate errors.

Before I get into the "how," I cover the "what" of errors. Multiple classes of error can sneak into your database design and each of them requires a different response. The best way to categorize an error in your database design is by asking two questions: "Is it good or bad?" and "Has it been released yet?"

I suppose there is one more indicator for a kind of error that could possibly happen: "Am I sweating, is there a lump in my throat, and do I have a sinking feeling in the pit of my stomach?" If the answer is "yes," then you probably have encountered a catastrophe. Catastrophic errors are things that have to be addressed using traditional database error-remediation tools such as restoring the backup you take before you upgrade a database from any version to any other.

You do that, right? Good.

Kinds of Errors

First, let's establish what an error is in the context of this book. An error in design is any time that a database has a behavior not specified by unit tests or whose history cannot be traced through transition tests.

If product management tells you to get rid of all the Social Security numbers in the database because having them on file is a liability, you confirm they mean "delete" as opposed to "encrypt," and then they are angry with you because you got rid of all the Social Security numbers on file, that's not the kind of error I'm talking about. If the phone number 503-555-0000 shows up correctly but the phone number 1-503-555-0000 shows up as 150-355-5000, that's the kind of development error I'm talking about.

The circumstances around an unspecified behavior govern what you are going to do with it, so categorizing it on two axes is important. The first axis is the good-or-bad axis. Some of the mistakes you make will be in the form of accidentally delivering some extra value. The second axis is the released-or-unreleased axis. You will often discover an error before it is irreversibly committed to a production environment. Others you won't.

Axis: Is the Error Good or Bad?

I know it's hard to believe, but if you develop a feature without having specified it in tests, you have made a mistake. That said, the impact of the mistake might not necessarily be bad. Thus, the first and most important axis of evaluation for any mistake you make is asking, "Is this actually a bad thing?" See Figure 8.1.

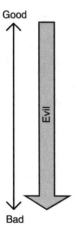

Figure 8.1 *The most important axis: Is the error good or bad?*

For this example, look at the design in Figure 8.2.

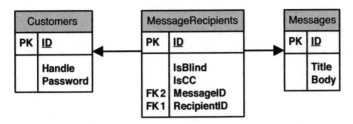

Figure 8.2 *A parties-and-messages design*

Suppose at some point I want to change the design in Figure 8.2 into something like Figure 8.3, perhaps as a refactor in preparation for another change.

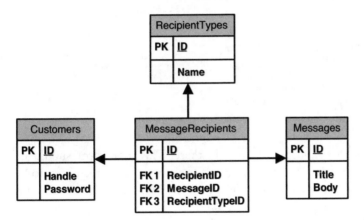

Figure 8.3 *A more sophisticated design*

Assuming I have transition tests specifying the change from the design in Figure 8.2 to that of Figure 8.3, suppose I write the following transition:

```
CREATE Table RecipientTypes(
   ID INT IDENTITY PRIMARY KEY,
   Name VARCHAR(20))

ALTER TABLE MessageRecipients ADD RecipientTypeID INT

DECLARE @ToID INT
DECLARE @CCID INT
DECLARE @BCCID INT
```

```
INSERT INTO RecipientTypes(Name) VALUES ('To')
SET @ToID = @@Identity;

INSERT INTO RecipientTypes(Name) VALUES ('CC')
SET @CCID = @@Identity;

INSERT INTO RecipientTypes(Name) VALUES ('BCC')
SET @BCCID = @@Identity;

UPDATE MessageRecipients SET RecipientTypeID = @ToID
  WHERE IsCC = 0

UPDATE MessageRecipients SET RecipientTypeID = @CCID
  WHERE IsCC = 1 AND IsBlind = 0

UPDATE MessageRecipients SET RecipientTypeID = @BCCID
  WHERE IsCC = 1 AND IsBlind = 1

ALTER TABLE MessageRecipients DROP COLUMN IsCC
ALTER TABLE MessageRecipients DROP COLUMN IsBlind

CREATE TABLE RecipientGroups(
  ID INT IDENTITY(1, 1) PRIMARY KEY,
  Name VARCHAR(50));

CREATE TABLE RecipientGroupMembers(
  ID INT IDENTITy(1, 1) PRIMARY KEY,
  GroupID INT,
  RecipientID INT);
```

There's a good error and a bad error in there. The good error should be easy to spot: There is also a feature allowing for canned lists of recipients to be maintained and associated with a message. Perhaps I was playing around with an idea and forgot to delete the unnecessary code.

The bad error is that some recipients who were shrouded by the blind bit before that transition are suddenly exposed. If this were a system for the CIA, that would be a catastrophe. Suppose it's a system for five-year-olds on a forum about cotton candy and most of them don't yet have the self-censorship required to even know why they would ever want to hide one recipient from another. So it's a little bad, but not "We're just making a quick stop in Guantanamo Bay" bad.

Axis: Is the Error Released or Not?

A version of your database class can mean two very different things. If it has been committed to an important database instance, it is an historical document explaining what has happened in the past. If not, it is a design document explaining what you intend to do in the near future. As a result, there's another question you have to ask yourself: "Has this been committed to production yet?"

The most innocuous combination of answers possible is that a mistake has a positive effect and was not yet released. The worst of the possible answers is that the effect is undesirable and that it has been committed to production. Figure 8.4 depicts these two axes together.

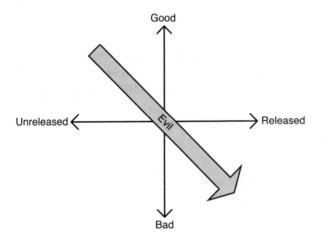

Figure 8.4 *Both axes of error together with an arrow telling you what to avoid*

When developing application logic, asking this question is not important, but for database development, it is critical. For application developers, every class file and every test is documentation of what you plan to do in the future. "When the next version deploys, this is what class A will do."

Like I wrote at the beginning of this section, for database developers, things are a lot different. After a version has been committed to a system that cannot be rolled back or destroyed and rebuilt, that version ceases to be a plan for the future and becomes historical fact.

That is why whether an error has been released or not is so important: Changing what you plan to do in the future is a lot easier than changing what you have already done. The former is almost trivial. With the technology available at the time of this writing, and I suspect for all technology to come, the latter is impossible, and you are left with repairing whatever damage you might have done as your only option.

Dealing with Good Errors

The happy accident is my favorite kind of mistake. I would like to say you should only make this kind of error, but I'm pretty sure that would be tempting fate. Anyway, you're not going to get rid of this feature unless there is absolutely no coupling to it whatsoever, so the solution is to specify the presence of the behavior that is already there.

Just Fix It

Having an extra feature that is desirable is a pretty good problem to have. It makes whether or not the defect has been released irrelevant, so both quadrants on the "good" side of the problem space have the same response (see Figure 8.5).

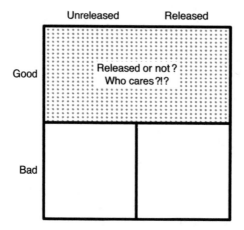

Figure 8.5 *It's okay if you released good mistakes*

Let's say you are working with the following database class for this section:

```
<Database>
  <Lenses>
    <Map Name="current" ToVersion="2" />
  </Lenses>
  <Version Number="1">
    <Script>
      <![CDATA[
CREATE TABLE Pants(
  ID INT
    IDENTITY(1, 1)
    CONSTRAINT PantsPK PRIMARY KEY,
```

```
    Name NVARCHAR(32),
    Color NVARCHAR(32));

CREATE TABLE Legs(
  ID INT
    IDENTITY(1, 1)
    CONSTRAINT LegsPK PRIMARY KEY,
  PantsID INT NOT NULL
    FOREIGN KEY REFERENCES
    PANTS(ID),
  Fabric NVARCHAR(120));
        ]]>
    </Script>
  </Version>
  <Version Number="2">
    <Interface>
      <Add Id="SearchView">
        <Add Id="PantsID" />
        <Add Id="Name" />
        <Add Id="Color" />
        <Add Id="LegCount" />
      </Add>
    </Interface>
    <Script>
      <![CDATA[
CREATE VIEW $SearchView AS
SELECT
  p.ID AS $SearchView.PantsID,
  p.Color AS $SearchView.Color,
  p.Name AS $SearchView.Name,
  COUNT(l.ID) AS $SearchView.LegCount
FROM
  Pants AS p INNER JOIN
  Legs AS l ON p.ID = l.PantsID
GROUP BY
  p.ID,
  p.Color,
  p.Name
        ]]>
    </Script>
  </Version>
</Database>
```

The defect is that the behavior of the view is not specified.

Document Behavior Now

Start by updating your unit test suite to demand the feature that already exists. Use the pinning technique discussed in Chapter 4, "Safely Changing Design," to do this. Write the unit test for the feature but make the expected results wrong.

```
[Test]
public void CanFindPantsByLegCount()
{
  var noisePantsID1 = InsertPants("Noisy Joes", "Paisley");
  var importantPantsID = InsertPants("Fancy", "Black");
  var noisePantsID2 = InsertPants("Screamin' Stevens", "Fire Truck Red");
  AddLeg(noisePantsID1, "Velvet");
  AddLeg(noisePantsID1, "Denim");
  AddLeg(noisePantsID1, "Troll Doll Hair");
  AddLeg(noisePantsID2, "Spandex");
  AddLeg(importantPantsID, "Wool");
  AddLeg(importantPantsID, "Wool");

  var actualResults = connection.ExecuteQuery(
    "SELECT * FROM " + design.SearchView + " WHERE LegCount = 2");

  Assert.That(actualResults.Count(), Is.EqualTo(0));
}
```

Run the test and get a failure with the actual result.

```
ErrorAndRemediation.Tests.PantsAndLegsTests.CanFindPantsByLegCount:
  Expected: 0
  But was:  1
```

Then update the test to expect what actually happens.

```
[Test]
public void CanFindPantsByLegCount()
{
  var noisePantsID1 = InsertPants("Noisy Joes", "Paisley");
  var importantPantsID = InsertPants("Fancy", "Black");
  var noisePantsID2 = InsertPants("Screamin' Stevens", "Fire Truck Red");
  AddLeg(noisePantsID1, "Velvet");
  AddLeg(noisePantsID1, "Denim");
  AddLeg(noisePantsID1, "Troll Doll Hair");
  AddLeg(noisePantsID2, "Spandex");
  AddLeg(importantPantsID, "Wool");
  AddLeg(importantPantsID, "Wool");

  var actualResults = connection.ExecuteQuery(
    "SELECT * FROM " + design.SearchView + " WHERE LegCount = 2");

  Assert.That(actualResults.Count(), Is.EqualTo(1));
  var resultRow = actualResults.ElementAt(0);
  Assert.That(
    resultRow[design.SearchView.PantsID],
    Is.EqualTo(importantPantsID));
}
```

Finally, see the test pass. If it turns out that the assertions that make the test pass were the wrong ones, you have to rethink whether or not this is a "good" bug. Even if it turns out that you decide the defect is really a problem and needs to be eradicated, you won't have wasted any effort here because getting a test that characterizes the current behavior is actually the first step of all three remediation processes.

Trace Feature Back to Its Genesis

After you have a unit test documenting the behavior you're happy you accidentally wrote, the next step is to document the life of the feature. Having a clear specification of how your feature grew and transformed over time is important, just like with any other feature.

In the case of this example, you would identify that the mistake was made in version 2 and you would put in place the following transition test to document that:

```
[Test]
public void PantsAndLegsViewIsThere()
{
   instantiator.UpgradeToSpecificVersion(connection, newDesign);

   var view = newDesign.SearchView;
   var descriptor = connection.GetStructureDescription(view);
   Assert.That(descriptor.GetColumn(view.PantsID).Exists);
   Assert.That(descriptor.GetColumn(view.Name).Exists);
   Assert.That(descriptor.GetColumn(view.Color).Exists);
   Assert.That(descriptor.GetColumn(view.LegCount).Exists);
}
```

In other, more complex scenarios, you will obviously end up generating more transition tests to document its origin.

You can use whatever form of analysis you like to do this, but the most reliable way to do it is to copy your unit test and start coupling it to earlier and earlier versions until it fails. There is construction logic in the transition between the earliest version in which your unit test passes and its predecessor. That behavior must be documented with a transition test, and you might also want to build a transition safeguard at that point.

If analysis indicates that the feature was not born in that transition but merely changed shape enough to cause the unit test to fail, change the unit test so that it passes and repeat the process. Continue doing this until you've documented the entire life of the bug. Figure 8.6 depicts this process.

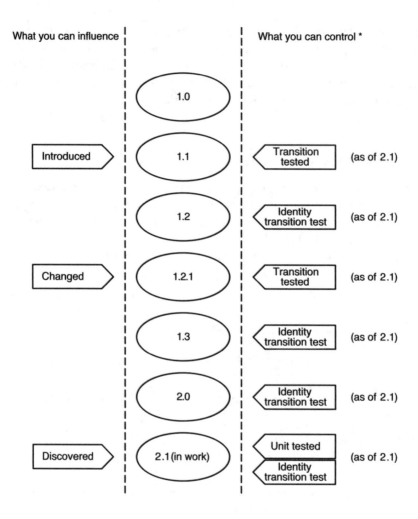

* To the extent that you can control anything

Figure 8.6 *Hunting the source of a beneficial, deployed defect*

Dealing with Bad Errors

Bad errors are undesirable behavior that resides in a database design with no tests specifying their existence. The two classes of bad errors are ones that haven't touched any production environments, and ones that have. The former case is easy to deal with; the latter represents a bit more work.

Unreleased Errors

The bad news is that you have a real defect on your hands, one that would make customers angry or sad if they saw it. The good news is that because it's unreleased, no customer will ever see it because you caught it before it got out into production. These kinds of problems tend to occupy one of the less painful but not totally pain-free quadrants of the problem space (see Figure 8.7).

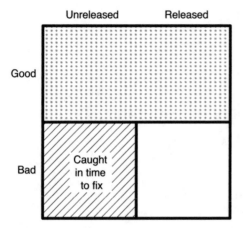

Figure 8.7 *Nobody has to know your shame*

This problem is an easy one to deal with: Change your unit tests to specify that the problem not be in your design, see the failure, fix the design, see the tests pass, and then forget the bug ever existed.

Let's walk through it once for good measure. Take a look at the following code:

```
<Database>
  <Lenses>
    <Map Name="current" ToVersion="2" />
  </Lenses>
  <Version Number="1">
    <Script>
      <![CDATA[
CREATE TABLE Fishes(
  ID INT
    IDENTITY(1, 1)
    CONSTRAINT FishesPK PRIMARY KEY,
  SpeciesName VARCHAR(200),
  Name VARCHAR(32));
```

```
CREATE TABLE Tanks(
  ID INT
    IDENTITY(1, 1)
    CONSTRAINT TanksPK PRIMARY KEY,
  Name VARCHAR(25),
  ViewMaterial VARCHAR(200),
  JoinMaterial VARCHAR(200),
  TrimMaterial VARCHAR(200));
        ]]>
    </Script>
  </Version>
  <Version Number="2">
    <Script>
      <![CDATA[
DECLARE @DefaultTankID INT;

SET IDENTITY_INSERT Tanks ON

INSERT INTO Tanks(ID, Name, ViewMaterial, JoinMaterial,
                  TrimMaterial)
VALUES(-1, '##Default', 'N/A', 'N/A', 'N/A');

SET IDENTITY_INSERT Tanks OFF

ALTER TABLE Fishes ADD TankID INT
  NOT NULL DEFAULT -1

ALTER TABLE Fishes
  ADD CONSTRAINT FishesToTanks
  FOREIGN KEY(TankID) REFERENCES Tanks(ID)
        ]]>
    </Script>
  </Version>
</Database>
```

The previous database class is mostly tested but has one little undesirable feature in it: The relationship between the `Fishes` table and the `Tanks` table is unnecessary as is the consequent creation of the "default" tank.

The first thing to do is specify how your class of databases works now. This can be done by either finding or writing the following test:

```
[Test]
public void FishCannotExistWithoutTank()
{
  var tankID = AddTank("Amazon Tributary", "air", "n/a", "silt");
  var fishID = AddFish("candiru", "Mr. Tickles");
  SetTank(fishID, tankID);

  try
  {
    DeleteTank(tankID);
  }
```

```
catch
{
  return;
}

Assert.Fail();
}
```

That test passes because that's the current behavior of the class. Next alter the test to specify the behavior you actually want. When it fails, turn your attention to the transition test suite for the current version. Some of the tests are probably along the lines of the following:

```
[Test]
public void ExistingFishAssignedToDefaultTank()
{
  var fishID = AddOriginalFish("clown fish", "joe");

  instantiator.UpgradeToSpecificVersion(connection, newDesign);

  var tankID = connection.ExecuteScalar(
    "SELECT TankID FROM Fishes WHERE ID = " + fishID);
  Assert.That(tankID, Is.EqualTo(-1));
}
```

Tear them down. I wouldn't bother writing tests for the opposite behavior. You already have a test specifying how your database class needs to change right now, and the assumption of any reader should be, "If a test is not there, the behavior should not be either." So, just delete those tests with all the ruthlessness you can muster.

Next, take a look at the transition logic for the current version:

```
DECLARE @DefaultTankID INT;

SET IDENTITY_INSERT Tanks ON

INSERT INTO Tanks(ID, Name, ViewMaterial, JoinMaterial,
                  TrimMaterial)
VALUES(-1, '##Default', 'N/A', 'N/A', 'N/A');

SET IDENTITY_INSERT Tanks OFF

ALTER TABLE Fishes ADD TankID INT NOT NULL DEFAULT -1

ALTER TABLE Fishes
  ADD CONSTRAINT FishesToTanks
  FOREIGN KEY(TankID) REFERENCES Tanks(ID)
```

Get rid of the stuff you don't want—in this case, all of it. In real life, you will probably have to be more judicious because most of the time you want to keep a lot of what you have written. In any event, your tests can tell you whether or not you cut too deep.

Getting rid of those construction steps will cause newly created databases to have the correct behavior and, consequently, make your unit test pass.

Figure 8.8 depicts the process for correcting these errors.

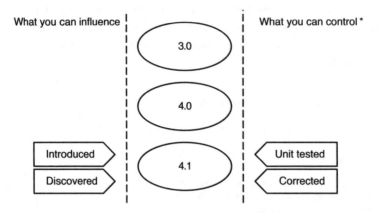

Figure 8.8 *Identifying and correcting unreleased problems*

Released Errors

The bad news is that the feature is unwanted. The really bad news is that it was released to production a couple months ago. The good news is that everyone on your team is still alive and healthy.

"For now," your manager reminds you (see Figure 8.9).

Imagine someone has employed the processes in this book and you are looking at the diffs of their changes in a source control server with no corresponding comments. You would have no idea whether he found a bad defect he wanted to eradicate or a good defect he wanted to document, and which he then decided to eradicate later. That's because the first part of dealing with any defect that has been deployed is always the same: Something actually happened. So, you have to establish a specification that accurately documents history.

I'll paint another little picture for you because I like to do that. Imagine you have a database containing home inspection details. Suddenly, 90 percent of your users cannot see log entries made by the other 10 percent. Some research reveals what happened.

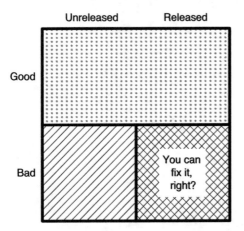

Figure 8.9 *You'll live but the clock is ticking*

A very junior programmer—let's call him "Tyler"—added an optional parameter to a stored procedure that marks log entries as being for "debug purposes." It was well intentioned enough; he wanted to be able to test his work and didn't know how to create a database of his own, so he added what he thought he needed to a version that got released into production. The problem is that, somehow, about one in ten end users have their client application set up to run in debug mode, so their log entries are invisible to other inspection workers.

Following is the body of the stored procedures the developer changed:

```
CREATE PROCEDURE $AddLogEntry
  $AddLogEntry.HomeID INT,
  $AddLogEntry.AuthorID INT,
  $AddLogEntry.InspectionTypeID INT,
  $AddLogEntry.Flag CHAR,
  $AddLogEntry.Notes TEXT,
  @IsDebug BIT = 0
AS
BEGIN
  DECLARE @RedFlag BIT
  DECLARE @YellowFlag BIT
  SET @RedFlag = 0
  SET @YellowFlag = 0

  IF $AddLogEntry.Flag = 'R' SET @RedFlag = 1
  IF $AddLogEntry.Flag = 'Y' SET @YellowFlag = 1

  INSERT INTO LogEntries(
    HomeID,
    AuthorID,
    InspectionTypeID,
```

```
      RedFlag,
      YellowFlag,
      Notes,
      IsDebug)
    VALUES(
      $AddLogEntry.HomeID,
      $AddLogEntry.AuthorID,
      $AddLogEntry.InspectionTypeID,
      @RedFlag,
      @YellowFlag,
      $AddLogEntry.Notes,
      @IsDebug)

    SELECT @@Identity
END

------------

CREATE PROCEDURE $ReadLogEntriesForHome
  $ReadLogEntriesForHome.HomeID INT,
  @IsDebug BIT = 0
AS
  SELECT
    ID AS $ReadLogEntriesForHome.ResultID,
    AuthorID AS $ReadLogEntriesForHome.ResultAuthorID,
    InspectionTypeID AS $ReadLogEntriesForHome.ResultInspectionTypeID,
    RedFlag AS $ReadLogEntriesForHome.ResultRedFlag,
    YellowFlag AS $ReadLogEntriesForHome.ResultYellowFlag,
    Notes AS $ReadLogEntriesForHome.ResultNotes
  FROM
    LogEntries
  WHERE
    HomeID = $ReadLogEntriesForHome.HomeID AND
    IsDebug <= @IsDebug
```

After feigning surprise and reassuring Tyler that the HR lady "probably just wants to make sure this incident is fully documented," you can start cleaning up the mess he's about to have left behind.

That begins by documenting the feature he added with some unit tests.

```
[Test]
public void DebugEntriesDoNotShowUpForNonDebugQueries()
{
  var homeID = 01;

  var entryID1 = WriteLogEntry(
    homeID, 11, 21, 'R', "There isn't even a roof!");
  var entryID2 = WriteLogEntry(
    02, 11, 21, 'R', "There isn't even a roof!");
  var entryID3 = WriteLogEntry(
    homeID, 12, 22, ' ', "Wiring looks fine.", isDebug: true);
```

```
  var entryID4 = WriteLogEntry(
    homeID, 13, 23, ' ', "Wall insulation is okay.");

  var entries = ReadEntriesForHome(homeID);

  var entryIDs = entries
    .Select(r => r[design.ReadLogEntriesForHome.ResultID]).ToArray();
  Assert.That(entryIDs, Is.EquivalentTo(new[] { entryID1, entryID4 }));
}
```

About the time security shows up and starts boxing up Tyler's personal effects, you'll want to start documenting the history of the feature he added by tracing it backward through the history of what was released to production as embodied by your database class. In this case, you might not need to run a copy of the unit test in every historical version until you find where it was added. Instead, you can just search the database class for @IsDebug and write transition tests for the version upgrade scripts in which it appears.

When writing the transition tests, you'll need to use the pinning method. Do not, under any circumstances, change the upgrade script for a deployed version of a database class. Rewriting history is fine when it doesn't matter, like when you're teaching children who discovered the Americas, but this is the definition of how you upgrade your database and how you build prototypes for it in test environments. There is no margin for error.

```
[Test]
public void ExistingEntriesGainAZeroDebugFlag()
{
  WriteLogEntry(100, 201, 309, 'R', "Some notes");
  WriteLogEntry(100, 203, 309, 'Y', "Some other notes");
  WriteLogEntry(101, 201, 300, ' ', "Some different notes");

  instantiator.UpgradeToSpecificVersion(connection, newDesign);

  var actualEntries = ReadEntries();
  Assertions.AssertRowsAreEqual(expectedEntries, actualEntries);
}
```

That test fails because its expectation is wrong, and running it tells you what the right one should be, so you update the test to reflect actual history:

```
[Test]
public void ExistingEntriesGainAZeroDebugFlag()
{
  WriteLogEntry(100, 201, 309, 'R', "Some notes");
  WriteLogEntry(100, 203, 309, 'Y', "Some other notes");
  WriteLogEntry(101, 201, 300, ' ', "Some different notes");
  var expectedEntries = ReadEntries();
  foreach (var row in expectedEntries)
```

```
   {
     row["IsDebug"] = false;
   }

   instantiator.UpgradeToSpecificVersion(connection, newDesign);

   var actualEntries = ReadEntries();
   Assertions.AssertRowsAreEqual(expectedEntries, actualEntries);
 }
```

About the time you hear Tyler's 1993 Subaru Justy with the wrong-colored door struggling to start in the parking lot, you'll be ready to start getting rid of his little gift. Ordinarily, that would start by altering the unit tests for AddLogEntry and ReadLogEntriesForHome. Yet, in this case, you want to eradicate the design structures used to create this scenario altogether. So, how do you drive this from tests?

The answer is to fall back on the basic test-driven development (TDD) advice: If there is no test, there should be no behavior. So if you want no behavior, you should make it so there's no test. Updating the specification for your class of databases is a matter of deleting the test you just wrote.

Writing a test and then turning around and deleting it might feel like a waste of time. If you're inclined not to write the test characterizing the bug, I ask you to remember that said test serves as a useful analysis tool while discovering transition tests that need to be written against historical versions of a database class.

It also is rarely the case that you want to delete a test and you might not know until it's time to remediate an error. Furthermore, you can check the test into source control before deleting it to document that you knew the feature was there and deleted it on purpose.

Use your best judgment.

Deleting the unit test frees you up to start working on the deconstruction logic for this bug by writing the transition test that indicates the AddLogEntry and ReadLogEntries procedures no longer have @IsDebug parameters and that the IsDebug column in your LogEntries table is gone.

```
[Test]
public void IsDebugFlagRemoved()
{
   WriteLogEntry(100, 201, 309, 'R', "Some notes");
   WriteLogEntry(100, 203, 309, 'Y', "Some other notes");
   WriteLogEntry(101, 201, 300, ' ', "Some different notes");
   var expectedEntries = ReadEntries();
   foreach (var row in expectedEntries)
   {
     row.Remove("IsDebug");
   }
```

```
    instantiator.UpgradeToSpecificVersion(connection, newDesign);

    var actualEntries = ReadEntries();
    Assertions.AssertRowsAreEqual(expectedEntries, actualEntries);
}
```

That transition test fails to compile, so add a new version, recompile, and rerun them. After you see it fail, add the transition logic to eliminate the unwanted structures.

```
  <Version Number="3">
    <Script>
      <![CDATA[
DROP PROCEDURE $AddLogEntry
DROP PROCEDURE $ReadLogEntriesForHome
ALTER TABLE LogEntries DROP CONSTRAINT DF_LogEntries_IsDebug
ALTER TABLE LogEntries DROP COLUMN IsDebug
    ]]>
    </Script>
    <Script>
      <![CDATA[
CREATE PROCEDURE $AddLogEntry
  $AddLogEntry.HomeID INT,
  $AddLogEntry.AuthorID INT,
  $AddLogEntry.InspectionTypeID INT,
  $AddLogEntry.Flag CHAR,
  $AddLogEntry.Notes TEXT
AS
BEGIN
  DECLARE @RedFlag BIT
  DECLARE @YellowFlag BIT
  SET @RedFlag = 0
  SET @YellowFlag = 0

  IF $AddLogEntry.Flag = 'R' SET @RedFlag = 1
  IF $AddLogEntry.Flag = 'Y' SET @YellowFlag = 1

  INSERT INTO LogEntries(
    HomeID,
    AuthorID,
    InspectionTypeID,
    RedFlag,
    YellowFlag,
    Notes)
  VALUES(
    $AddLogEntry.HomeID,
    $AddLogEntry.AuthorID,
    $AddLogEntry.InspectionTypeID,
    @RedFlag,
    @YellowFlag,
    $AddLogEntry.Notes)
```

```
    SELECT @@Identity
END
      ]]>
    </Script>
    <Script>
      <![CDATA[
CREATE PROCEDURE $ReadLogEntriesForHome
  $ReadLogEntriesForHome.HomeID INT
AS
  SELECT
    ID AS $ReadLogEntriesForHome.ResultID,
    AuthorID AS $ReadLogEntriesForHome.ResultAuthorID,
    InspectionTypeID AS $ReadLogEntriesForHome.ResultInspectionTypeID,
    RedFlag AS $ReadLogEntriesForHome.ResultRedFlag,
    YellowFlag AS $ReadLogEntriesForHome.ResultYellowFlag,
    Notes AS $ReadLogEntriesForHome.ResultNotes
  FROM
    LogEntries
  WHERE
    HomeID = $ReadLogEntriesForHome.HomeID
      ]]>
    </Script>
  </Version>
```

That code makes the test pass, so you can check your changes into the source code repository and try to forget that the problem ever happened.

Figure 8.10 depicts the process of tracking down and eradicating a released bug.

Catastrophic Errors

It's always possible that something will go horribly, horribly awry and for it to happen in production. Having it happen without your knowing should be nearly impossible. If it happens, do what you always would have done.

If you are disciplined, and you take backups before upgrading a database's structure, then cancel the deployment, restore the backup, and get ready to start figuring out what went wrong. If you are undisciplined and you allow any changes to happen without a proper backup being taken first, then cry, go home, find a good lawyer, and doctor up your resume to make it look like you've been in prison so nobody asks whether you're "that guy from [wherever you work]."

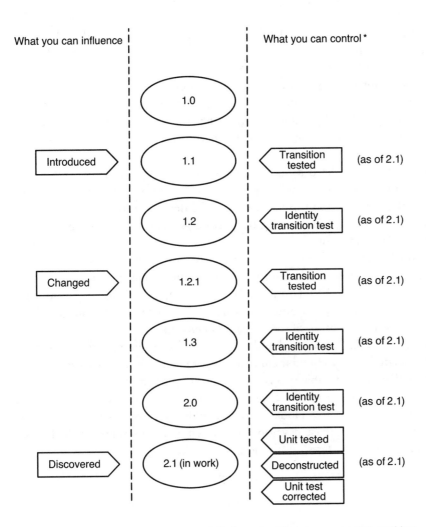

What you can influence | What you can control*

1.0

Introduced   1.1   Transition tested   (as of 2.1)

1.2   Identity transition test   (as of 2.1)

Changed   1.2.1   Transition tested   (as of 2.1)

1.3   Identity transition test   (as of 2.1)

2.0   Identity transition test   (as of 2.1)

Unit tested

Discovered   2.1 (in work)   Deconstructed   (as of 2.1)

Unit test corrected

* To the extent that you can control anything

Figure 8.10 *Documenting and destroying a committed bug*

Summary

Up until this chapter, I've focused on helping you not make mistakes. That's important. The cheapest mistakes are the ones you don't make. However, sometimes people get a little bit of tunnel-vision in regard to preventing error—so focused on not making a mistake that absolutely no provisions exist for the eventuality of something going wrong.

What I want you to do is make the right amount of preparation for each kind of error. There are four basic categories: unreleased, good-and-released, bad-and-released, and catastrophic.

You need not make any preparation for unreleased errors. When you find them, you fix them and nobody has to even know they happened. Good errors—features you accidentally implemented without a test—that make it out into production are also not a big problem. All you have to do is document their existence with tests.

You do, however, need to have plans in place to deal with bad errors that leak out into production. Catastrophic errors that cause a loss of data or an unacceptable interruption of service need to be dealt with the "old-fashioned" way: restoring backups and fishing out lost data, writing repair scripts, rolling back upgrades, and so on.

The smaller errors require a more measured approach. A subtle defect that has been in your database design for, say, six months, has become part of that design's character. Don't try to pretend it never happened. Instead, write tests that show that it *did* happen, and then write more tests to drive resolution of any data issues and elimination of the unwanted behavior.

Now you should have a good understanding of how database designs should be encapsulated, how to build them to allow for change, and how to address the problems that are inevitable in any human effort. That means you have a basic understanding of how to make classes of database and how to maintain them. In Chapter 9, "Design," you look at how to apply what you know about object-oriented design to database development, which is the beginning of the last leg of the TDD tour: how tests inform design.

Chapter 9

Design

Some design principles discovered by people developing application logic can pretty easily be applied to database design. When you're done adapting these techniques, you'll have a system of tools that give you something like the same kind of testability as you might find in an object-oriented language.

A class of databases won't have the flexible, fluid, reusability of a truly modern language such as C#, Ruby, or Java, but you can at least come up with something akin to C++. That's a huge step up from what a lot of people do now, which most closely parallels programming in something a little less primitive than assembly language.

To start this conversation, I hope to drive the final wedge between the concept of a database's design and its physical structure, forever separating the ideas in your mind. My position is that the design of a database class lives in its test. Actual structures in a particular database instance, such as tables or stored procedures, are more like machine code—execution details, not design.

When actually instantiated, an object's innards are highly exposed to one another—remember, it's all just ones and zeroes when it's running. The same is true of a database. Inside a database instance, it's okay if everything could potentially couple to everything. The reason is because design elements can still be encapsulated from one another and physical structures are derived from design elements.

For a developer, the process of creating a design is the process of encapsulating things from one another. In general, encapsulation is the process of dividing problems into their constituent concerns and protecting them from changes in each other. A particularly interesting kind of encapsulation is encapsulation of variation. When writing technical specifications (unit tests), test-driven development makes heavy use of this kind of encapsulation to ensure a test only tests what it is actually about.

Two primary means exist for encapsulating the design details of one database design element from another. One is aggregation, in which one database instance delegates to another to do a certain amount of work. Another is composition, in which one physical database instance is comprised of several logical components.

At one point in time, there was a belief that one of the principal benefits of object-oriented development was reuse. Following in the evolutionary footsteps of the object-oriented development movement, I'll point out that one of the obvious applications of aggregation and composition is reuse. With such tools, you could start building reusable database components that are shared by numerous database designs, or coupled to by separate database instances.

Another, much more powerful way exists to apply these kinds of tools, though: abstraction. Abstraction enables you to encapsulate variation. At the time of this writing, it is not likely that people will start taking design patterns into account, but what you can do is employ one of the most important patterns of all: the mock object pattern, discussed in Chapter 10, "Mocking."

This chapter, however, focuses on the basic principles of design.

Structures Versus Design

The structures that live in a database aren't what you, the database developer, are responsible for building. The fact that you have to deal directly with the structures that get made is an ugly detail of your job, not the goal.

In the context of database design, you are on the hook for making a good design, from which those structures can be derived. The problem is that there aren't good tools for describing database design, like there are for the design of some classes in a .NET or Java application. Excellent tools exist for considering a database's structure but not for design itself.

Structures: Execution Details

For decades, developers have been satisfied working with databases in what amounts to assembly code. Sure, a more readable syntax and more validation tools are available, but that's not important. Besides, I was not referring to the absence of those things. I'm talking about the near-parity between DDL statements and physical structures.

Assembly programming was marked by the virtually one-to-one mapping between instructions in the "human readable" text file and machine-code instructions in the assembled output. Take a look at some data definition scripts and think about whether or not that sounds familiar:

```
CREATE TABLE Allocations(
   ID INT IDENTITY NOT NULL,
   AllocatedHandleID INT NOT NULL,
   AllocatedResourceID INT NOT NULL,
   LeaseRenewedAt DATETIME NOT NULL,
   LeaseLengthInMilliseconds INT NOT NULL);

ALTER TABLE Allocations
   ADD CONSTRAINT AllocationsPK
   PRIMARY KEY(ID);

CREATE TABLE Handles(
   ID INT NOT NULL,
   Name VARCHAR(20) NOT NULL);

ALTER TABLE Handles
   ADD CONSTRAINT HandlesPK
   PRIMARY KEY(ID);

CREATE TABLE Resources(
   ID INT NOT NULL,
   Name VARCHAR(20) NOT NULL,
   EndpointUri VARCHAR(4000) NOT NULL);

ALTER TABLE Resources
   ADD CONSTRAINT ResourcesPK
   PRIMARY KEY(ID);

ALTER TABLE Allocations
   ADD CONSTRAINT AllocatedHandleIDs
   FOREIGN KEY (AllocatedHandleID)
   REFERENCES Handles(ID);

ALTER TABLE Allocations
   ADD CONSTRAINT AllocatedResourceIDs
   FOREIGN KEY (AllocatedResourceID)
   REFERENCES Resources(ID);

CREATE UNIQUE INDEX HandleAllocationusUnique
   ON Allocations(AllocatedHandleID);

CREATE UNIQUE INDEX ResourceAllocationsUnique
   ON Allocations(AllocatedResourceID);
```

The preceding code contains numerous instructions. Each of those instructions corresponds directly to a structural aspect of a database instance. Did I drag it out a little? Sure, but only in that I didn't use shorthand. I could have made that sample a little shorter, but not really any better.

In the previous code sample, I express the details of instantiating a database and leave it to you to infer what my intent was. For comparison, consider what an object model in a "normal" programming language might look like:

```
public class Handle {
  public string Name { get; set; }
}

public class Resource {
  public string Name { get; set; }
  public string EndpointUri { get; set; }
}

public class Allocations {
  public List<Handle> Handles { get; set; }
  public List<Resources> Resources { get; set; }
  public Dictionary<Handle, Resource> HandleToResources { get; set; }
  public Dictionary<Resource, Handle> ResourceToHandles { get; set; }
}
```

Of course, that's far worse than anything one would actually write in a middle tier language, but I was trying to maintain some correspondence between both examples' level of encapsulation. The thing that should strike you upon reading the previous code sample is how much more obvious it makes the intent of the code.

Although this code offers a slight benefit in the form of your not having to spend as much time typing and reading, that is really the side benefit. The real power of something that expressive is that it lets you think about fewer things. Most people have a limit to the number of entities they can model and consider in their head. Being able to think about three classes with some easily described relationships frees you up to make more important, and consequently better, design decisions.

I am certainly not arguing that you shouldn't create tables or relationships. A database needs those things to do its job. I just want to make it clear that data definition languages are extremely implementation-centric. They do nothing to abstract away implementation details.

When a document is mired down in such details, there is really no way you can expect anyone to give design the proper treatment in that document. What is needed is another place to store design.

Tests and Class Information

Fortunately, developers have exactly that—at least, some semblance of it. Dividing a database's construction logic into transitions and proper transition testing enables you to think only about construction when it is time to think about construction. They also let you not think about construction when it is time to think about design.

Unit tests specify behavior and interactions between various entities. Interface specification defines how objects can relate to a database. Defining behavior, relationships, and public coupling opportunity are the basic components of an object-oriented design. So, maybe those are the places where a database's design should live.

What Is Design?

I have no idea what you think is important about design or even what you think it means. The term is so heavily overloaded that I feel like we should find a new one. I can tell you what I think is important about design and that's what I'm going to do right now.

Design is about encapsulating unrelated things from one another. When a requirement changes, if you only have to change the tests and behaviors directly related to that requirement, then you are working with an excellent design. If requirements changes send shockwaves rippling throughout the system, causing weeks of follow-up work, you have a terrible design on your hands. A lot of designs live in the middle space.

The way to go about creating a good design is to divide concepts into "buckets." In object-oriented programs, those buckets tend to be classes. The idea is to keep strongly related concepts close together, while funneling interactions between less-related concepts through the narrowest interface possible.

Test-driven development not only helps you build designs like this, it absolutely requires that you do so. If you don't have a good way of insulating behaviors from one another, you will find that certain prolific behaviors infiltrate numerous tests. When those behaviors have to change, you'll have to update all the tests that touch them, which would constitute a pretty bad design given the measure of design quality I just gave you.

Buckets of Concepts

The key to design is encapsulation, which is about dividing a problem into the appropriate chunks and ensuring only the right chunks can see each other. Consider the design shown in Figure 9.1.

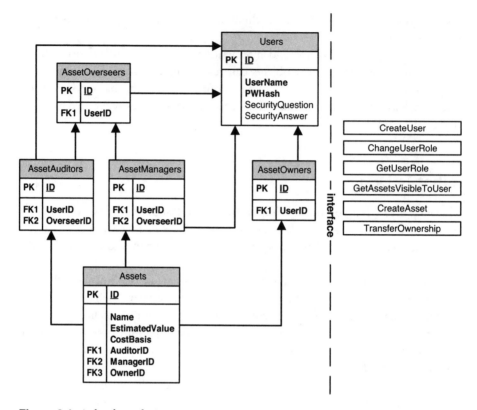

Figure 9.1 *A database design*

Breaking it down into the behaviors produces a list something like the following, in no particular order:

- Create user
- Make user an asset owner
- Make user an overseer
- Make user an asset auditor
- Asset auditors must have an overseer

- Make user an asset manager

- Asset managers must have an overseer

- Users may only ever be in one role

- Get user role

- Overseer with asset managers may not have asset auditors

- Overseer with asset auditors may not have asset managers

- Create asset

- Assets must have an owner

- Assets must have a manager

- Assets must have an auditor

- Transfer ownership of an asset

- Get list of assets visible to a manager, auditor, or owner

Some of those behaviors are very strongly related to one another, such as creating a user and setting that user's role. Some of the behaviors are not related at all, such as associating a manager with an overseer and finding the list of assets visible to a user.

When you draw how the behaviors relate to one another, you get something like Figure 9.2.

Note how there are two "lumps" of behaviors. In each lump are numerous connections and interactions, even in a simplified diagram of a simplified database's behaviors. Yet between the lumps are comparatively few relationships. That means that the lumps are cohesive, which is a strong indicator that they could be made into separate concerns.

Figure 9.3 depicts the same set of behaviors divided among two classes of database. The complexity of the relationships between these two classes is far lower than what you find inside either class. This is a strong indicator that many of the behaviors in either class are private concerns and could be modified without impacting the design of the other class.

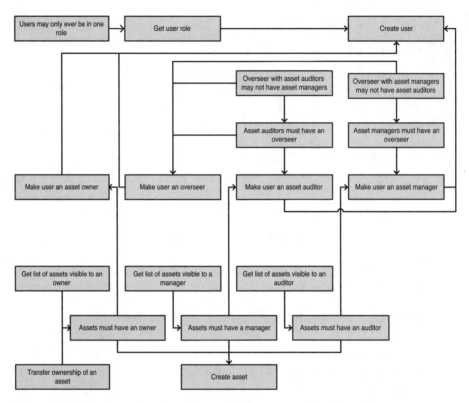

Figure 9.2 *Behaviors of assets-and-users database mapped by dependency*

Mandatory Part of True TDD

At this point, the separation of behaviors into two categories is purely theoretical. That is, I've taken an existing design and shown where the boundaries should be. That is going to have to change in order to support any kind of true, sustainable test-driven development effort against this design.

The reason is that the dependencies between behaviors will corrupt any test suite that tries to specify them. For instance, getting the list of assets visible to an asset manager is impossible without first setting up a whole host of records with a complex arrangement. This means that you cannot test how assets are created and retrieved without also testing the security model.

Over the course of this chapter and the next, I show you how to change the way you design databases to enable you to test each of these bodies of highly related features independently. You could take it further and find a way to test every feature independently, and I won't discourage you from that, but at this point I just want everyone to start breaking down database designs into insular components.

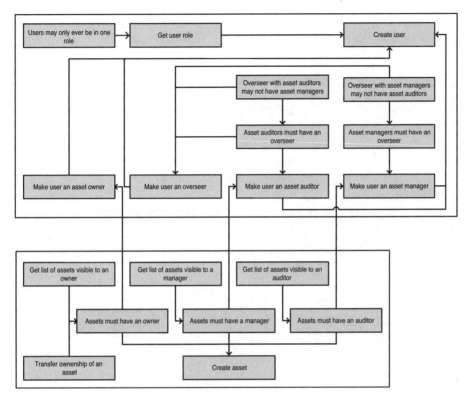

Figure 9.3 *Like behaviors grouped together*

Composition and Aggregation

Two relevant design tools can be easily ported over from the object-oriented design world. One of them is called *composition*. Composition relies on there being a distinction for you between what you consider to be a logical database and your actual, physical database deployments. I believe composition to be, far and away, the most appropriate and widely applicable tool given the level of technology available at the time of this writing.

The other tool is *aggregation*. In modern software development environments, this is the most popular mechanism by a very wide margin. In some languages, it's really the only option that's even available. When you use aggregation, you have two distinct objects interacting with one another. The major advantage is that many objects can all share a reference to a single object and, therefore, they can all aggregate its behavior into the solution they provide their clients.

Aggregation's applications in database design are not nearly as broad as composition's, but it can still have its uses. So, I will teach you both.

Composition: One Thing with Multiple Parts

Both composition and aggregation make it possible for you to think of your database offering as several classes of database. Composition enables you to do so without introducing the overhead of multiple database instances. This is because each database class is only separate in a logical sense. When actually constructing a database, you build all the components into the same instance in a predictable order.

Take a look at composing one object out of two others in the classic, middle-tier design sense. Figure 9.4 is a UML (Unified Modeling Language) diagram of how the composite class relates to its two components.

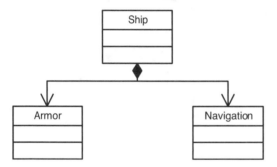

Figure 9.4 *A class composed of two other classes*

The black diamond indicates that instances of Ship own their instances of Armor and Navigation, and that the means of ownership is composition. In code form, written in languages that I know pretty well, composition is most easily recognizable in C++.

```
class Armor {
public:
      int getDamage(int force);
};

class Navigation {
public:
      double getHeading(double latitude, double longitude);
};

class Ship
{
private:
```

```
      Armor myArmor;
      Navigation myNavigation;
  public:
      void applyDamage(int amount);
      void setCourse(double latitude, double longitude);
  };
```

That code declares three classes: `Armor`, `Navigation`, and `Ship`. Instances of the `Ship` class have member variables called `myArmor` and `myNavigation` that are instances of `Armor` and `Navigation`, respectively. In C++, member variables are composed unless otherwise specified. If I were to instantiate a `Ship` object, enough room will be created for its `myArmor` component and its `myNavigation` component, and the `Armor` and `Navigation` constructors would be called on their corresponding regions in memory.

Database composition might look something like Figure 9.5, when depicted graphically.

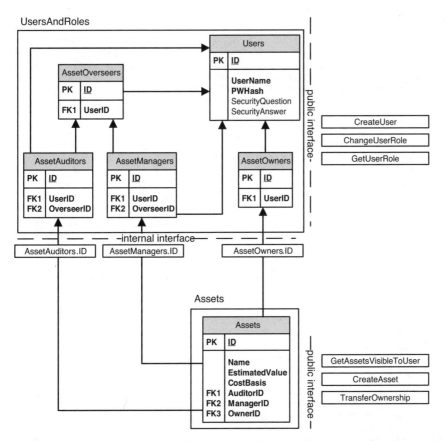

Figure 9.5 *Behaviors distributed between two classes with extra interface for coupling*

The database class file for the UsersAndRoles virtual database might look something like the following:

```
<Database Name="UsersAndRoles">
  <Version Number="1">
    <Interface>
      <Add Id="AssetManagers">
        <Add Id="Identity" Value="ID" />
      </Add>
      <Add Id="AssetAuditors">
        <Add Id="Identity" Value="ID" />
      </Add>
      <Add Id="AssetOwners">
        <Add Id="Identity" Value="ID"/>
      </Add>
    </Interface>
    <!-- Create encapsulated tables -->
    <Script>
      <![CDATA[
CREATE TABLE $AssetManagers(
  $AssetManagers.Identity INT PRIMARY KEY,
  UserID INT,
  OverseerID INT);

CREATE TABLE $AssetAuditors(
  $AssetAuditors.Identity INT PRIMARY KEY,
  UserID INT,
  OverseerID INT);

CREATE TABLE $AssetOwners(
  $AssetOwners.Identity INT PRIMARY KEY,
  UserID INT,
  OverseerID INT);
      ]]>
    </Script>
    <!-- Build stored procedures -->
  </Version>
</Database>
```

The file for the UsersRolesAndAssets virtual database would probably look like this:

```
<Database Name="UsersRolesAndAssets">
  <Version Number="1">
    <Interface>
      <Add Id="AssetManagers">
        <Add Id="Identity" Value="ID" />
      </Add>
      <Add Id="AssetAuditors">
        <Add Id="Identity" Value="ID" />
      </Add>
      <Add Id="AssetOwners">
        <Add Id="Identity" Value="ID"/>
```

```
      </Add>
    </Interface>
    <Upgrade
      TypeName="UsersAndRoles" InstanceName="users" TargetVersion="1" />
    <Script>
      <![CDATA[
CREATE TABLE Assets(
  ID INT IDENTITY,
  Name NVARCHAR(200),
  EstimatedValue NUMERIC(12, 2),
  CostBasis NUMERIC(12, 2),
  AuditorID INT,
  ManagerID INT,
  OwnerID INT);
      ]]>
    </Script>
    <Script>
      <![CDATA[
ALTER TABLE Assets
  ADD CONSTRAINT AssetsToAuditors FOREIGN KEY (AuditorID) REFERENCES
    $users.AssetAuditors($users.AssetAuditors.Identity);
      ]]>
    </Script>
    <Script>
      <![CDATA[
ALTER TABLE Assets
  ADD CONSTRAINT AssetsToManagers FOREIGN KEY (ManagerID) REFERENCES
    $users.AssetManagers($users.AssetManagers.Identity);
      ]]>
    </Script>
    <Script>
      <![CDATA[
ALTER TABLE Assets
  ADD CONSTRAINT AssetsToOwners FOREIGN KEY (OwnerID) REFERENCES
    $users.AssetOwners($users.AssetOwners.Identity);
      ]]>
    </Script>
    <!-- Build stored procedures -->
  </Version>
</Database>
```

In this case, because there is a dependency in the UsersRolesAndAssets class on UsersAndRoles, I made the UsersRolesAndAssets database class depend on UsersAndRoles.

Note how you have to take into account certain things that weren't important when doing classic object-oriented programming (OOP). For instance, each version of the asset class must explicitly declare when it is dependent upon a new version of the UsersAndRoles database. This way, the database build engine will know that version 3 of the UsersRolesAndAssets database class requires its Users database to be updated to version 2.

This alone doesn't enable you to start testing the behaviors of UsersRoles
AndAssets independently of those in Users, but it does get you a step closer by
isolating those behaviors into two distinct classes.

Aggregation: Connecting Distinct Things

Another way to separate database classes is by aggregation. To aggregate databases, you would define two distinct database classes and make the aggregator
have some kind of connection to the aggregated database class. To fulfill certain
needs, the container database would then execute queries or stored procedures
on the contained database and merge the results into its response to its clients.

Back in the old days of OOP, programmers would push back on delegation
because an indirect function call took an extra ten or so clock ticks. That was
an absurd argument even then and, now, hardly anyone even brings up the performance argument.

In the database world, however, the performance cost of delegation can be a
lot more significant. There's no way to put an exact price on it, but must be high
relative to that of composition. Furthermore, the developer experience for building two related database instances tends to give people nightmares. Over time, I
predict both of those costs will vanish and, even now, they might end up being
negligible when measured against the benefits of this kind of design.

First, let me show you in Figure 9.6 how an aggregation relationship might
work in a classically object-oriented environment.

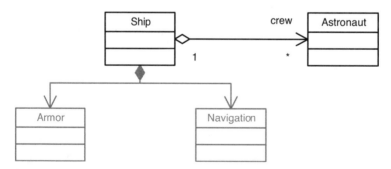

Figure 9.6 *Ship with armor, navigation, and crew*

A spaceship carries a crew but they are not part of it. They can embark and
debark under various circumstances. Thus, I use the white diamond to describe
that a ship can logically contain some people but that they are not components
of it. Following is the C++ code that corresponds with Figure 9.6:

```
class Astronaut {
public:
    bool canBreath(std::string const compound);
};

class Ship
{
private:
    std::vector<Astronaut*> crew;
    Armor myArmor;
    Navigation myNavigation;
public:
    void applyDamage(int amount);
    void setCourse(double latitude, double longitude);
    void addCrew(Astronaut* crewman);
    void removeCrew(Astronaut* crewman);
};
```

When a Ship is created, its armor and navigation objects are created with it, but all that is allocated for the crew is a place to put a list of pointers. Crew-members have to be instantiated and added to or removed from a ship object separately.

Let's consider how an aggregation relationship might work between the UsersRolesAndAssets and UsersAndRoles database classes. With the possible exception of upping the encapsulating by adding some extra stored procedures, the class definition for UsersAndRoles would not change because it is the contained object and doesn't know anything about its container. Figure 9.7 depicts this slightly different design. I don't use it much until near the end of the book, so I defer showing you a code example until then.

In this example, I create a SQL linkage between the UsersRolesAndAssets class of databases and an instance of the UsersAndRoles class. That linkage is used to enforce relationships between asset objects and users.

The major, obvious downside of this approach is the additional cost of an extra database. Where there once was one database, there now are two. Your deployment process becomes more complex as a result. In addition, although this might not matter in the case of the particular design I used as an example, every query against the UsersRolesAndAssets database involves a subordinate query against a UsersAndRoles's database instance. In high-traffic scenarios, that might be a fatal flaw.

There are upsides to be considered as well. What if, for contractual reasons, data about your company's clients' assets must be stored in the same country as the assets they model? That is, it is legal for people to access this data in an application but no permanent storage of the data for an asset can occur outside an asset's country. In that case, aggregation would go from being a bane to a boon.

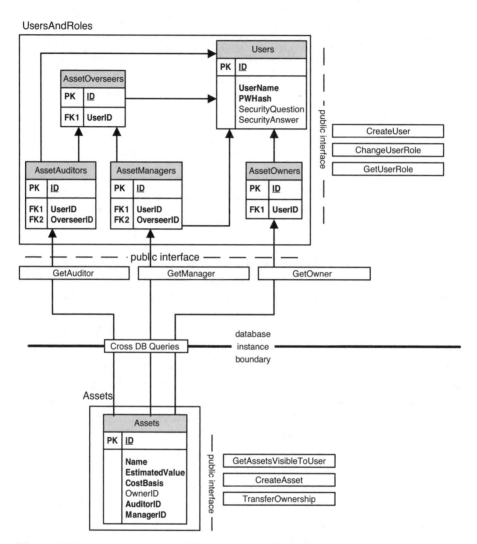

Figure 9.7 UsersAndRoles *residing in its own database instance*

That's a pretty unlikely case, though. The big benefits of aggregation come from the dynamism it offers at runtime. It lets you easily vary the behavior or structure of one database instance without touching the other one. If you have a large suite of unit tests for a particular database class, only having to rebuild the instance you are testing and not the ones upon which it depends is an inexpensive way to make your tests run much more quickly.

Reuse

Early in the days of object-oriented programming, these tools were thought of as a means of reuse, meaning the reuse of code. Achieving code reuse is important, valuable, and doable. However, other factors are even more important when you are developing application code.

Another kind of reuse is the reuse of objects. In the application-development domain, this kind of reuse is paid almost no attention. Objects are cheap and plentiful. It frequently costs more to even consider object reuse than could ever be paid back in the form of memory footprint and CPU time. With databases, however, it is far from the case.

In this section, I show you how to leverage composition and aggregation to achieve both reuse of design and reuse of instances.

Avoid Developing the Same Thing Twice

It's not frequent that different database classes might want to share some amount of design, but it is hardly rare either. Imagine that you have two database designs, as shown in Figure 9.8 and Figure 9.9.

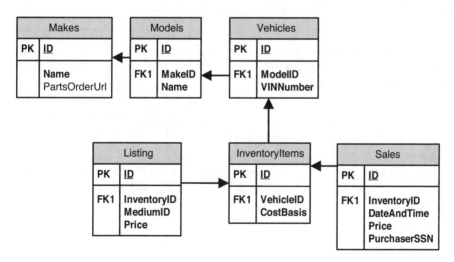

Figure 9.8 *An inventory database with makes and models of cars*

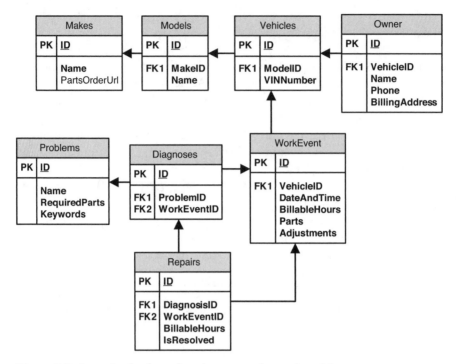

Figure 9.9 *A repairs database that also uses makes and models*

Regardless of the actual mechanism, it would be nice if there were a way to avoid rewriting the makes and models part of those designs and not just because you want to avoid copying and pasting or retyping some scripts. If you have those behaviors duplicated in two database classes, you have to maintain them together. Because the duplicates model the same thing, it is extremely likely you are going to want to keep their designs synchronized.

You can accomplish this with the design in Figure 9.10.

Note that I put neither a solid nor an empty diamond in that diagram. The potential for reuse is there regardless of how you choose to implement it. The mechanism you choose will be a consequence of the forces in the problem you are solving.

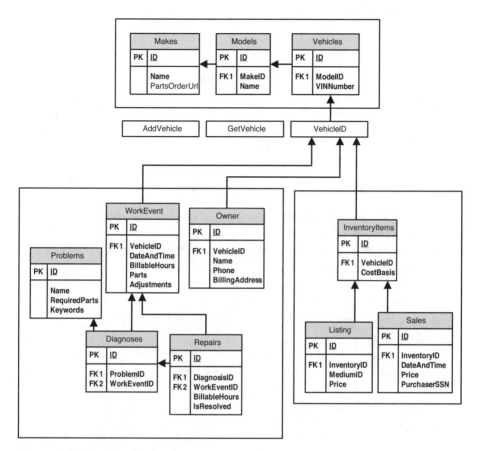

Figure 9.10 *Two similar databases reusing code*

Reuse by Composition or Aggregation

Composition is one mechanism you might use to accomplish reuse. Its advantages are undeniable. Integrating two logical databases when you know they are going to live in the same place is easier than when they live in different database instances. You also avoid the additional operational and performance costs associated with an extra database in production and in all your test environments.

On the other hand, databases are objects that gather knowledge over time. You might want to share knowledge across many downstream database instances. If you are going to reuse a class and a need exists to share data among several instances of a class, then aggregation is really your only choice. The same is true of databases. If you might need to share some core pieces of data between two or more databases, then aggregation is the way to go.

Abstraction

The true power of dividing responsibilities among classes comes from the ability to create abstractions. Abstractions let you hide variation by creating numerous classes of objects that all fulfill the same contract but do so in different ways.

This, in turn, means that a class can be truly encapsulated from the behaviors in its dependencies and opens up the door to the most powerful and soon to be most prolific design pattern in the world: the mock object pattern.

Identifying Opportunities for Abstraction

When hiding the potential for variation, the first thing you need to do is figure out how you're going to talk to multiple objects with variant behavior as if they are interchangeable. That means the dependency must be drawn against a reliable interface rather than implementation details.

For aggregation type relationships, this problem is easy to solve. Databases designed into that kind of relationship are stand-alone objects. A new client could come and couple directly to them, so they need a nice, clean, information-oriented interface.

Composition offers more choices. You might want to make certain tables or views into points of interaction so you can leverage most database engines' natural ability to make tables work together, as with a join. You might also want to force all interactions to go through an information-oriented interface so that a composed object can easily be migrated into being an aggregated one.

Given the `UsersRolesAndAssets` and `UsersAndRoles` classes of database, I choose composition because that's the more complex of the two choices. Figure 9.11 shows that the `AssetOwner`, `AssetManager`, and `AssetAuditor` tables make ideal points of interface. Access is read-only from outside the `UsersAndRoles` class of database to those tables, and I could hide practically any design I wanted behind those structures if I turned them into views.

What I want to do is factor the abstraction part—the interface for users and roles—away from the implementation part, which is the underlying database for users and roles. The design should look like something in Figure 9.12.

In Figure 9.12, assets are coupled to an abstract idea. That is, I've set up the `RoleAssignments` class of databases as an interface with three tables in it: `AssetAuditors`, `AssetManagers`, and `AssetOwners`. These tables are also abstract; they have specified interfaces but no implementations.

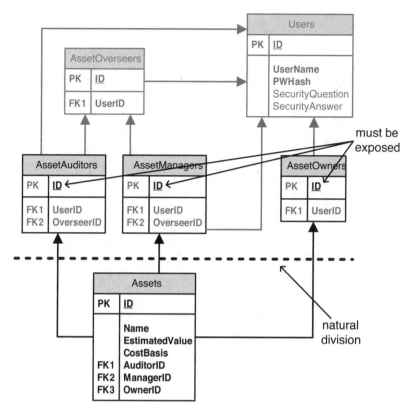

Figure 9.11 *Opportunities to create an abstraction*

I'll get into exactly how this is done soon, but the short version is this—while doing design work, you couple to abstract things, but when you are building an actual database, you couple its structures to the concrete implementations of those abstract things. It's the same basic idea as late-binding a function call in object-oriented programming which, I'm pretty sure, was a good idea before it was a bad one.

Encapsulating Behaviors

Suppose you want to create a new `Assets` database class that delegates to another database. In this way, you can have a number of deployment options. The default deployment adds a `UsersAndRoles` component to the database being deployed. An alternate deployment creates a `UsersAndRoles` database that forwards requests to another `UsersAndRoles` database hosted in a different instance.

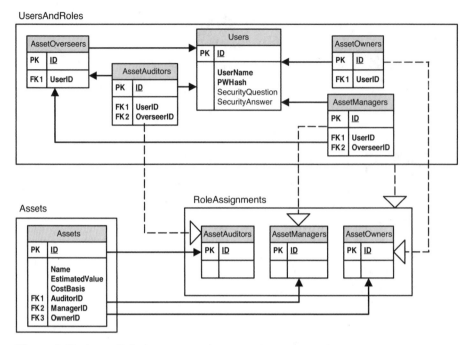

Figure 9.12 *Assets linked to users and groups via an abstraction*

Start by creating an abstract class of databases that only has interface definitions. It would look like this:

```
<Database Name="Abstraction.UsersAndRoles" IsAbstract="true">
  <Version Number="1">
    <Interface>
      <Add Id="IsValidAssetManager">
        <Add Id="Identity" Value="@id" />
      </Add>
      <Add Id="IsValidAssetAuditor">
        <Add Id="Identity" Value="@id" />
      </Add>
      <Add Id="IsValidAssetOwner">
        <Add Id="Identity" Value="@id"/>
      </Add>
    </Interface>
  </Version>
</Database>
```

Now look at how an `Assets` database that consumes the services of a `UsersAndRoles` database would look:

```
<Database Name="Abstraction.Assets">
  <Version Number="1">
    <Interface>
```

```
        <Add Id="AssetManagers">
          <Add Id="Identity" Value="ID" />
        </Add>
        <Add Id="AssetAuditors">
          <Add Id="Identity" Value="ID" />
        </Add>
        <Add Id="AssetOwners">
          <Add Id="Identity" Value="ID"/>
        </Add>
      </Interface>
      <Upgrade TypeName="Abstraction.UsersAndRoles"
        InstanceName="users" TargetVersion="1" />
      <Script>
        <![CDATA[
CREATE TABLE Assets(
  ID INT IDENTITY,
  Name NVARCHAR(200),
  EstimatedValue NUMERIC(12, 2),
  CostBasis NUMERIC(12, 2),
  AuditorID INT NOT NULL,
  ManagerID INT NOT NULL,
  OwnerID INT NOT NULL);
        ]]>
      </Script>
      <Script>
        <![CDATA[
ALTER TABLE Assets
  ADD CONSTRAINT AssetsToManagers
  CHECK(dbo.$users.IsValidAssetManager(ManagerID) = 1)
        ]]>
      </Script>
      <Script>
        <![CDATA[
ALTER TABLE Assets
  ADD CONSTRAINT AssetsToAuditors
  CHECK(dbo.$users.IsValidAssetAuditor(AuditorID) = 1)
        ]]>
      </Script>
      <Script>
        <![CDATA[
ALTER TABLE Assets
  ADD CONSTRAINT AssetsToOwners
  CHECK(dbo.$users.IsValidAssetOwner(OwnerID) = 1)
        ]]>
      </Script>
    </Version>
</Database>
```

That example contains a database class that stores asset records with references to the users associated with them. A reference to a user record is validated abstractly via a check constraint that calls the IsValidAssetManager, IsValidAssetAuditor, or IsValidAssetOwner methods of the users component database.

This setup gives you a lot of flexibility in how the innards of a UsersAnd
Roles implementation are structured, but at the price of not being able to use
some built-in database features such as foreign key constraints. It also requires
more infrastructure than would make sense to put in this chapter of this book.
For instance, to get the full effect of a foreign key constraint, you would also
need to have a way for the UsersAndRoles implementation to check whether,
say, it was okay to change a user out of his role.

Whether the juice is worth the squeeze for something like this is a decision
you have to make, and you will have to make it for every relationship, probably
several times for some. However, the point of this section is to show you how to
create variation of behavior and hide it behind an abstraction, not to advise you
on which design decisions to make and when.

Next, build an implementation of that abstraction for the hosted Users
AndRoles database class.

```
<Database Name="Abstraction.UsersAndRolesImpl"
  Implements="Abstraction.UsersAndRoles">
  <Version Number="1" Implements="1">
    <!-- Create encapsulated tables -->
    <Script>
      <![CDATA[
CREATE TABLE AssetManagers(
  ID INT IDENTITY PRIMARY KEY, UserID INT, OverseerID INT);

CREATE TABLE AssetAuditors(
  ID INT IDENTITY PRIMARY KEY, UserID INT, OverseerID INT);

CREATE TABLE AssetOwners(
  ID INT IDENTITY PRIMARY KEY, UserID INT, OverseerID INT);
      ]]>
    </Script>
    <Script>
      <![CDATA[
CREATE FUNCTION $BaseVersion.IsValidAssetManager(
  $BaseVersion.IsValidAssetManager.Identity INT)
RETURNS BIT
AS
BEGIN
  RETURN (SELECT
    CASE COUNT(*) WHEN 0 THEN 0 ELSE 1 END
    FROM AssetManagers(ID)
    WHERE ID =
      $BaseVersion.IsValidAssetManager.Identity)
END;
      ]]>
    </Script>
    <Script>
      <![CDATA[
```

```
CREATE FUNCTION $BaseVersion.IsValidAssetAuditor(
  $BaseVersion.IsValidAssetAuditor.Identity INT)
RETURNS BIT
AS
BEGIN
  RETURN (SELECT
    CASE COUNT(*) WHEN 0 THEN 0 ELSE 1 END
    FROM AssetAuditors(ID)
    WHERE ID =
      $BaseVersion.IsValidAssetAuditor.Identity)
END;
    ]]>
    </Script>
    <Script>
    <![CDATA[
CREATE FUNCTION $BaseVersion.IsValidAssetOwner(
  $BaseVersion.IsValidAssetOwner.Identity INT)
RETURNS BIT
AS
BEGIN
  RETURN (SELECT CASE
    CASE COUNT(*) WHEN 0 THEN 0 ELSE 1 END
    FROM AssetOwners(ID)
    WHERE ID =
      $BaseVersion.IsValidAssetOwner.Identity)
END;
    ]]>
    </Script>
    <!-- stored procedures for populating tables -->
  </Version>
</Database>
```

Note all the `Implements` attributes. For database classes, that is how I indicate that the class implements an abstraction. For versions, that's how I tell the database build system that comes with this book what version of the abstraction it implements.

> **Note**
>
> Sprinkled throughout the example is the token `$BaseVersion`. That's how I access the design elements of the abstract version being implemented.

The preceding database class builds a database that contains data for users and groups. It also exposes some functions that can be used to validate a proposed link to a user in a role. This essentially translates those check constraints in the containing `Assets` database into selects against a primary key.

After that, build the other implementation, which forwards the requests to a foreign database. I don't deal with the specifics of calling a dynamically referenced foreign database in this example as that's not really the point. Instead, I use the syntax FOREIGN (expression) to represent delegating to a foreign database the task of executing an expression.

```
<Database Name="Abstraction.UsersAndRolesRef"
  Implements="Abstraction.UsersAndRoles">
  <Version Number="1" Implements="1">
    <Script>
      <![CDATA[
/* Set up cross database connection stuff */
      ]]>
    </Script>
    <Script>
      <![CDATA[
CREATE FUNCTION $BaseVersion.IsValidAssetManager(
  $BaseVersion.IsValidAssetManager.Identity INT)
RETURNS BIT
AS
BEGIN
  RETURN FOREIGN($BaseVersion.IsValidAssetManager(
    $BaseVersion.IsValidAssetManager.Identity))
END;
      ]]>
    </Script>
    <Script>
      <![CDATA[
CREATE FUNCTION $BaseVersion.IsValidAssetAuditor(
  $BaseVersion.IsValidAssetAuditor.Identity INT)
RETURNS BIT
AS
BEGIN
  RETURN FOREIGN($BaseVersion.IsValidAssetAuditor(
    $BaseVersion.IsValidAssetAuditor.Identity))
END;
      ]]>
    </Script>
    <Script>
      <![CDATA[
CREATE FUNCTION $BaseVersion.IsValidAssetOwner(
  $BaseVersion.IsValidAssetOwner.Identity INT)
RETURNS BIT
AS
BEGIN
  RETURN FOREIGN($BaseVersion.IsValidAssetOwner(
    $BaseVersion.IsValidAssetOwner.Identity))
END;
      ]]>
    </Script>
  </Version>
</Database>
```

This gives you the basic structures you need to build flexible database designs that hide variation of behavior. Hiding variable behavior is probably not the most important design decision you'll have to make when deciding how to structure a production database but, as you'll see in Chapter 10, "Mocking," it is absolutely critical to test-driven development.

Finding Ways to Allow Variation in Dependencies

If you already have the capability to do composition and aggregation in your engine, all you need to add is the capability to vary the classes that are used as the composed or aggregated database classes. One way might be to make any class that depends on an abstraction inherently abstract and put another structure in place to tie together dependents and dependencies.

```
<DatabaseImplementation
  Name="ConcreteAssets"
  TypeToBuild="Abstraction.Assets" />
  <InstanceMapping Name="users" Type="Abstraction.UsersAndRolesImpl" />
</DatabaseImplementation>
```

Another way to do it would be for your database build mechanism to accept dependency classes as parameters when it is asked to construct a new instance and then to have it track what choices were made in the database so that future upgrades can follow the right track.

```
var library = new[] {
  DatabaseDescriptor.LoadFromFile("Abstraction.UsersAndRoles.xml"),
  DatabaseDescriptor.LoadFromFile("Abstraction.UsersAndRolesImpl.xml"),
  DatabaseDescriptor.LoadFromFile("Abstraction.UsersAndRolesRef.xml"),
};
var instantiator = Instantiator.GetInstance(
  DatabaseDescriptor.LoadFromFile("Abstraction.Assets.xml"),
  library);
instantiator.BindInstanceType("users", "Abstraction.
UsersAndRolesMock");
```

In this solution, you load up a library of database classes from the various files in which they live. You then create a database instantiator object for the class of object you want to construct. Finally, you configure that instantiator to tell it the concrete types of component instances.

The former solution is slightly easier to implement, but I tend toward the latter solution because it is a lot more flexible in the long run. In any event, your circumstances might call for an entirely different implementation, and I don't want to color any decision you make.

I am enough against the first way of doing things that I didn't bother to put example code in the companion zip file for it. If you have a compelling reason to take that road, I'm sure you will figure out a way to do so, though I must point out that those circumstances seem incredibly unlikely. This is because you can always build a solution that takes inputs as shown in the former example on top of the mechanism that supports the latter example.

Dealing with the Time Problem

You might have noticed you have to deal with a little bit of trickiness when building a database that isn't there for application logic classes. Interfaces evolve over time, but the implementations behind them might evolve as well. Figure 9.13 depicts the problem of these two things happening over time.

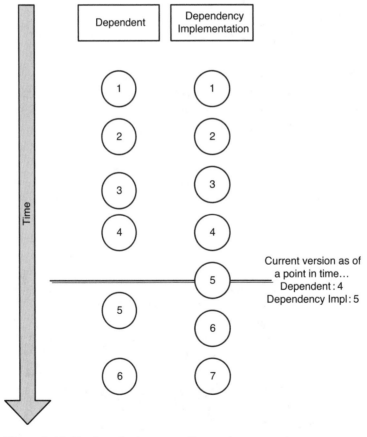

Figure 9.13 *Versions don't necessarily match up over time*

If the dependency were direct, it wouldn't be that hard to keep everything in sync. Just draw a line from the dependency to the version of the dependent it needs. Because you have an intermediate class that serves as an abstraction, it gets a little more complicated. The key is to allow each version of an implementation database to declare what version of the abstraction it is implementing and to express dependencies in terms of the abstract version needed rather than the concrete one, as shown in Figure 9.14.

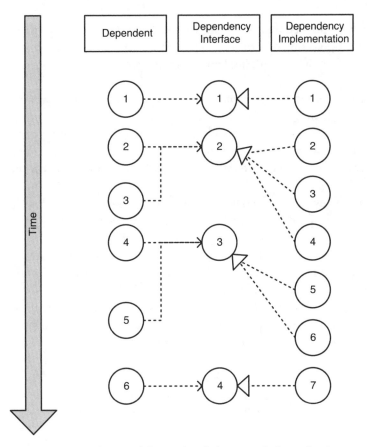

Figure 9.14 *Evolution of three related classes with dependencies properly specified*

In case you aren't familiar with UML-esque notation, the dashed arrow with the winged head means "depends on." It's saying that, for instance, version 6 of the dependent database class needs something that conforms to version 4 of the dependency interface.

The dashed arrow with the triangular head means "realizes." So version 7 of the dependency implementation realizes the contract embodied in version 4 of the dependency interface class. Anywhere you want to use version 4 of the interface class, you can use a version 7 instance of the implementation class instead.

When actually upgrading the dependent database resolving an abstract version to the lowest concrete version that supports it is a pretty simple matter. For example, in Figure 9.14, version 6 of the dependent database wants version four of its abstract dependency, which translates to version seven of the concrete dependency.

You probably have noticed that this creates a "problem" in the form of gaps. That is, in Figure 9.14, version 4 of the dependent database requires version 3 of its dependency interface, which isn't implemented until version 5 of the concrete implementation.

Why this is a problem is that version 5 of the dependency implementation database doesn't exist until after the thing that needs it exists. If that gap is measured in minutes, it's probably not a big deal. In fact, that's how I recommend people work. However, if the gap is measured in months, you have a real problem because the dependent database is in an unreleasable state for the duration.

That problem, however, is not really a derivative of managing coupling in this way. Instead it is a function of bad process, probably something like not working on whole feature slices or working on too many things at a time.

In the case of prior examples, the realizations are represented in the form of the Implements attributes in a version XML element. The dependencies are defined by the Upgrade XML elements.

So, for instance, the following XML shows that version one of some database class depends on version one of some dependency abstraction, while versions two and three of the consumer class depend on version two of the abstraction:

```
<Database Name="Consumer">
  <!--
    builds an instance DB named 'dep' of type
    DependencyInterface, version 1
  -->
  <Version Number="1">
    <Upgrade
      TypeName="DependencyInterface"
      InstanceName="dep"
      TargetVersion="1" />
  </Version>
  <!--
    dep should already be at DependencyInterface version 1.
    this version upgrades it to version 2.
  -->
```

```
<Version Number="2">
  <Upgrade
    TypeName="DependencyInterface"
    InstanceName="dep"
    TargetVersion="2" />
</Version>
<!--
  This version doesn't change dep but dep has already been built
  to version 1.  Hence, a v2 component DB is inherited by this
  version
-->
<Version Number="3" />
</Database>
```

Likewise, the following database definition shows an implementation of `DisplayInterface` that supports version one and version two of the abstract interface:

```
<Database
  Name="DependencyImplementation"
  Implements="DependencyInterface"
  IsAbstract="true">

  <!-- v1 Implementation is a v1 Interface -->
  <Version Number="1" Implements="1" />

  <!--v2 Implementation is a v1 Interface -->
  <Version Number="2" Implements="1" />

  <!--v3 Implementation is a v2 Interface -->
  <Version Number="3" Implements="2" />
</Database>
```

That information is sufficient to enable your database build engine to validate the coupling between two proposed upgrades in two logical database instances. Determining which versions of an interface are backward compatible with one another is pretty easy, so the range of valid versions for a dependency class is easy to calculate.

This gives you a lot of flexibility in how you assemble a system of database objects. In production, you might not want that flexibility, but taking a flexible system and making it rigid is extremely easy. Doing the opposite is pretty hard. I recommend that you create a database build tool that hard-codes all the database classes and versions. That tool can be used by your test organization. The same binary image of the tool that was tested could then be used when doing production promotions.

The flexibility, as you'll see in Chapter 10, is critical to creating a simple, healthy suite of unit tests for your various database classes.

Summary

At least two kinds of design exist, in object-oriented terms: how the internal details of a class are arranged, and how a class relates to other classes. Both are important.

In the database world, a large body of work surrounding how a database instance's innards should work already exists. So in this chapter, I focused on how classes of databases should relate to one another. That might be a foreign concept to you, but it is necessary to get the full effect of test-driven development. Part of TDD is finding the right design and defining the right level of modularity.

The basic thought-tool used in object-oriented design work is dividing concepts into related buckets. Things that are cohesive—strongly related to one another—should be placed "near" one another. Things that are weakly related should be kept as separate as possible.

In terms of mechanisms, you have two main ways to go about this: composition and aggregation. Those terms might both be practically archaic in the application development world, but they still mean a lot in regard to designing systems of database instances.

When an object is composed of another object, they are logically separate but physically adjacent, like fields in a record. When an object is an aggregate of other objects, both logical and physical separation exist, like two records related by a foreign key. Each has advantages and disadvantages and, at this formative stage of developing database technology, composition is probably a lot easier to achieve than aggregation.

In either event, separating a design into several related classes puts you in a position to do what object-oriented designs really let you do well: create abstractions. Abstractions allow a class to couple to a role, rather than a specific type. After the class is coupled to a role, developers can fill that role with any object able to do the job.

You might wonder why this is important. After all, no need exists for a lot of variation in database designs right now, right? For one thing, that might not really be true. It might simply be that developers' inability to easily create abstractions discourages their use.

The more sapient response is that a need actually does exist for variation in database behavior in the form of mocking. The next chapter provides a look at why mocking is important and how the ability to create abstractions helps you mock out behaviors you don't want to cover in a particular test.

Chapter 10

Mocking

Useful systems tend to have multiple behaviors. If a system only has one behavior, one could argue that test-driven development is not really necessary for that system.

Test-driven development is a means by which you document the behaviors that live in a system in tests. The trick is finding a way to test any one behavior separately from the others.

In classic object-oriented environments, the techniques for doing this are well established. In a nutshell, they all boil down to this: Hide dependency behaviors behind abstractions and then create implementations of those abstractions that have constant behavior. You can also use a rich host of tools to make such processes a lot easier.

My proposal is that the technique for mocking out dependencies in a class of databases is the same as when doing so in the object-oriented world. Create an abstract class of databases behind which the dependent behaviors are hidden. In integrated environments, connect the real dependency to its dependent. In unit testing environments, use a mock implementation of that abstraction to test the dependent class of databases.

I believe that if developers start doing this, a bounty of tools will spring up around the activity, the same as what happened with object-oriented languages.

Testing Individual Behaviors

For any reasonably complex system, the million-dollar question is invariably "How do I test each behavior without the influence of others?" This is an easy problem to solve for two behaviors that are not related: Write tests for each without regard of the other. When the behaviors are related, for instance if one depends on another, that's where the going gets tough.

Why do you want to do this? One answer is "because you want people to care about your test suites." Another is "for the same reason you want to encapsulate any other two unrelated things." If a test suite is seen as a house of cards that crumbles as soon as any changes are made, then people won't care when they fail. If nobody cares when your tests fail, then you really haven't gotten much from writing them.

Tests specify all that which can affect their outcome but they do not control. So if you have a test that specifies how one behavior operates by including an assumption about how another behavior will work, you are actually testing both those behaviors with that single artifact.

The good news is that tests can control an awful lot. In test-driven development, designs are side-effects of valid tests and not the other way around. So your tests can *force* a design that allows it to test each behavior independently of one another.

After a behavior has had all of its direct dependencies broken and replaced with indirect ones, you can use mock objects to isolate that behavior from all of its concrete dependencies.

Why Encapsulate

Encapsulation is a good thing. It is of great value to you as a developer and, ultimately, to your customers that any two unrelated things not affect one another. Many people accept this with regard to object-oriented designs involved in creating application logic, though some interpret it differently from others. I sincerely hope that I've instilled this belief in you with regard to databases by this point. So it should be an easy leap that this is how things should be with tests.

The most practical and obvious application of how it harms you to not encapsulate behaviors from one another while testing is what happens to a suite of tests when you don't. If people are being good about writing or changing tests in advance of developing production code and their changes frequently cause dozens of other tests to fail, they will eventually start to consider the test suite to be more of a burden than a boon.

What do developers do with code that is burdensome? The best ones fix or replace it. The worst ignore it. Most live somewhere in between. Having a suite of tests that everyone ignores is not desirable, and I can tell you from personal experience, it is excruciating to have a suite of tests that everyone ignores but you.

Tests Test Everything Not Under Their Control

A test does not magically specify what you want it to specify. It specifies the behavior of every relevant thing it does not control. Consider the following middle-tier code (C#):

```
[TestFixture]
public class FilteredItemsTests
{
  [Test]
  public void FilteredItemCount()
  {
    var server = new FilteredItemsServer();

    Assert.That(
      server.GetItems("live human", 98.5, 98.7).Length,
      Is.EqualTo(1));
  }
}

public class FilteredItemsServer
{
  public Item[] GetItems(
    string query,
    double lowTemperatureF,
    double highTemperatureF)
  {
    var items = new ItemsServer().GetItems(query);

    return items
      .Where(i => i.TemperatureF >= lowTemperatureF)
      .Where(i => i.TemperatureF <= highTemperatureF)
      .ToArray();
  }
}
```

This test looks like it specifies the `FilteredItemsServer.GetItems` method, but it doesn't. It demands something from both `ItemsServer` and `FilteredItemsServer`. It just happens to query the former indirectly via the latter.

Tests test all the parts of what they measure that are not known in advance. There is an interesting correlation to be drawn here. Information is all the data that is not known in advance by the recipient. A test tests all the parts of its expectations that it doesn't already know to be true. One could argue that, by definition, tests test all the information they receive. This fits very nicely with the way clients like tests should interact with database instances—via a narrow, information-oriented interface.

Controlling Irrelevant Behaviors from Tests

The tricky bit of isolating behaviors is making sure that tests only receive information from one behavior at a time. The nice thing about test-driven development is that tests are not only first-class citizens of a code base, they are the only first-class citizens of a code base. Tests exist to specify what should be there. Product code exists to make tests pass.

You have two ways to ensure a test doesn't receive information from a behavior. One way is to ensure that behavior isn't invoked in the course of running a test. Another way is to know in advance what that behavior's contribution is going to be to the data a test will receive.

Sometimes you can isolate two behaviors by doing something as simple as measuring one behavior's result and then including that measurement in the expectations of your test for another behavior. This is demonstrated in the following code:

```
[Test]
public void FilteredItemCount_Shielded()
{
  var items = new ItemsServer().GetItems("live human");
  var server = new FilteredItemsServer();

  Assert.That(
    server.GetItems("live human", 98.5, 98.7).Length,
    Is.EqualTo(items.Count(i =>
      i.TemperatureF >= 98.5 && i.TemperatureF <= 98.7)));
}
```

The previous example shows how a test might go about insulating itself from a behavior it's not trying to test.

Mocking Controls Behaviors

Other times, it's not so simple as measuring a part of a process and then using the result of that measurement to evaluate the whole. Even in the cases where measuring the outcome of a behavior works, you still run a small risk of one behavior affecting the tests for another. For instance, if in the previous example, the `ItemsServer.GetItems` method were to start crashing, the test for `FilteredItemsServer.GetItems` would fail.

That risk is small and probably not worth worrying about, but a very real chance exists that a behavior could develop an outside dependency—especially if you aren't regularly isolating dependencies into separate classes. Outside dependencies make the measure-and-adjust-expectations technique not work because they could be slow, unreliable, or unpredictable.

Mocking is another technique that enables you to substitute a production behavior that will likely grow, change, and acquire dependencies of its own with a test-only behavior that will only ever change as a consequence of changes in the contract between the behavior you intend to specify and its dependencies.

Mocking in Object-Oriented Programming

"Classic" mocking is firmly rooted in modern test-driven development. There are always little retro-revolutions that tell you not to mock; that you shouldn't break behaviors down into manageable pieces; or that you should start wearing bell-bottoms and preaching peace, love, and understanding.

Wear whatever you want and activate for all the peace you like, but don't let anyone convince you that mocking is a bad idea. Mocking is here to stay. In case you aren't familiar with the technique, let's look at how it works in the application-logic world.

This example starts with a small design, two classes with a dependency from one to the other, and then shows a test suite for each of them. Variation in the dependent class is not a problem. However, variation in the dependency will cause all the dependent class's tests to fail even though the behaviors they supposedly specify haven't changed.

You then see how to decouple the dependent behavior from its dependency. This involves switching the dependent class's relationship with its dependency over to an abstraction with the same interface. After you do that, you'll be free to define another implementation of the abstraction that has a well-known behavior defined by its test. Using that behavior when testing the dependent class completely decouples one behavior from another.

The final step is using integration tests to ensure that everything plays nicely together. If you are an experienced developer working in a statically typed language, this is not a super important step. If you are on the steep part of the learning curve or you are using a more weakly typed language, this becomes critical. Either way, it's valuable to do.

Setup

Let's say you have the design shown in Figure 10.1.

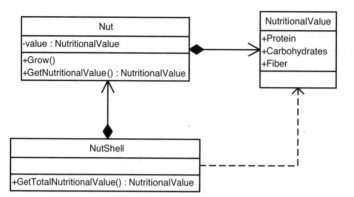

Figure 10.1 Nut, Nutshell, *and* NutritionalValue

NutritionalValue is a data object with no behavior. Its implementation is shown in the following code:

```
public class NutritionalValue
{
  public double Protein { get; set; }
  public double Carbohydrates { get; set; }
  public double Fiber { get; set; }
}
```

Nut objects have a (somewhat) complex, fractal mechanism for determining their nutritional value. The test specifying how this works is as follows:

```
[Test]
public void NutGrowthTest()
{
  var nut = new Nut(4);

  Assert.That(
    nut.GetNutritionalValue(),
    Is.EqualTo(NutritionalValue.Zero));

  GrowAndAssertValue(nut, 0.1, 0.001, 0.005);
  GrowAndAssertValue(nut, 0.2089, 0.0017, 0.010);
  GrowAndAssertValue(nut, 0.3282, 0.0020, 0.0150);
  GrowAndAssertValue(nut, 0.4598, 0.0023, 0.0200);
  GrowAndAssertValue(nut, 0.4598, 0.0023, 0.0200);
}

private static void GrowAndAssertValue(
    Nut nut,
    double expectedProtein,
    double expectedCarbohydrates,
    double expectedFiber)
```

```
{
  nut.Grow();

  var actualValue = nut.GetNutritionalValue();
  Assert.AreEqual(expectedProtein, actualValue.Protein, 0.0001);
  Assert.AreEqual(expectedCarbohydrates, actualValue.Carbohydrates,
    0.0001);
  Assert.AreEqual(expectedFiber, actualValue.Fiber, 0.0001);
}
```

That test drives an implementation as follows:

```
public class Nut
{
  private NutritionalValue value;
  private int generations;

  public Nut(int growthGenerations)
  {
    this.value = NutritionalValue.Zero;
    this.generations = growthGenerations;
  }

  public NutritionalValue GetNutritionalValue()
  {
    return value;
  }

  public void Grow()
  {
    if (generations == 0)
    {
      return;
    }

    generations--;

    value = new NutritionalValue
    {
      Protein =
        (Math.Pow(1 + value.Protein, 1.08) - 1) +
        (value.Carbohydrates / 2) +
        0.1,
      Carbohydrates =
        (Math.Pow(1 + value.Carbohydrates / 2, 1.3) - 1)
        + 0.001,
      Fiber = value.Fiber + 0.005
    };
  }
}
```

Nutshells add a constant amount of fiber to the nutritional value of the nuts they contain and have a way of yielding the underlying nut. Following is the test that specifies that behavior:

```
[Test]
public void AddsASmallAmountOfFiber()
{
  var shell = new Nutshell();
  var nut = shell.GetNut();
  var nutNutritionalValue = nut.GetNutritionalValue();

  Assert.That(
    shell.GetNutritionalValue(),
    Is.EqualTo(
      new NutritionalValue
      {
        Protein = nutNutritionalValue.Protein,
        Carbohydrates = nutNutritionalValue.Carbohydrates,
        Fiber = nutNutritionalValue.Fiber + 1
      }));
}
```

Having that test would in part drive the development of the following class:

```
public class Nutshell
{
  private readonly Nut nut;

  public Nutshell()
  {
    var generations = 10;
    nut = new Nut(generations);

    for (var i = 0; i < generations; ++i)
    {
      nut.Grow();
    }
  }

  public Nut GetNut()
  {
    return nut;
  }

  public NutritionalValue GetNutritionalValue()
  {
    var result = new NutritionalValue
    {
      Protein = nut.GetNutritionalValue().Protein,
      Carbohydrates = nut.GetNutritionalValue().Carbohydrates,
      Fiber = 1 + nut.GetNutritionalValue().Fiber
    };
```

```
      return result;
   }
}
```

These tests work fine. If Nutshell changes, let's say to add a small amount of protein to the nutritional value of the underlying nut, you have a nice clean process for doing this. Start by changing the test as shown in the following snippet:

```
Assert.That(
   shell.GetNutritionalValue(),
   Is.EqualTo(
     new NutritionalValue
     {
       Protein = nutNutritionalValue.Protein + 0.3,
       Carbohydrates = nutNutritionalValue.Carbohydrates,
       Fiber = nutNutritionalValue.Fiber + 1
     }));
```

When that test fails, change the Nutshell class as in the following code:

```
var result = new NutritionalValue
{
   Protein = 0.3 + nut.GetNutritionalValue().Protein,
   Carbohydrates = nut.GetNutritionalValue().Carbohydrates,
   Fiber = 1 + nut.GetNutritionalValue().Fiber
};
```

The tests pass and that works great. Let's say you want to change the Nut class so that it calls out to an external service to get its random numbers.

Luckily, the service provides a handy test implementation that offers a simple progression of numbers. The first time you invoke it within a session, you get a 1. The next time, you get a 2, then a 3, and so on. So predictability is not a problem, and you can easily change your Nut tests to work with the web service and point it to your service provider's mock web service.

However, the service provider chose to host the mock service on the other side of the world. Each query takes a nanosecond to compute but has an extra tenth of a second added to it in the form of a round trip. This makes instantiating the Nut class extremely expensive. That, in turn, makes any test that creates a Nut object expensive to use in tests.

Decoupling

You can no longer build a Nut object in any of your tests. In fact, none of the current tests would even compile after you made the previous change because the way nuts are made has changed, which means that the way you make nutshells must change as well.

Because you have to change all of this stuff anyway, hide the problem so you never have to make this kind of change in your tests again. What you want to do is factor the construction and behavior of nuts away from the `Nutshell` class, as shown in Figure 10.2.

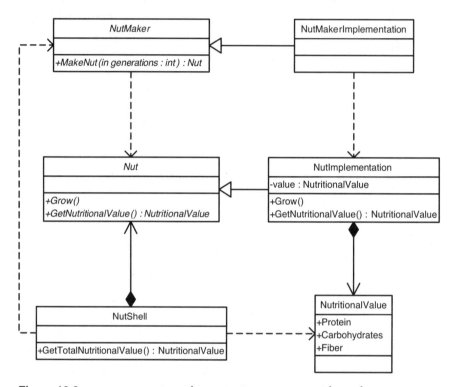

Figure 10.2 `Nut`, `Nutshell`, *and* `NutritionalValue` *with an abstraction*

The new design hides instantiation of a `Nut` behind an instance of the new `NutMaker` type, makes both `Nut` and `NutMaker` abstract, and moves all the old behaviors into two new types: `NutImplementation` and `NutMakerImplementation`.

The advantage of this new design is that you can preserve all the old behaviors, such as `NutShell` being responsible for deciding when a new `Nut` is created, while being able to isolate each behavior from its dependencies.

You learn how the actual isolation happens in a bit, but first, refactor to the new design:

```
public abstract class NutMaker
{
    public abstract Nut MakeNut(int generations);
```

```
}

public class NutMakerImplementation : NutMaker
{
  public override Nut MakeNut(int generations)
  {
    return new NutImplementation(generations);
  }
}

public abstract class Nut
{
  public abstract void Grow();
  public abstract NutritionalValue GetNutritionalValue();
}

public class NutImplementation : Nut
{
  public NutImplementation(int growthGenerations)
  {
    this.value = NutritionalValue.Zero;
    this.generations = growthGenerations;
  }

  /* the rest is the same as for the old Nut class */
}
```

That refactor causes a compiler error everywhere that an instance of Nut was created. To get things compiling, just switch all the new Nut expressions to new NutImplementation for now.

The next thing to do is give yourself a way to vary Nut behaviors. You accomplish this by routing construction of Nut objects through the NutMaker interface. In C#, you can easily do this without affecting existing code. This is shown in the following example:

```
/* create a new constructor that uses NutMaker */
public Nutshell(NutMaker maker)
{
  var generations = 10;
  nut = maker.MakeNut(generations);

  for (var i = 0; i < generations; ++i)
  {
    nut.Grow();
  }
}

/* make the old constructor delegate to the new one */
public Nutshell() : this(new NutMakerImplementation()) { }
```

That gets you the flexibility you need to be able to test two things separately from one another. Next, you need to take advantage of the new abstractions to isolate each behavior from the other.

Isolation

Now create a MockNut class that returns a constant amount of protein and categories, as shown in the following code:

```
public class MockNut : Nut
{
  public override void Grow()
  {
  }

  public override NutritionalValue GetNutritionalValue()
  {
    return new NutritionalValue()
    {
      Protein = 0.567,
      Carbohydrates = 0.891,
      Fiber = 0.234
    };
  }
}
```

This requires a MockNutMaker class, which is shown in the next code snippet:

```
public class MockNutMaker : NutMaker
{
  public override Nut MakeNut(int generations)
  {
    return new MockNut();
  }
}
```

Now it's easy to change the Nutshell tests so that they specify just the behavior of Nutshell and its contract with Nut, without regard for how NutImplementation works. This change follows:

```
var shell = new Nutshell(new MockNutMaker());
```

Now the unit tests for the Nutshell class are completely resilient to changes in the Nut class.

Integration

In some cases, especially when complex networks of classes are working together to deliver a unit of value to a customer, ensuring more than just individual behaviors and the contracts between them is necessary. Ensuring that the behaviors all "line up" correctly and produce the value the customer needs is also important.

If you have a good suite of acceptance tests, you'll already have something that does that. If not, I recommend creating integration tests. Even if you do have a good suite of acceptance tests, creating integration tests in addition is sometimes valuable because they tend to run fairly quickly when compared to acceptance tests and the faster you get feedback from a suite of tests, the more valuable it is.

An integration test is responsible for ensuring that multiple behaviors, typically in multiple classes, work together. They can run from the "ceiling" of a design, just below the user interface, to its "floor," just above any persistence services. They could also include just two classes. They could also include two behaviors in a single class without any insulation between the two of them. They are there to help you, the developer, figure out what went wrong in a complex system.

Using the mock testing service offered by the service provider ensures that the whole system has a stable, if slow, cumulative behavior. That, in turn, allows you to pin such behaviors down with tests.

Mocking in Database Design

Databases have the exact same problems as object-oriented programs. Why shouldn't they? They have behaviors. Certain behaviors have to couple to other behaviors to make a useful system. Because they have the same basic problem, the basic solution is the same: mocking.

Because databases are at the pre-C++ level of development technology and developers are just now adding the C++-like mechanisms, the different kinds of ways you can arrange objects have an impact on how you choose to mock.

Composition designs provide a lot of power in how you combine the features of various classes. They also provide a lot of potential runtime performance benefits that might well matter in certain deployments. On the other hand, you have to create a new database to inject a new kind of mock. This will have a big impact on how you write your tests and how long they take to run.

Aggregation designs are almost the exact opposite. Their relationship with consumers is much stricter than when arranging by composition. This has performance implications in production environments and an impact on how you write your tests. On the other hand, setting up test environments that require a lot of variation in mocks is probably a lot easier because you can keep rebuilding your mocked database without rebuilding the database you are testing.

Example Problem

Let's look at a database that has some dependencies between its behaviors. Consider a database that backs a smart phone app that helps people escape from a burning building. Figure 10.3 shows this database.

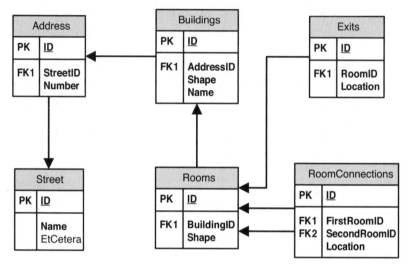

Figure 10.3 *Emergency routing application database*

This design has three entities of interest. A Building is the thing you want very much to not be in when you fire up your app. A Room is a part of a building connected to other rooms and also connected to an EmergencyExit.

The app uses the Building to group together all the rooms, through which an escape route might be planned. It uses the connections between Rooms to help the user plan an escape route to the nearest EmergencyExit.

The behaviors in the database are as follows:

- Add building
- Add room to building
- Add emergency exit to room
- Add emergency to room

- Remove emergency from room

- Connect room to another room

- Get room by coordinate

- Get building by room

- Get all rooms for building

- Get all rooms for room

- Get all emergency exits for room

- Get all emergencies for room

On the server-side, this is used to build a block of XML, which is then passed back to the application. The application proactively gathers data and plans an escape route whenever you change locations, so performance is not really a concern.

It's a reasonable design for the function of the application, but it makes testing annoying by way of coupling. You have to have at least one `Building` to test the relationship between a `Room` and an `EmergencyExit` or an `Emergency`.

Example Solution

Abstractly, I'm sure you've already guessed that the solution is mocking. Without classes of databases, mocking for databases is hard. It's not hard from a technology standpoint; many clever and interesting solutions exist for the technical problems. Instead, determining what you need to mock is difficult.

With classes, it's easier. Mock out the behaviors in one class when testing another. If two behaviors need to be decoupled, put them in different classes. In this case, a building's structure is one logical thing and the various traits of a room are part of another thing.

In this case, you want to separate the structure of a `Building` from the features of a `Room` and then mock out the structure when testing features. You can do this through composition, as shown in Figure 10.4.

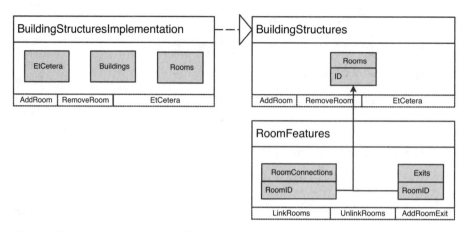

Figure 10.4 *Structures and room features broken into separate classes*

As you would when inverting any dependency, start by adding an abstraction (following):

```
<Database Name="BuildingStructures" IsAbstract="true">
  <Version Number="1">
    <Interface>
      <Add Id="Rooms">
        <Add Id="Identity" Value="ID" />
      </Add>
    </Interface>
  </Version>
</Database>
```

Next, create the default concrete implementation of that abstract database class, shown in the following snippet:

```
<Database
  Name="BuildingStructuresImplementation"
  Implements="BuildingStructures">
  <Version Number="1" Implements="1">
    <Script>
      <![CDATA[
CREATE TABLE Buildings(
  ID INT IDENTITY(1, 1)
    CONSTRAINT BuildingsPK PRIMARY KEY,
  Address NVARCHAR(300),
  Shape BINARY
  /*other dependencies*/)

CREATE TABLE $BaseVersion.Rooms(
  $BaseVersion.Rooms.Identity INT IDENTITY(1, 1)
    CONSTRAINT RoomsPK PRIMARY KEY,
  RoomID INT NOT NULL
```

```
   CONSTRAINT RoomsToBuildingsFK
   FOREIGN KEY REFERENCES Buildings(ID),
 Shape BINARY)
      ]]>
    </Script>
  </Version>
</Database>
```

Then, when writing tests for the RoomFeatures class, you can create a mock BuildingStructures class that has only a Rooms table with only the Identity column, which is all that the RoomFeatures class needs. This is shown in the following code:

```
<Database
  Name="BuildingStructuresMock"
  Implements="BuildingStructures">
  <Version Number="1" Implements="1">
    <Script>
      <![CDATA[
CREATE TABLE $BaseVersion.Rooms(
  $BaseVersion.Rooms.Identity INT PRIMARY KEY)
      ]]>
    </Script>
  </Version>
</Database>
```

It's interesting to note that dependencies between data records flow in exactly the opposite direction as they tend to between middle-tier objects; that is, child rows point to their parents whereas parent objects tend to point to their children. As a consequence, the abstractions and mockeries required are also reversed. If you started your professional life as a database person, that probably feels normal. If you are mostly an object-oriented developer, it will probably feel weird and backward, but you will get used to it.

Having that mock available gives you the capability to write tests for the RoomFeatures class of database, as demonstrated in the following:

```
[Test]
public void AddRoomAssociationsAndGetBackUniqueListOfAssociatedRooms()
{
  var instantiator = Instantiator.GetInstance(
    DatabaseDescriptor.LoadFromFile("RoomFeatures.xml"),
    DatabaseDescriptor.LoadFromFile("BuildingStructures.xml"),
    DatabaseDescriptor.LoadFromFile("BuildingStructuresMock.xml"));
  instantiator.BindInstanceType("structures", "BuildingStructuresMock");
  instantiator.UpgradeToLatestVersion(connection);
  MockRooms(5);

  AssociateRooms(1, 2);
  AssociateRooms(1, 3);
```

```
    AssociateRooms(4, 1);
    AssociateRooms(1, 4);

    var design = new RoomFeatures.v1();
    var readProcedure = design.GetAssociatedRooms;

    var rows = connection.ExecuteStoredProcedure(
      readProcedure,
      new Dictionary<string, object>
      {
        { readProcedure.RoomIdentity, 1 }
      });

    Assert.That(
      rows.Select(r => r[readProcedure.ResultID]).ToArray(),
      Is.EquivalentTo(new[] { 2, 3, 4 }));
  }

  private void AssociateRooms(int room1, int room2)
  {
    var design = new RoomFeatures.v1();
    var writeProcedure = design.AssociateRooms;
    connection.ExecuteStoredProcedure(
      writeProcedure,
      new Dictionary<string, object> {
        {writeProcedure.Room1Identity, room1},
        {writeProcedure.Room2Identity, room2}
      });
  }

  private void MockRooms(int p)
  {
    connection.ExecuteSql("DELETE Rooms");

    for (var i = 1; i <= p; ++i)
    {
      connection.ExecuteSql("INSERT INTO Rooms VALUES(" + i + ")");
    }
  }
```

You can repeat that pattern as often as needed.

Composition

An object that is composed of other objects has an inherently more intimate relationship with its components than an aggregate does with its parts. This is a double-edged sword.

If you relax the encapsulation between two components of an object, you have all kinds of opportunities. When those two components are sets of tables and the object is a database, those opportunities include leveraging a database engine's natural ability to relate data records living in different structures, like tables.

The ability for one class's behavior to join with data from another class is a distinct advantage in the database world. Notwithstanding the performance benefits, which I believe will evaporate over the course of the next two to three decades, it allows developers to use powerful querying language features that we have developed over a substantial period and with which we all have a great deal of affinity.

Consider the following code snippet, which finds all the Foo rows that have at least one Bar row associated with them:

```
SELECT Foo.* FROM Foo INNER JOIN Bar ON Bar.FooID = Foo.ID
```

Now compare it with the next snippet that does the same thing, as might be required to reach across databases:

```
-- Database 1 & 2
CREATE TYPE IdentityList AS TABLE(ID INT);

-- Database 1
DROP PROCEDURE GetBarsByIds;
CREATE PROCEDURE GetBarsByIds
  @ids IdentityList READONLY
AS
  SELECT b.* FROM Bar b INNER JOIN @ids i ON B.ID = i.ID

-- Database 2
DECLARE @BarIds IdentityList;
DECLARE @Bars TABLE (ID INT, X CHAR);

INSERT INTO @BarIds
  SELECT DISTINCT BarID FROM Foo;

INSERT INTO @Bars
  EXECUTE GetBarsByIds @BarIds

SELECT f.* FROM Foo f INNER JOIN @Bars b ON f.BarID = b.ID;
```

My firm belief is that the runtime for either of the two previous examples will eventually converge until they are the same, if it's not already that way by the time this book prints. It will happen one way or another.

What will take work is to make the latter as readable as the former. It can be done. As the performance concerns dissipate, developers might eventually start working on it but someone has to take up the flag and lead the charge.

The downside can be described using the exact same words used to describe the advantages. Composition creates all kinds of opportunities to couple. An opportunity to create coupling is to an undisciplined developer as those little plastic rings from the top of a milk jug is to a kitten: irresistible. It doesn't matter why. That's just the way it is.

The dynamic nature of most database engines exacerbates this problem. It does so by exposing anything and everything to everything and anything as long as the developer knows the name of the thing to which he wants to couple.

Aggregation

The best way to create an impenetrable interface between two database classes is to make sure they are always instantiated into separate database instances. If you do that, then you can make misbehavior difficult enough that junior developers will find respecting the boundary between the two classes easier than violating them.

That said, any barrier between two databases that is firm enough to prevent bad discipline also prevents use of interesting, natural, and expressive language features. Technology is getting better about allowing us to encapsulate without losing fluency. At the time of this writing, a few database platforms are making great strides in allowing for very natural but still properly encapsulated relationships between two database instances. I just don't believe we are there yet.

Designing for Testability

The capability to mock out a behavior is all the justification you need to break one database class into two. Allow me repeat that. The capability to mock out a behavior is *all* the justification you need to break one database class into two.

History has shown me that an extreme minority of the abstractions you create to support testability end up existing solely to support testability by the time you release. That is, the best tool for predicting where behavior will need to vary is where it already needs to vary for tests.

Even if that weren't true, testability is the foundation of agility. A database will never fit into an agile process unless it is properly tested.

Summary

Test-driven development is unsustainable without mocking. There are those who would tell you otherwise. I have been tempted by the call of the "test that covers everything." It's a mirage. There's a good chance you will need to find that out for yourself.

When you do, you'll want to start mocking out dependency behaviors so that your tests can be useful to you. The great thing about this is that it forces you to make the kinds of design decisions you already should have made: encapsulating loosely related ideas from one another, coupling to abstractions rather than concrete behaviors, and so on.

Mocking in the database world is going to be a lot like mocking in the object-oriented world. When you have two behaviors with a dependency, you start by coupling the dependent behavior to an abstraction rather than directly to the dependency. You then create an alternate implementation of that abstraction with a constant, simple, and symbolic behavior. The key is that it is easy to measure that the dependency behavior was invoked and that its output was appropriately consumed by the dependent behavior.

Having a clear array of executable technical specifications in the form of unit tests telling you exactly what your database classes do and don't do is nice. That requires things to be broken out so that each behavior can be exposed and independently measured.

Yet, you don't want to create arbitrary divisions in advance of any actual need. So, what do you do when you started out with two behaviors in a single class and you discover they ought to live in separate classes, or vice versa? You refactor, and that's the topic of the next chapter.

Chapter 11

Refactoring

This book isn't directly about refactoring, but I feel that it's worth a little bit of discussion to at least provide you with a frame of reference for the coming chapters. So, I've added this "mini chapter" to help set some context.

The word *refactor* is bandied about a lot, and much of the time it is misused. Many of the people who use it actually mean "change" even though the definition is much narrower than that. Refactoring is changing design without changing behavior. It is a disciplined way of introducing change that minimizes the risks of injuring existing behavior. In the data world, that can be extended to include knowledge as well as behavior.

Of course, all changes should have a purpose. If you're changing design and not behavior, then you had better have a good reason. For the purpose of this book, let's assume the reason is always to make room for a new feature to be added in the very near future.

Refactoring happens in the context of passing tests. You start with a bunch of passing tests and you should end with the same tests passing. If you're doing something other than that, like changing design in a way that requires your tests to change or driving in new behavior from a failing test, you probably shouldn't call it refactoring.

Each kind of change carries a different amount of risk with it. Changing how structures are organized into classes of databases is very low risk. Likewise, changing how classes of databases relate to one another as would happen when injecting an abstraction is fairly safe. By contrast, changing as in reshaping knowledge into a new data format is dangerous.

The level of risk involved in a change along with the amount of test coverage you already have should help you determine whether you are in a position to safely perform a given refactor. Documenting all the individual refactoring operations and their associated levels of risk is outside the scope of this book.

What Refactoring Is

Refactoring is a highly structured way of changing design. In the object-oriented development world, it's been refined to the point where many of the refactoring operations can be completely automated in a decent IDE. I don't think that we are there yet in the database world, but we're working on it.

Fundamentally, refactoring is the process of changing design without changing behavior. Take, for instance, the merger of two tables into a single table. If the tables were part of a database class's public interface, then that would not be a refactor because you are changing the set of interface constructs visible to clients of your database. Again, there's no reason to change something without the intent of improving it, so let's assume that we are talking about improving design.

Of course, it's nice to say that you aren't changing behavior, but how do you actually know whether you are changing behavior? Fortunately, you can use these nifty little things called *tests* that tell you whether or not a class has a behavior. If you have a complete specification for a class of databases in the form of tests, then you know a change was a refactor if the same tests passed after the change as before.

Changing Design Without Changing Behavior

A lot of changes are safe. A subset of those, known to be extra safe, are changes that change only design and changes that change only behavior. The former are called refactors. Changing design is a risky thing in the object-oriented world. Reducing the scope of any change that affects design to affect design only is one way to cut down on that risk.

> **Note**
>
> Changes that affect only behavior and not design I've heard called *transitions* by Robert Martin. That's not why I call the changes from one version of a database to another *transitions*—I have been calling them that since 2005—but it's a really cool coincidence.

Even more importantly, keeping design and behavior changes as separate as possible forces you to implement a certain degree of encapsulation. After all, if every aspect of your implementation is publicly visible, then how could you change design without affecting apparent behavior?

Consider the design in Figure 11.1.

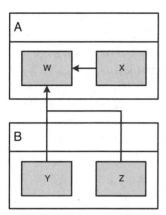

Figure 11.1 *Two database classes:* A *and* B

Figure 11.2 shows an example of a refactored design.

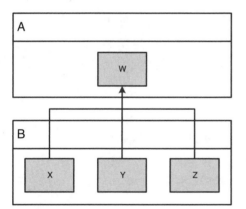

Figure 11.2 W *moved from* A *to* B

Assuming that all the publicly visible stored procedures behave exactly as they did before, that change in design would constitute a refactoring because table X was moved from class A to class B.

In the Context of Passing Tests

Refactoring is hard to do without tests—so hard that I would argue there is no point in even calling a change a refactoring if you don't have adequate test coverage to validate it. Sure, you can and probably have made changes that you felt were pretty secure, but don't call them refactors.

Instead, say that to refactor, you have to start with an adequate executable specification of the behaviors that are living in a design and that all of those tests must be passing. Furthermore, the same tests must pass afterward. I hope that's a clear enough statement that you won't need any examples.

Refactoring is a much simpler thing if you have a good enough suite of tests. Let's try another case. What do you do if you need to change design and there is not adequate test coverage? You don't refactor and, by that, I don't mean you do a change that is pretty safe and just don't call it refactoring. I mean, you realize that you aren't ready to refactor and go do something else to get ready to refactor.

Consider the test suite in Listing 11.1.

Listing 11.1 Animal *Database Class Tests*

```
[Test]
public void AddAndGetPuppies()
{
  var add = design.AddPuppy;
  var get = design.GetPuppyByIdentity;

  var id = connection.ExecuteStoredProcedureScalar(add,
    new Dictionary<string, object>
    {
      { add.Name, "Rex" },
      { add.Color, "Brown" }
    });

  var row = connection.ExecuteStoredProcedure(get,
    new Dictionary<string, object>
    {
      {get.Identity, id }
    });

  Assertions.AssertRowsAreEqual(
    new[]
    {
      new Dictionary<string, object>
      {
        { get.ResultName, "Rex" },
        { get.ResultColor, "Brown" }
      }
    },
    row);
}

[Test]
public void AddAndGetDogs()
{
  var add = design.AddDog;
  var get = design.GetDogByIdentity;
```

```
  var id = connection.ExecuteStoredProcedureScalar(add,
    new Dictionary<string, object>
    {
      { add.Name, "Sparky" },
      { add.Color, "White" }
    });

  var row = connection.ExecuteStoredProcedure(get,
    new Dictionary<string, object>
    {
      {get.Identity, id }
    });

  Assertions.AssertRowsAreEqual(
    new[]
    {
      new Dictionary<string, object>
      {
        { get.ResultName, "Sparky" },
        { get.ResultColor, "White" }
      }
    },
    row);
}

[Test]
public void AddAndGetCats()
{
  var add = design.AddCat;
  var get = design.GetCatByIdentity;

  var id = connection.ExecuteStoredProcedureScalar(add,
    new Dictionary<string, object>
    {
      { add.Name, "Nightshade" },
      { add.Color, "Black" }
    });

  var row = connection.ExecuteStoredProcedure(get,
    new Dictionary<string, object>
    {
      {get.Identity, id }
    });

  Assertions.AssertRowsAreEqual(
    new[]
    {
      new Dictionary<string, object>
      {
        { get.ResultName, "Nightshade" },
        { get.ResultColor, "Black" }
      }
    },
    row);
  }
```

Now let's add in the database class from Listing 11.2.

Listing 11.2 Animal *Database Class*

```
<Database
  Name="Animals"
  >
  <Lenses>
    <Map Name="Current" ToVersion="1" />
  </Lenses>
  <Version Number="1">
    <Interface>
      <Add Id="AddPuppy">
        <Add Id="Name" Value="@name" />
        <Add Id="Color" Value="@color" />
      </Add>
      <Add Id="GetPuppyByIdentity">
        <Add Id="Identity" Value="@id" />
        <Add Id="ResultName" />
        <Add Id="ResultColor" />
      </Add>
      <Add Id="AddDog">
        <Add Id="Name" Value="@name" />
        <Add Id="Color" Value="@color" />
      </Add>
      <Add Id="GetDogByIdentity">
        <Add Id="Identity" Value="@id" />
        <Add Id="ResultName" />
        <Add Id="ResultColor" />
      </Add>
      <Add Id="AddCat">
        <Add Id="Name" Value="@name" />
        <Add Id="Color" Value="@color" />
      </Add>
      <Add Id="GetCatByIdentity">
        <Add Id="Identity" Value="@id" />
        <Add Id="ResultName" />
        <Add Id="ResultColor" />
      </Add>
      <Add Id="AddKitten">
        <Add Id="Name" Value="@name" />
        <Add Id="Color" Value="@color" />
      </Add>
      <Add Id="GetKittenByIdentity">
        <Add Id="Identity" Value="@id" />
        <Add Id="ResultName" />
        <Add Id="ResultColor" />
      </Add>
    </Interface>
    <Script>
      <![CDATA[
```

```
CREATE TABLE Puppies(
  ID INT IDENTITY PRIMARY KEY,
  Name VARCHAR(30),
  Color VARCHAR(10));

CREATE TABLE Dogs(
  ID INT IDENTITY PRIMARY KEY,
  Name VARCHAR(30),
  Color VARCHAR(10));

CREATE TABLE Cats(
  ID INT IDENTITY PRIMARY KEY,
  Name VARCHAR(30),
  Color VARCHAR(10));

CREATE TABLE Kittens(
  ID INT IDENTITY PRIMARY KEY,
  Name VARCHAR(30),
  Color VARCHAR(10));
      ]]>
    </Script>

    <Script>
      <![CDATA[
CREATE PROCEDURE $AddPuppy
  $AddPuppy.Name VARCHAR(30),
  $AddPuppy.Color VARCHAR(10)
AS
BEGIN
  INSERT INTO Puppies(Name, Color)
  VALUES($AddPuppy.Name, $AddPuppy.Color)

  SELECT @@Identity;
END;
      ]]>
    </Script>
    <Script>
      <![CDATA[
CREATE PROCEDURE $GetPuppyByIdentity
  $GetPuppyByIdentity.Identity INT
AS
  SELECT
    Name AS $GetPuppyByIdentity.ResultName,
    Color AS $GetPuppyByIdentity.ResultColor
  FROM Puppies
  WHERE ID = $GetPuppyByIdentity.Identity
      ]]>
    </Script>
    <Script>
      <![CDATA[
CREATE PROCEDURE $AddDog
  $AddDog.Name VARCHAR(30),
  $AddDog.Color VARCHAR(10)
```

```
AS
BEGIN
  INSERT INTO Dogs(Name, Color)
  VALUES($AddDog.Name, $AddDog.Color)

  SELECT @@Identity;
END;
    ]]>
  </Script>
  <Script>
    <![CDATA[
CREATE PROCEDURE $GetDogByIdentity
  $GetDogByIdentity.Identity INT
AS
  SELECT
    Name AS $GetDogByIdentity.ResultName,
    Color AS $GetDogByIdentity.ResultColor
  FROM Dogs
  WHERE ID = $GetDogByIdentity.Identity
    ]]>
  </Script>
  <Script>
    <![CDATA[
CREATE PROCEDURE $AddCat
  $AddCat.Name VARCHAR(30),
  $AddCat.Color VARCHAR(10)
AS
BEGIN
  INSERT INTO Cats(Name, Color)
  VALUES($AddCat.Name, $AddCat.Color)

  SELECT @@Identity;
END;
    ]]>
  </Script>
  <Script>
    <![CDATA[
CREATE PROCEDURE $GetCatByIdentity
  $GetCatByIdentity.Identity INT
AS
  SELECT
    Name AS $GetCatByIdentity.ResultName,
    Color AS $GetCatByIdentity.ResultColor
  FROM Cats
  WHERE ID = $GetCatByIdentity.Identity
    ]]>
  </Script>
  <Script>
    <![CDATA[
CREATE PROCEDURE $AddKitten
  $AddKitten.Name VARCHAR(30),
  $AddKitten.Color VARCHAR(10)
AS
BEGIN
```

```
  INSERT INTO Kittens(Name, Color)
  VALUES($AddKitten.Name, $AddKitten.Color)

  SELECT @@Identity;
END;
      ]]>
    </Script>
    <Script>
      <![CDATA[
CREATE PROCEDURE $GetKittenByIdentity
  $GetKittenByIdentity.Identity INT
AS
  SELECT
    Name AS $GetKittenByIdentity.ResultName,
    Color AS $GetKittenByIdentity.ResultColor
  FROM Kittens
  WHERE ID = $GetKittenByIdentity.Identity
      ]]>
    </Script>
  </Version>
  </Database>
```

Now given the full test coverage for the Dogs and Puppies tables, if I wanted to factor out the variation between a dog and a puppy and merge those tables together, I'm in great shape—at least figuratively. However, no tests touch the Kittens table, do they? So, if I want to collapse the Cat and Kittens table, I need some tests for kittens.

```
[Test]
public void AddAndGetKittens()
{
  var add = design.AddKitten;
  var get = design.GetKittenByIdentity;

  var id = connection.ExecuteStoredProcedureScalar(add,
    new Dictionary<string, object>
    {
      { add.Name, "Nightshade" },
      { add.Color, "Black" }
    });

  var row = connection.ExecuteStoredProcedure(get,
    new Dictionary<string, object>
    {
      {get.Identity, id }
    });

  Assertions.AssertRowsAreEqual(
    new[]
    {
      new Dictionary<string, object>
      {
```

```
        { get.ResultName, "Nightshade" },
        { get.ResultColor, "Black" }
      }
    },
    row);
}
```

With the tests in place, I'm free to collapse those tables together. I could even go as far as collapsing all four tables into a single table with a `Species` field and a `LifecycleState` field, if I so desired.

Of course, any such change should also be protected by transition tests and/or transition safeguards.

Lower and Higher Risk Design Changes

An entire spectrum of changes can be made to a database's design ranging from very safe to very dangerous. The risk level associated with a change should feed into your decision making when deciding whether or not the existing level of test coverage is sufficient to permit refactoring. For databases that were test-driven from the very get-go, it probably won't matter: Coverage will always be adequate. As you'll see in the next chapter, this becomes very important in maintaining legacy databases.

Listing all the known database refactoring operations is outside the scope of this book. Instead, I break down the spectrum into three broad categories of risk. The lowest-risk category is changing things about database classes themselves without altering the structure of an instantiated database. The next level of danger lives in altering how the behaviors that live in things such as stored procedures and views are factored. The highest level of risk is intrinsic to any change that alters the structure of a container for data.

Lower Risk: Changing Class-Level Design

A class of changes exists that only affects the database classes themselves. That is, for them to affect behavior is nearly impossible because they affect only how classes relate to database structures instead of changing the actual design of any given database structure.

This includes things such as moving tables from one class to another, adding abstractions so you can mock, or adding a new public interface item that exposes an existing behavior. They are kind of like changing the namespace of a class in a C# design. The feedback loop is very, very tight and the odds of causing any real havoc are low but still extant.

Consider the database design in Figure 11.3.

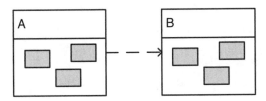

Figure 11.3 *Two database classes:* A *and* B

Now, imagine I want to be able to mock out database class B when testing class A. That would require me to add an abstraction between A and B, as shown in Figure 11.4.

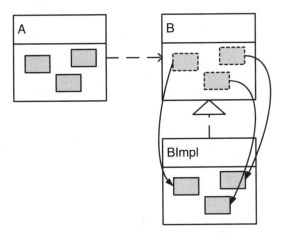

Figure 11.4 B *renamed to* BImpl *with an abstraction left in its place*

This change would fall into the lowest risk category. In these kinds of cases, it is extremely unlikely that a behavior will be created or destroyed. Any level of testing that exercises the relationships between affected structures and their dependents is sufficient.

Medium Risk: Rearranging Behavior Logic

The next level of risk exists in how various behaviors are arranged within a database's logical structure. This might include extracting some instructions from one stored procedure and putting them in another procedure to which the original procedure delegates.

Consider the following views:

```
-- Batch #1
CREATE VIEW NonDeleted AS
SELECT
  f.ID AS FooID,
  b.ID AS BarID,
  f.Code AS Code,
  b.AltCode AS AltCode,
  f.A AS A,
  f.B AS B,
  b.C AS C
FROM Foo AS f INNER JOIN Bar AS b ON f.ID = b.FooID
WHERE b.Del = 0

-- Batch #2
CREATE VIEW Deleted AS
SELECT
  f.ID AS FooID,
  b.ID AS BarID,
  f.Code AS Code,
  b.AltCode AS AltCode,
  f.A AS A,
  f.B AS B,
  b.C AS C
FROM Foo AS f INNER JOIN Bar AS b ON f.ID = b.FooID
WHERE b.Del = 1
```

Let's assume that I don't want the duplication therein and want to move to the following implementation:

```
CREATE VIEW FooBar AS
SELECT
  f.ID AS FooID,
  b.ID AS BarID,
  f.Code AS Code,
  b.AltCode AS AltCode,
  f.A AS A,
  f.B AS B,
  b.C AS C,
  b.Del AS Del
FROM Foo AS f INNER JOIN Bar AS b ON f.ID = b.FooID
GO
CREATE VIEW NonDeleted AS
SELECT
  FooID, BarID, Code, AltCode, A, B, C
FROM FooBar
WHERE Del = 0
GO
CREATE VIEW Deleted AS
```

```
SELECT
  FooID, BarID, Code, AltCode, A, B, C
FROM FooBar
WHERE Del = 1
```

Eradicating the duplication between the preceding views is relatively low risk in that it is unlikely to damage any existing data in a database. However, a very real chance exists that such a factoring could break one or both of those views in a subtle way.

In such a case, I would want to have some tests that exercised the views in an interesting way. That's not to say that a complete and perfect specification of their behaviors is required, but I want more than just proof that the right tables are involved.

In the case of the previous examples, I would want to test the following:

- `Foos` without `Bars` don't show up.

- Deleted `Bars` don't show up in `NonDeleted`.

- Non-deleted `Bars` don't show up in `Deleted`.

- The relationship between a `Foo` and multiple `Bars` is reflected.

- All the other data columns show up in both views.

As I just mentioned, a near-perfect test suite is unnecessary. A few tests that populate a database with some reasonably rich data and check all the results from their respective views will do.

Higher Risk: Altering Knowledge Containers

The highest category of risk includes changes that alter how data is stored. Even if you are changing constraints, risk exists. The biggest risk to these kinds of changes comes from damaging the knowledge stored in a database. You'll want to mitigate that risk with a full regimen of transition tests and transition safeguards.

The other risk you run is damaging a client's ability to add new knowledge to your database. The mitigation for that is to make sure you have a comprehensive specification of a class of databases' behaviors in the form of a unit test suite. If that's impossible, then do the best you can.

This Is Not an Invitation to Skip Testing

By delineating the various categories of risk and the minimum level of testing required to support refactoring, I am not suggesting that you avoid writing tests. If you do everything test-driven, you will probably always exceed the minimum level of testing required. This section is more of an "in case of emergency, break glass" kind of thing. You should already have the testing you need, but this section shows how you evaluate whether or not you really do and what to do if you need more.

Summary

Refactoring is one of the last pieces of the puzzle. Up to this chapter, you've been told "don't plan too far ahead, just deal with things as they come." This is how you deal with things as they come. Make design changes independent of your behavior changes.

Of course, knowing whether or not you've really only impacted behavior is difficult. That's where tests come into play. If you have a healthy suite of tests, you can change design, see that all your tests still pass, check in your changes, and finally adjust your tests to specify the more granular design.

Even with tests, though, all changes imply a certain degree of risk. That level of risk should provide guidance as to how many risk-mitigating activities you need to perform.

For instance, rearranging whole classes of databases without altering any of their contents is probably the lowest-risk kind of refactor so you don't need to do much to mitigate. On the other end of the spectrum is performing "surgery" on a table that contains vital data. In that case, you must dot all of your "i's," cross all of your "t's," and make sure you write plenty of transition tests.

In any event, knowing the scale of risks is not really a good reason to hold back on testing. You should have a full suite of tests for everything you write all the time anyway. If you do, you probably have most of your risks covered already and you don't need to do any extra work in preparation for a refactor.

Where the scale of risk becomes really useful is in dealing with legacy database designs, where a hearty suite of tests is not a foregone conclusion. Chapter 12, "Legacy Databases," deals with that topic directly.

Chapter 12

Legacy Databases

No process can be whole until it has a way to enlist artifacts created before its discovery. In the application world—where designs are relatively easy to change or dispose of—this is true. In the database world—where knowledge adds weight to deployed designs—it goes double.

Legacy databases are typically enormous wads of unspecified behavior. The way they are built and upgraded tends to not conform to the standards set by this book. Before you can think about maintaining any legacy database, you have to coerce it into a class of databases so that you can later write tests.

Rarely does such a design have strong encapsulation and only expose the behaviors that are actually needed. You'll want to work toward good encapsulation over time, but that will be hard because of all the clients using your database in production. After you have a class of databases, you will want to control how applications couple to it.

After you have a handle on coupling, the next problem will be change. Remember, you still don't have tests that would support rapid change. To solve this problem, put forces in place that drive test coverage upward. Most importantly, institute a rule that the test coverage around any given artifact be made satisfactory before any changes are made to it.

A vital skill is the ability to decompose a legacy database into components. One technique, the obvious one, is to look for things that are logically related to one another. Such natural groupings can often be formed into components, and that division will serve you well. Another technique is to look for so-called "seams," which are areas in the system where coupling is weaker and can more easily be replaced with abstraction.

Promoting to a Class

Step one of wrestling a legacy database into submission is gaining control over how it is upgraded and giving yourself the ability to instantiate new, test instances at will. This involves recognizing that, for the purposes of this book, the behavior of your legacy database is unspecified. Chapter 8, which covers error and remediation, talks about how to handle unspecified behavior, so this section focuses on how that applies in legacy database scenarios.

Start by making a new database class. The very first version of this class is just a script that can turn an empty database into one with the same design as a currently deployed legacy database. It can also detect that said design is already present and do nothing.

Next you want to pin the behavior of that transition script with some kind of transition test. The exact implementation details are not important. Two solutions come to mind, though. One is comparing the result of building a new database to some kind of standard such as the result of restoring a backup. Another one, and this is super-easy, is to simply pin a hash of the script used to build version 1 of your legacy database class.

Deducing Initial Version

Suppose I have a legacy database with a design, as shown in Figure 12.1.

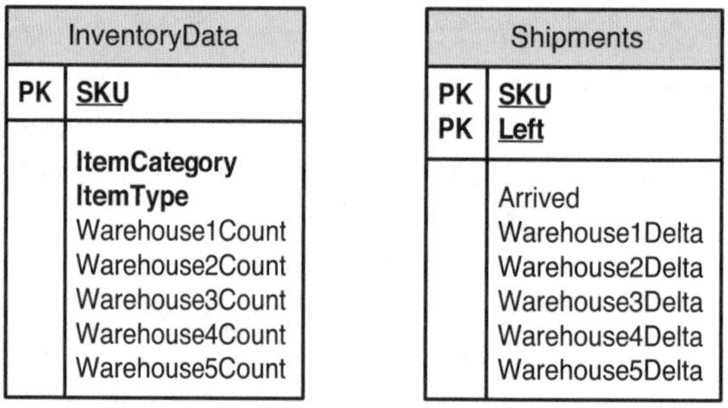

Figure 12.1 *The omni-table design*

Really, having a different design for this database would be nice. In a perfect world, I would probably prefer something like Figure 12.2.

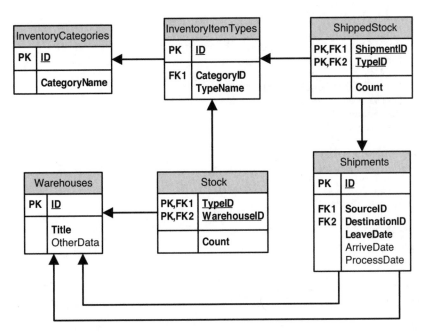

Figure 12.2 *A better factored database*

I would want the item data to be broken out into their own table, as well as the item type information. I would also want warehouses to be in their own table and for there to be a `Stock` entity that connects an item type to a warehouse and includes a count of items on hand.

There are just too many clients to the design in Figure 12.1, though. So, I have to go a different route for now. I start by putting that design into its own database class. This requires a script that is smart enough to imbue upon an empty database some new design elements and do nothing to databases that already have the legacy designs.

I should point out that every database engine worth any attention has some way of getting a script with exactly that ability. In SQL Server, for instance, you simply have to right-click on a database in SQL Manager or SQL Management Studio for an option to generate such scripts for that database. Using that, I can quickly build a database class as follows:

```
<Database Name="Warehouse">
  <Version Number="1">
    <Script>
      <![CDATA[
IF NOT EXISTS (
  SELECT * FROM sys.objects
  WHERE object_id = OBJECT_ID(N'[dbo].[Shipments]') AND type in
➥(N'U'))
```

```
BEGIN
CREATE TABLE [dbo].[Shipments](
       [SKU] [char](24) NOT NULL,
       [Left] [datetime] NOT NULL,
       [Arrived] [datetime] NULL,
       [Warehouse1Count] [int] NULL,
       [Warehouse2Count] [int] NULL,
       [Warehouse3Count] [int] NULL,
       [Warehouse4Count] [int] NULL,
       [Warehouse5Count] [int] NULL,
PRIMARY KEY CLUSTERED
(
       [SKU] ASC
))
END
     ]]>
   </Script>
   <Script>
     <![CDATA[
IF NOT EXISTS (
  SELECT * FROM sys.objects
  WHERE object_id = OBJECT_ID(N'[dbo].[InventoryData]') AND type in
➡ N'U'))
BEGIN
CREATE TABLE [dbo].[InventoryData](
       [SKU] [char](24) NOT NULL,
       [ItemCategory] [nvarchar](24) NOT NULL,
       [ItemType] [nvarchar](24) NOT NULL,
       [Warehouse1Count] [int] NULL,
       [Warehouse2Count] [int] NULL,
       [Warehouse3Count] [int] NULL,
       [Warehouse4Count] [int] NULL,
       [Warehouse5Count] [int] NULL,
PRIMARY KEY CLUSTERED
(
       [SKU] ASC
))
END
     ]]>
   </Script>
 </Version>
</Database>
```

Note how I'm trying to keep variation in construction to a minimum. Version 1 might take two paths, but it can still always be described in linear terms: Check to see whether the initial design is there and put it there if it is not.

The next step in making a legacy database maintainable is to ensure that this version, which has already been committed to production, never changes.

Pinning the Transition Behavior with Tests

You can do this however you like, but I discourage doing anything that requires substantial effort on your part. The primary objective is to make sure that this version of the database class is not corrupted by some would-be lookie loo who accidentally hit the spacebar with his thumb and didn't notice. You can write better, more granular transition tests later, when they will matter to you.

One mechanism is to compare the result of running that script against an empty database to the result of restoring a structure-only backup. This is a fair amount of work because you have to write or find the tool that compares two schemas. However, you only have to pay the price once, and I usually don't care about such costs when they are reasonable.

However, another technique is even simpler and at least as strict: run the version 1 upgrade script through a hashing algorithm and then assert that said hash never changes. The odds of fooling such a test are astronomically low; probably lower than the odds of finding some corner of design that isn't tested by your schema comparison tool. The infrastructure to do this is trivial. The constraints are draconian.

I think this is an ideal test for an historical transition. In fact, I do it for every version just before it is committed to production, even when I've built the database from the ground-up using test-driven development.

Having such a test completes a foundation from which I can build new versions and alter design safely.

Controlling Coupling

After you have a class of databases, you'll want to start regulating how applications use it. This is important because you are probably going to want to change your legacy database's public interface over time. To avoid interruption of service when doing this, you must have a high degree of certainty in your knowledge of who is using what.

You first must lock down permissions so that nobody can use your database in a way they aren't using it now. At least, you need to do that for any part of your design that you think you'll want to change in the future.

You next must change your process so that you don't allow new coupling to interfaces you want to change. Of course, you need to let new clients access the value in your legacy database. I'm not saying, "Don't let new clients couple to your database." I'm saying, "Don't let new clients couple to interfaces with which you are not satisfied." Satisfy new needs by offering a new, unrestricted interface that encapsulates all the stuff you want hidden.

Identifying and Locking Down to Existing Uses

Start by auditing how your legacy database is used. You have a finite number of credentials that can log on to the system, a finite number of actions that can be taken, and a finite number of artifacts upon which those users can take those actions. Let's look at a broader version of the inventory database I've been working with in Figure 12.3.

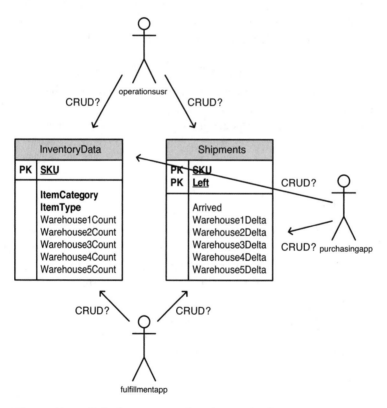

Figure 12.3 *All the known users for a legacy database*

Note how there are three users. Two of them are applications and one of them is an operations worker. Further investigation reveals the following:

1. The `purchasingapp` user only ever inserts into the `Shipments` table.

2. The `purchasingapp` user never touches the `InventoryData` table.

3. The `fulfillmentapp` user only ever selects and deletes from the `Shipments` table.

4. The `fulfillmentapp` user selects, inserts, and updates the `InventoryData` table.

5. The `operationsusr` user needs full access to both tables.

After I'm confident in the accuracy of my audit, I lock down each user's permissions accordingly, as shown in Figure 12.4.

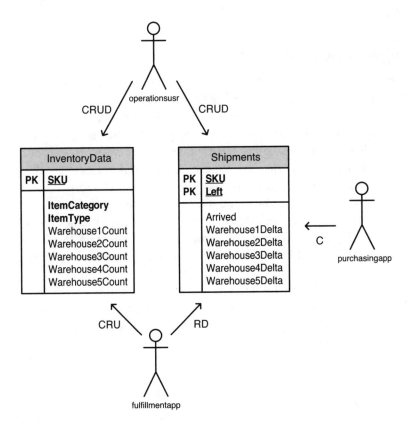

Figure 12.4 *Locked-down permissions*

This creates at least a little pressure on developers to couple to my new system, especially developers working on new applications. There will need to be a grace period to account for the inherent inaccuracy of any audit process.

Let's say that a reporting service was logging in as purchasingapp and needs the ability to select against both the InventoryData and the Shipments table, but the developer for that application didn't speak up during the auditing process. In that case, I wouldn't find out until the reporting service was used, perhaps at the end of the month after I do my lockdown.

There has to be a way to protect customers from significant service interruption, so I would have to relax the access-constraints to support that reporting application. Ideally that would happen by giving the application its own user with exactly the permissions it needs, but the implementation details aren't that important.

Aside from that kind of request, no additional access should be granted on my old interface, ever. The challenge going forward will be standing up to people and saying "no." If that's not something you are good at, get good at it now. It's a very important skill.

Encapsulating on Demand

I've locked down all the privileges in the production database. A new development group wants to access a feature in it that they weren't using before. What do I do? I create the interface I wish I had to expose the features I already have.

In concrete terms, imagine that the new development group is responsible for an enterprise-wide reporting engine. They want to pull in my shipments and inventory data. Of course, what they are requesting is the right to SELECT from both of those tables. I'll say "no" and then ask what they really need.

After a little bit of hemming and hawing, they tell me they need the data for each of those tables as separate blocks so that they can perform whatever analyses they want. I applaud their desire for encapsulation and tell them I will add GetAllInventoryItems and GetAllShipments stored procedures for them shortly.

Over time, a rich and meaningful interface will emerge in this way. Developers will migrate away from the old interface toward the new one. Eventually, I will have no more users that directly connect with my InventoryData table, and I can make it a private part of my design.

Controlling Change

In the previous section, I glossed over how one actually implements a new feature in a legacy database. Every situation is different, so the order of events cannot be codified in a book. However, I can tell you what things you need to do and let you find a sequence that works well for you.

One thing that has to be done often is pinning. Every time you touch or think you might touch the behavior of something that is publicly visible, you need to pin its behavior in tests. Likewise, you must pin a knowledge container's ability to retain knowledge across the transition from one version to the next. Of course, you have to drive the new behaviors and exposures of existing behaviors from tests.

Test-Driving New Behaviors

Usually, I start by writing tests for the new behavior I am implementing or exposing. I do this because it sets context and helps me decide what other tests I have to write.

I'll use the example from the previous section of this chapter: I am going to add a `GetAllInventoryItems` stored procedure. That test follows:

```
[Test]
public void GetAllInventoryItemsRetrievesAllInventoryItems()
{
   connection.ExecuteSql(
@"INSERT INTO InventoryData(
   SKU, ItemCategory, ItemType,
   Warehouse1Count, Warehouse3Count, Warehouse5Count)
VALUES('abcd', 'x', 'y', 9, 14, 108)");
   connection.ExecuteSql(
@"INSERT INTO InventoryData(
   SKU, ItemCategory, ItemType,
   Warehouse1Count, Warehouse2Count, Warehouse3Count,
Warehouse4Count)
VALUES('efg', 'r', 'j', 91, 11, 17, 83)");
   var procedure = design.GetAllInventoryItems;

   var actualRows = connection.ExecuteStoredProcedure(
      procedure,
      new Dictionary<string, object> { });

   Assertions.AssertRowsAreEqual(
      new[]
      {
         GetInventoryItem("abcd", "x", "y", -1, 9),
         GetInventoryItem("abcd", "x", "y", -3, 14),
         GetInventoryItem("abcd", "x", "y", -5, 108),
         GetInventoryItem("efg", "r", "j", -1, 91),
```

```
            GetInventoryItem("efg", "r", "j", -2, 11),
            GetInventoryItem("efg", "r", "j", -3, 17),
            GetInventoryItem("efg", "r", "j", -4, 83),
        },
        actualRows);
}

private Dictionary<string, object> GetInventoryItem(
    string sku, string category, string type, int warehouseID, int
➡ count)
{
    var procedure = design.GetAllInventoryItems;

    return
        new Dictionary<string, object>
            {
                { procedure.ResultWarehouseID, warehouseID },
                { procedure.ResultSKU, sku },
                { procedure.ResultCategory, category },
                { procedure.ResultType, type },
                { procedure.ResultCount, count }
            };
}
```

To get the test to compile and run, I add the following version script to my legacy database class:

```
<Version Number="2">
  <Interface>
    <Add Id="GetAllInventoryItems">
      <Add Id="ResultSKU" />
      <Add Id="ResultCategory" />
      <Add Id="ResultType" />
      <Add Id="ResultWarehouseID" />
      <Add Id="ResultCount" />
    </Add>
  </Interface>
  <Script>
    <![CDATA[
CREATE PROCEDURE $GetAllInventoryItems
AS
BEGIN
  SELECT NULL AS $GetAllInventoryItems.ResultSKU
END
    ]]>
  </Script>
</Version>
```

It enables me to see the test fail.

Pinning Construction on Demand

Another thing that you must do is to pin how your legacy database class behaves when upgrading from one version to the next. The level of aggressiveness I demonstrate next is probably more than you actually need. That is, I could probably get away without pinning the construction behaviors of my legacy database at this stage, and I freely admit that doing so is a little bit contrived. That said, I've never once been bitten by writing a few pinning tests a little bit too early—but I have by writing none or writing them too late.

Any time I want to make a change to my database class that touches an untested structure—even if only by way of a SELECT—I pin the construction behaviors surrounding that structure. In this case, my GetAllInventoryItems stored procedure pulls data out of the InventoryData table. So I put in place safeguards against changes to the InventoryData table, as follows:

```
<Safeguards>
  <Add Name="InventoryData">
    <Sample>
      <![CDATA[
SELECT TOP 3 * FROM InventoryData
ORDER BY SKU
      ]]>
    </Sample>
  </Add>
</Safeguards>
```

That safeguard can serve as the basis for a transition test as well.

```
[Test]
public void InventoryDataPreservationTest()
{
  connection.ExecuteSql(
@"INSERT INTO InventoryData(
  SKU, ItemCategory, ItemType,
  Warehouse1Count, Warehouse3Count, Warehouse5Count)
VALUES('abc', 'q', 'r', 1, 2, 3)");
  connection.ExecuteSql(
@"INSERT INTO InventoryData(
  SKU, ItemCategory, ItemType,
  Warehouse1Count, Warehouse2Count, Warehouse3Count,
Warehouse4Count)
VALUES('def', 's', 'r', 2, 9, 1, 81)");
  connection.ExecuteSql(
@"INSERT INTO InventoryData(
  SKU, ItemCategory, ItemType,
  Warehouse5Count)
VALUES('xyz', 't', 'u', 11)");
```

```
instantiator.UpgradeToSpecificVersion(connection, newVersion);

   Assert.Pass();
}
```

I now know that I can safely make changes to my legacy database without jeopardizing any important data collected in the `InventoryData` table.

Pinning Behavior on Demand

Ensuring that the behaviors clients have come to expect are specified by tests is also necessary. Again, you do this by writing pinning tests. The behavior I think most people would expect is that, when they put a piece of data into the `InventoryData` table, they will be able to retrieve it later by identity. So, I start by writing that test.

```
[Test]
public void PinInventoryDataBehavior()
{
   connection.ExecuteSql(
@"INSERT INTO InventoryData(SKU, ItemCategory, ItemType,
   Warehouse1Count, Warehouse2Count, Warehouse3Count, Warehouse4Count,
   Warehouse5Count)
VALUES('xyz', 'b', 'a', 5, 4, 3, 2, 1)");

   var actualRows = connection.ExecuteQuery("SELECT * FROM
➥InventoryData");

   Assertions.AssertRowsAreEqual(
      new[]
      {
         new Dictionary<string, object>
         {
            { "SKU", "xyz".PadRight(24, ' ') },
            { "ItemCategory", "b" },
            { "ItemType", "a" },
            { "Warehouse1Count", 5 },
            { "Warehouse2Count", 4 },
            { "Warehouse3Count", 3 },
            { "Warehouse4Count", 2 },
            { "Warehouse5Count", 1 },
         }
      },
      actualRows);
}
```

I'll go through the process of seeing it fail and changing the assertion to make it pass as always. You can go as far as you want with pinning behaviors before adding new ones. If you are making complex changes to something's behavior, you'll probably want a lot of tests. If you are leaving a table be, you'll probably just want a test that says, "It's a table." Use your best judgment.

Implementing New Behavior

After you have enough tests to protect you from accidental loss of functionality or data, you can finish the cycle of change by adding the behavior demanded by your unit test. In the case of the example for this section, I would do this with the following script:

```
CREATE PROCEDURE $GetAllInventoryItems
AS
BEGIN
  SELECT *
  FROM
  ((SELECT
    RTRIM(LTRIM(SKU)) AS $GetAllInventoryItems.ResultSKU,
    ItemCategory AS $GetAllInventoryItems.ResultCategory,
    ItemType AS $GetAllInventoryItems.ResultType,
    -1 AS $GetAllInventoryItems.ResultWarehouseID,
    Warehouse1Count AS $GetAllInventoryItems.ResultCount
  FROM InventoryData
  WHERE Warehouse1Count IS NOT NULL)
  UNION ALL
  (SELECT
    RTRIM(LTRIM(SKU)) AS $GetAllInventoryItems.ResultSKU,
    ItemCategory AS $GetAllInventoryItems.ResultCategory,
    ItemType AS $GetAllInventoryItems.ResultType,
    -2 AS $GetAllInventoryItems.ResultWarehouseID,
    Warehouse2Count AS $GetAllInventoryItems.ResultCount
  FROM InventoryData
  WHERE Warehouse2Count IS NOT NULL)
  UNION ALL
  (SELECT
    RTRIM(LTRIM(SKU)) AS $GetAllInventoryItems.ResultSKU,
    ItemCategory AS $GetAllInventoryItems.ResultCategory,
    ItemType AS $GetAllInventoryItems.ResultType,
    -3 AS $GetAllInventoryItems.ResultWarehouseID,
    Warehouse3Count AS $GetAllInventoryItems.ResultCount
  FROM InventoryData
  WHERE Warehouse3Count IS NOT NULL)
  UNION ALL
  (SELECT
    RTRIM(LTRIM(SKU)) AS $GetAllInventoryItems.ResultSKU,
    ItemCategory AS $GetAllInventoryItems.ResultCategory,
    ItemType AS $GetAllInventoryItems.ResultType,
    -4 AS $GetAllInventoryItems.ResultWarehouseID,
    Warehouse4Count AS $GetAllInventoryItems.ResultCount
  FROM InventoryData
  WHERE Warehouse4Count IS NOT NULL)
  UNION ALL
```

```
(SELECT
  RTRIM(LTRIM(SKU)) AS $GetAllInventoryItems.ResultSKU,
  ItemCategory AS $GetAllInventoryItems.ResultCategory,
  ItemType AS $GetAllInventoryItems.ResultType,
  -5 AS $GetAllInventoryItems.ResultWarehouseID,
  Warehouse5Count AS $GetAllInventoryItems.ResultCount
FROM InventoryData
WHERE Warehouse5Count IS NOT NULL)) v
ORDER BY
  v.$GetAllInventoryItems.ResultSKU,
  v.$GetAllInventoryItems.ResultWarehouseID DESC
END
```

Is it ugly? Yes, it is, but having some well-encapsulated ugly code that presents the right interface is better than casting little bits of ugliness all over your organization by way of a bad interface.

After all my tests passed, I could start the cycle again with another behavior. Note how this pattern of work doesn't ask too much of you at any one point in time, yet it sets in motion a machine that slowly covers the most important parts of your database design with tests.

Finding Seams and Components

A hallmark of legacy systems is scarce encapsulation. Typically, though, you can exploit natural boundaries to create encapsulation with a comparatively small amount of risk and effort. This additional encapsulation greatly improves the testability of your database design.

Finding Seams

So-called "seams" are places in a software design where encapsulation can be inserted with little cost or risk. My experience has shown that such places are typically parts of your design where little coupling exists between one body of design elements and another.

Take a look at Figure 12.5. It shows how the elements of a legacy database class's design might look if left totally unorganized, as might happen if you simply laid them out in alphabetical order.

It's all jumbled up, isn't it? The way everything is piled together makes it hard to see where one class of databases might want to be divided into two. Rearranging things so that there are as few crossing lines as possible results in the much clearer picture represented by Figure 12.6.

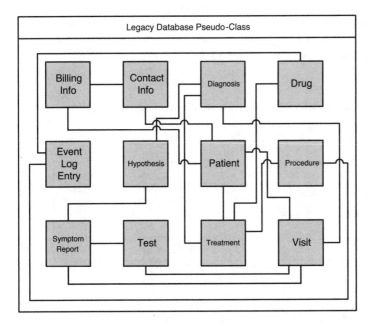

Figure 12.5 *Design elements ordered as they occurred to developer*

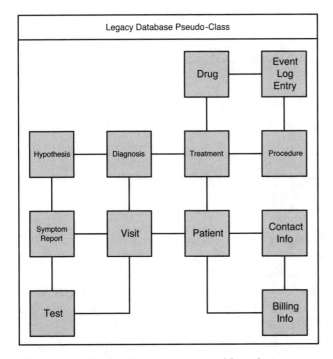

Figure 12.6 *Design elements rearranged by cohesion*

Note how clusters of items with many internal relationships are linked together by just a few lines. Those voids crossed by a small number of dependencies are the seams in your system. Figure 12.7 shows the design with the seams drawn in it.

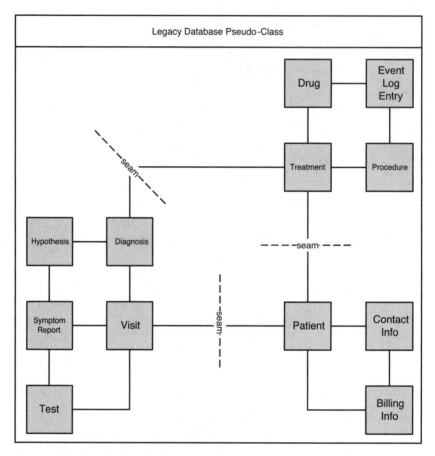

Figure 12.7 *Pseudo-class broken apart by seams*

The clusters of strongly related objects each represent a component of your database. The places where relationships cross each seam represent not only the relationship between two tables but also the relationship between two components. The dependency structures represent the public interface of the components in which they live. Figure 12.8 shows this design redrawn to show the various components with their public interfaces.

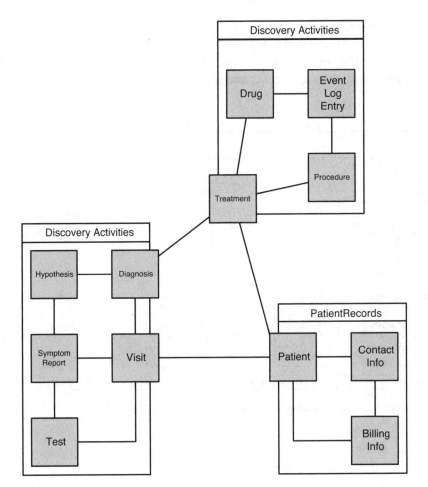

Figure 12.8 *Concepts broken into classes along seams*

Doing this kind of analysis sets you up to start encapsulating each component of a database from the others.

Encapsulating Components

Even if you are not in a position to hide the innards of a component from clients to your database, and many readers will not be to start, there is value to you in hiding a database design's components' contents from each other.

The basic argument for doing this is that mockability and testability are strongly related. Take the design in Figure 12.9. To test attachments, you would have to create a valid message, sender, and recipient. This means you would have to set up an entire security model that gives the sender rights to send to the recipient.

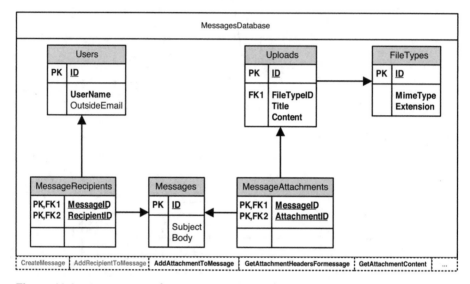

Figure 12.9 *Messages, attachments, recipients, and so on*

The spider web that extends from a message is bigger than I want to test. I want all relationships to be enforced in production but don't care about how everything works together in a unit-testing environment. Having the ability to mock the attachments component allows me to test how associating attachments with messages works independently of how uploading attachments works.

Figure 12.10 shows the proposed new design.

Let's assume that I already have the code to create the database in Figure 12.9. In that case, the safest way to divide it into classes would be to write pinning tests for the entire legacy system before making any changes. That's probably more work than I can reasonably do, though.

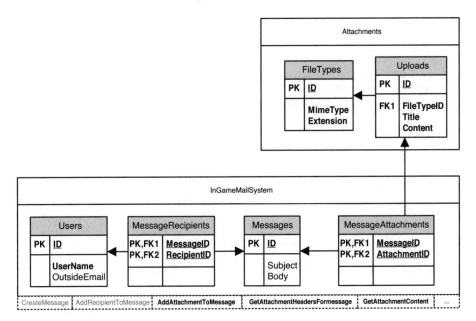

Figure 12.10 *A design that supports mocking*

An alternative is to build a small, focused suite of pinning tests. These tests would target behaviors that invoke behaviors in the component I intend to segregate. For instance, if I am going to break attachments into its own component, I would write some tests that create messages, add some attachments, and then check that the attachments are properly associated with their parent message. This is shown in the following example:

```
[Test]
public void CreateMessageAddAndGetAttachment()
{
  var messageID = connection.ExecuteStoredProcedureScalar(
    "CreateMessage",
    new Dictionary<string, object>
    {
      { "@subject", "hey!" },
      { "@body", "How's it going?" }
    });

  var attachmentID = connection.ExecuteStoredProcedureScalar(
    "AddAttachmentToMessage",
    new Dictionary<string, object>
    {
      { "@messageID", messageID },
      { "@mimeType", "text/plain" },
```

```
        { "@title", "textfile.txt" },
        { "@content", new byte[] { 1, 2, 3, 4 } }
    });

    var rows = connection.ExecuteStoredProcedure(
      "GetAttachmentHeadersForMessage",
      new Dictionary<string, object>
      {
        { "@messageID", messageID }
      });

    Assertions.AssertRowsAreEqual(
      new[]
      {
        new Dictionary<string, object>
        {
          { "ID", attachmentID },
          { "Title", "textfile.txt" },
          { "MimeType", "text/plain" },
        }
      },
      rows);

    var content = connection.ExecuteStoredProcedureScalar(
      "GetAttachmentContent",
      new Dictionary<string, object>
      {
        { "@attachmentID", attachmentID }
      });

    Assert.That(
      content,
      Is.EqualTo(new byte[] { 1, 2, 3 ,4 }));
}
```

I could go a lot further but doing so is not really necessary. The point of this kind of test is to mitigate risk, not specify behavior, and the risk of moving a structure from one component to another component starts out really low.

It mainly exists in the form of accidentally breaking coupling between two structures. If you have a test that demonstrates one behavior leveraging another, you're getting rid of the primary source of risk. Going beyond that is certainly an option you have but not one that I employ very often.

For this new class of databases I am creating—the attachments database—there are necessarily two ways to be created. One way is to be built into an empty database as is done in test environments and new deployments. Another way is to take ownership of certain structures that live in a live database, as happens when a production system is upgraded.

Absolutely no variation of any kind can be permitted among the outputs of these two paths. This means that transition testing is non-trivial. In this case, what I would do is write a test that generates a legacy database that will be treated as an input to the newly factored-out component database, then compare it to a freshly instantiated component database instance.

I would then check the schemas of every non-system structure to make sure they matched exactly as well as all relationships. Tools are available that you can leverage to do this, but I like to roll my own solution, as shown in the following example:

```
[Test]
public void
AttachmentsDatabaseBuiltOffOfInGameMailHasSameSchemaAsIf
➥BuiltFromScratch()
{
  attachmentsInstantiator.UpgradeToSpecificVersion(
    connection, attachmentsNewVersion);
  var attachmentsDescription = connection.Describe();
  RecycleDatabase();

  instantiator.UpgradeToSpecificVersion(connection,
    inGameMailNewVersion);
  attachmentsInstantiator.UpgradeToSpecificVersion(
    connection, attachmentsNewVersion);

  Assertions.AssertRowsAreAccountedFor(
    attachmentsDescription,
    connection.Describe());
}
```

The definition of Describe() is outside the scope of this book but is available in the example code associated with this book (in C#, for SQL Server).

With that test in place, refactoring my structures so that they live in different components is safe. This is mostly a matter of adding interface declarations for the public attachments tables to the attachments component database and updating my stored procedures to use those interface declarations as I've already shown in previous chapters.

From there, injecting an abstraction and mocking out the behavior of the attachment component is a very tractable problem. Having the ability to test attachments independently enables me to fully specify its behavior in unit tests should the need arise.

Summary

It seems like adoption of any new TDD process is going be slow at best, unless a way exists to apply it to software written prior to its introduction. For that reason, I have made how to do TDD database development for a legacy database part of this book.

If a database is totally "wild"—as in you have not touched it since you started implementing the processes in this book—then you will have to start by inferring a class of databases from what you already have.

After you have a database class, you next must control how people couple to it. Audit your existing deployed databases and restrict access to them so that no client developers can modify their systems to do anything they couldn't already do. You'll probably want to repeat this process several times, taking away access when it is no longer needed.

After you've limited access to the legacy structures as best you can, it's time to start processing the database design into something that is no longer legacy— that is, something that is covered in automated tests and can be changed with little cost. This is accomplished by refactoring but, of course, you probably don't have any tests, so you need to use pinning tests to lock down transition logic and database behavior before implementing any changes.

Doing only the pinning you need to do is important. If you're going to make a change around an area, lock down its behavior with pinning tests. If not, leave it be.

This way of doing things can make accessing new behavior hard for client developers. After all, you're probably removing more privileges on a quarterly basis than you are adding. In Chapter 13, I cover the façade pattern, which both eases that burden and entices application developers away from coupling to a legacy database.

Chapter 13

The Façade Pattern

A major problem with legacy designs, be they Java class systems, C# assemblies, C libraries from antiquity, or old database designs, is that they tend to have interfaces that get in the way of writing good tests.

The façade pattern lives in such problems and advises you on how to solve them. I will show you how it applies to database design. The first step is encapsulating the old database design behind a new one.

If you decide to go the façade route, you want to slowly "strangle" the old interface over time. You accomplish this using the same techniques you would employ to migrate clients over from direct table access to the use of stored procedures and views.

When embracing the façade pattern to implement a controlled rewrite, you must resist the urge to add behavior to your legacy database. One reason is political: If you add behaviors to a legacy database, you remove an incentive that would drive clients to the newer interface. Another reason is technical: You are doing a controlled rewrite for a reason and that reason is probably that the legacy system is very hard to modify.

So, be sure to test drive all new behaviors into your façade database. Over time, it will grow to be the "real thing" and the legacy database will hollow out until it is just an adapter.

Encapsulation with a Façade

Public interfaces are very hard to change. One reason is that there are usually many points of coupling. Also, in the case of a legacy database, the feedback loop is extremely long because you usually don't have anything in place to tell you where all those points of coupling actually live.

In such cases, developers often have a very strong impulse to rewrite the legacy thing. "I know better now," you tell yourself. "I won't make the same mistakes again."

That's actually true. You won't make the same mistakes again. You'll make new ones, which is why many people resist every rewrite impulse they have after the very first. Rewrites are expensive, have a high rate of failure, and take a long time before they can start adding value.

The Façade pattern lives in this problem and tells you that, instead of rewriting something all at once, you should put in place a new design that starts off as a prettier interface for the old design. All new work can be coupled to the new design, new behavior can be added to the new design, and old behavior can gradually be transferred to the new design.

It's a way of getting all the good stuff from a rewrite without any of the disadvantages. I show you how to do this when building a database using both composition, which I discourage in this case, and aggregation, which I recommend.

Rewriting via a façade is optional. In this chapter, I show how to employ it but you won't always want to do that. Sometimes you will want to stick with the process in Chapter 12, "Legacy Databases," and simply bring an existing design under control.

Regarding the question of which route is best, I say, "Trust your gut."

Explanation of Façade Pattern

When you have the urge to rewrite something, you have a façade-type problem. Fundamentally, the façade pattern says that you shouldn't rewrite things and, instead, should set up forces that cause bad things to be gradually decommissioned and replaced with good things.

Let's first look at a façade problem in application logic design. Consider the interface depicted in Figure 13.1.

This design has a capabilities interface. What I want is a needs interface. To accomplish this in a manner consistent with the advice gotten from the façade pattern, I would create a new class that supports the needs of whatever client I am working on at the time. That class doesn't really have any interesting behaviors. It exists exclusively to put a pretty face on an ugly design. Figure 13.2 shows this new design.

However, over time it is probably true that clients to the old design would have new demands of the system that is encapsulated by the façade. Rather than changing the legacy classes to support the new features, I would just add the new features to the façade layer and coerce those clients into using it, as shown in Figure 13.3.

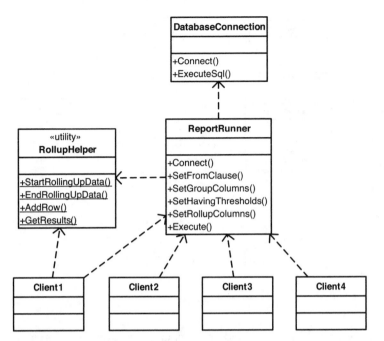

Figure 13.1 *A capabilities interface*

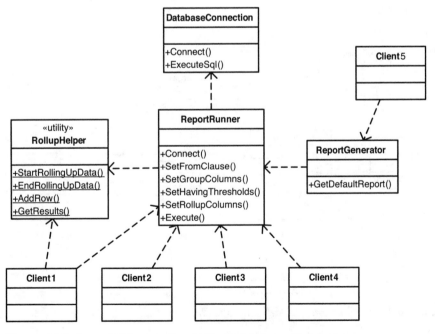

Figure 13.2 *A capabilities interface hidden behind a needs interface*

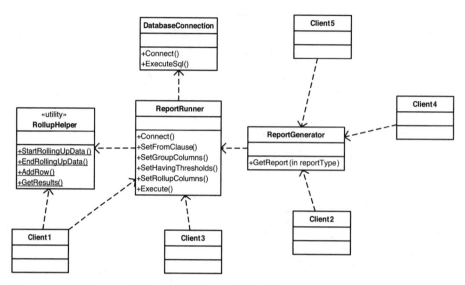

Figure 13.3 *Clients with altered needs coupled to façade*

Sometimes those new demands would cause changes to existing behaviors. When that happens, the thing to do is transfer the behavior from the legacy system to the façade and change the legacy system to delegate to the façade (see Figure 13.4).

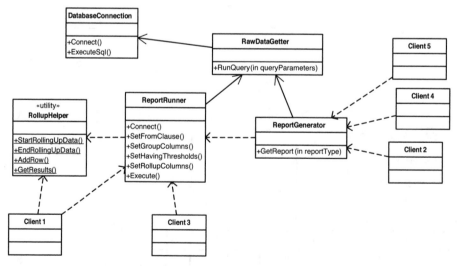

Figure 13.4 *Legacy classes now delegate to the façade*

Over time, what was the façade grows into the first-class system and what was the legacy system grows into a system of adapters to the façade (see Figure 13.5).

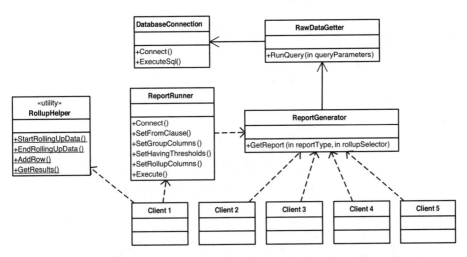

Figure 13.5 *Legacy classes are now just adapters for the façade.*

This process, if adhered to in a disciplined way, sets up forces that simultaneously encourage stability and discourage coupling to the old system. As shown in Figure 13.6, an ever-increasing number of behaviors accessible only through the new, test-driven, needs-oriented interface drive clients away from the legacy system and toward the new system.

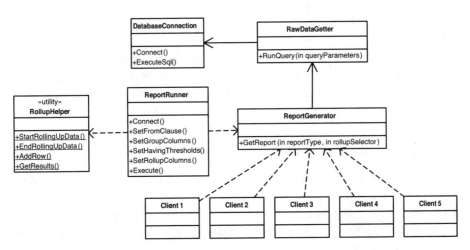

Figure 13.6 *All clients use the new interface.*

Only ever adding functionality to the new system encourages developers to transfer coupling from the new system to the old. When a legacy class has no more clients, you remove it (see Figure 13.7), further widening the rift in functionality between the new system and the legacy system.

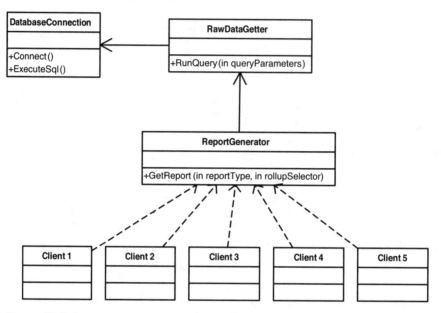

Figure 13.7 *Legacy system goes away entirely*

This manner of changing behavior and design has a very high rate of success. After all, eventually the legacy code is nothing more than a bunch of hollowed-out adapters pointing to the non-legacy code, you really don't care if it ever goes away.

On the other hand, substantial and compounding forces work to eradicate the legacy code, and therein lies the irony: If you attempt to rewrite legacy code, you will probably fail, but, if you are disciplined and patient, you can set up a system that enables a legacy system to simply vaporize over time.

New Test-Driven Façade Database

All the forces that cause me to resist a rewrite of an application-logic module are present in database designs and are exacerbated by the presence of vital, knowledge-containing data. Let's assume that I have a good reason for wanting to ultimately rewrite my inventory database from Chapter 12, but I know enough to not try doing it wholesale.

Instead, I want to encapsulate it behind a façade. Assume that I've already implemented in version 1 a way to link a façade to a legacy database. In version 2, I exposed the legacy behavior through a `GetAllInventoryItems` method that makes the data look normalized, like the procedure I showed in Chapter 12.

Presumably, there are some needs to fulfill for a new or changing client. In this case, I'm going to say that I want to be able to dynamically add warehouses. This means I also need the ability to store inventory on a per dynamically created warehouse basis as well.

I start by writing tests for the `AddWarehouse` behavior:

```
[Test]
public void AddAndGetWarehouse()
{
  var address = "123 Main Street.";
  var title = "Central America";

  var addWarehouse = facadeDesign.AddWarehouse;
  var id = facadeConnection.ExecuteStoredProcedureScalar(
    addWarehouse,
    new Dictionary<string, object>
    {
      { addWarehouse.Address, address },
      { addWarehouse.Title, title},
    });

  var getWarehouse = facadeDesign.GetWarehouse;
  var rows = facadeConnection.ExecuteStoredProcedure(
    getWarehouse,
    new Dictionary<string, object>
    {
      { getWarehouse.ID, id },
    });

  Assertions.AssertRowsAreEqual(
    rows,
    new[]
    {
      new Dictionary<string, object>
      {
        { getWarehouse.ResultTitle, title },
        { getWarehouse.ResultAddress, address }
      }
    });
}
```

After getting all the class and transition-test stuff in order, I can alter my façade class of database to make my test pass as follows:

```
<Version Number="3">
  <Interface>
    <Add Id="AddWarehouse">
```

```
            <Add Id="Title" Value="@title" />
            <Add Id="Address" Value ="@address" />
          </Add>
          <Add Id="GetWarehouse">
            <Add Id="ID" Value="@id" />
            <Add Id="ResultTitle" />
            <Add Id="ResultAddress" />
          </Add>
      </Interface>
      <Script>
        <![CDATA[
CREATE TABLE Warehouses(
  ID INT IDENTITY CONSTRAINT WarehousesPrimaryKey PRIMARY KEY,
  Title VARCHAR(200),
  Address VARCHAR(300))
        ]]>
      </Script>
      <Script>
        <![CDATA[
CREATE PROCEDURE $AddWarehouse
  $AddWarehouse.Title VARCHAR(200),
  $AddWarehouse.Address VARCHAR(300)
AS
BEGIN
  INSERT INTO Warehouses(Title, Address)
  VALUES($AddWarehouse.Title, $AddWarehouse.Address);

  SELECT @@Identity;
END;
        ]]>
      </Script>
      <Script>
        <![CDATA[
CREATE PROCEDURE $GetWarehouse
  $GetWarehouse.ID INT
AS
BEGIN
  SELECT
    Title AS $GetWarehouse.ResultTitle,
    Address AS $GetWarehouse.ResultAddress
  FROM Warehouses
  WHERE ID = $GetWarehouse.ID
END;
        ]]>
      </Script>
    </Version>
```

I also need the capability to specify the item-related details (category and type) associated with a particular SKU. I leave it to your imagination how I did that, but you can always just look at the companion code and see how I did it if you want.

Next, I add the capability to create warehouse-specific stock records as specified in the following test. Keep in mind that this test will be a little ugly, but it is really just the ugliness of the problem that has been created at some point in the past. The solution will also be ugly—even uglier than the test. When you choose to use the Façade pattern, you are choosing to pay the price for ugliness so that you can limit its effect and lifespan.

```
[Test]
public void MergesRecordsFromFacadeAndLegacyDatabase()
{
  var sku = "foo";
  var category = "category text 17243";
  var type = "type text 19423";
  var facadeItemCount = 18213;

  legacyConnection.ExecuteSql(
@"INSERT INTO InventoryData(SKU, ItemCategory, ItemType,
➥Warehouse1Count)
VALUES('foo', 'x', 'y', 805)");
  var warehouseID = AddWarehouse("new location", "new warehouse");
  SetSKUDetails(sku, category, type);
  SetStock(warehouseID, sku, facadeItemCount);
  SetStock(-4, sku, 21);
  var getProcedure = facadeDesign.GetAllInventoryItems;

  var actualRows = facadeConnection.ExecuteStoredProcedure(
    getProcedure,
    new Dictionary<string, object> { });

  Assertions.AssertRowsAreEqual(
    new[]
    {
      GetInventoryItem(sku, category, type, warehouseID,
➥facadeItemCount),
      GetInventoryItem(sku, "x", "y", -1, 805),
      GetInventoryItem(sku, "x", "y", -4, 21),
    },
    actualRows);
}

private void SetStock(object warehouseID, string sku, int
➥facadeItemCount)
{
  var addProcedure = facadeDesign.SetStock;
  facadeConnection.ExecuteStoredProcedure(
    addProcedure,
    new Dictionary<string, object>
```

```
    {
        { addProcedure.SKU, sku },
        { addProcedure.WarehouseID, warehouseID },
        { addProcedure.Count, facadeItemCount }
    });
}
```

Note how that test demands the existence of a reference to one of the legacy database instances. The link is specified in two ways. First, it is required that data from the legacy database show up in the new interface. Second, it is required that when stock information is set through the new interface, it updates the counts for those warehouses in a way that preserves the item type and category in the legacy database.

I could go further and require that the records be updated in the legacy database. If I were really building this kind of design, I probably would do that. I would also write a lot more tests to make sure all the complexity is covered. I recommend you do the same. I'm not going to show any of that here, though, because it is pretty tedious and would slow down the pace of the book significantly.

Employing the façade pattern is like writing a Lovecraftian horror story. Typically, an evil lurks just outside of what you want to see with a thin buffer between you and it that, itself, is somewhat frightening. The horror is the legacy code you want to hide and the frightening buffer is the façade itself.

Where a horror story and the façade pattern differ, however, is in the ending. Instead of hopelessly railing against an inevitable tragedy, you are setting up forces to limit the effect of and ultimately destroy the great evil embodied in legacy code. You do this by saying, "This (your legacy code) is all the ugliness I am going to allow and this (your façade) is the line across which bad design is not permitted to cross."

After that test fails, I can use transition testing to drive the following change into my façade class. I start with the Stock table because it's easy to show.

```
<Script>
  <![CDATA[
CREATE TABLE Stock(
  SKU VARCHAR(24) NOT NULL,
  WarehouseID INT NOT NULL CONSTRAINT StockToWarehouses
    FOREIGN KEY REFERENCES Warehouses(ID),
  Count INT NOT NULL,
  CONSTRAINT StockPrimaryKey PRIMARY KEY(SKU, WarehouseID));
  ]]>
  </Script>
```

Next, I deal with inserting records. That's a bit complex because if the ID maps to a warehouse in the Façade database, I want to create a Stock record, but if it maps to a legacy warehouse, I want to update my legacy database. Listing 13.1 shows that bit of nastiness.

Listing 13.1 SetStock *Stored Procedure*

```
CREATE PROCEDURE $SetStock
  SKU VARCHAR(24) NOT NULL,
  WarehouseID INT NOT NULL CONSTRAINT StockToWarehouses
    FOREIGN KEY REFERENCES Warehouses(ID),
  Count INT NOT NULL,
  CONSTRAINT StockPrimaryKey PRIMARY KEY(SKU, WarehouseID));
      ]]>
    </Script>
    <Script>
      <![CDATA[
CREATE PROCEDURE $SetStock
  $SetStock.SKU VARCHAR(24),
  $SetStock.WarehouseID INT,
  $SetStock.Count INT
AS
BEGIN
  IF $SetStock.WarehouseID >= 0
  BEGIN
    DELETE Stock
    WHERE SKU = $SetStock.SKU
    AND WarehouseID = $SetStock.WarehouseID

    INSERT INTO Stock(SKU, WarehouseID, Count)
    VALUES(
      $SetStock.SKU,
      $SetStock.WarehouseID,
      $SetStock.Count);
  END
  ELSE
  BEGIN
    DECLARE @wh1Val INT
    DECLARE @wh2Val INT
    DECLARE @wh3Val INT
    DECLARE @wh4Val INT
    DECLARE @wh5Val INT
    DECLARE @error VARCHAR(2000);

    SET @wh1Val = NULL;
    SET @wh2Val = NULL;
    SET @wh3Val = NULL;
    SET @wh4Val = NULL;
    SET @wh5Val = NULL;

    IF $SetStock.WarehouseID = -1
      SET @wh1Val = $SetStock.Count
    ELSE IF $SetStock.WarehouseID = -2
      SET @wh2Val = $SetStock.Count
    ELSE IF $SetStock.WarehouseID = -3
```

```sql
      SET @wh3Val = $SetStock.Count
    ELSE IF $SetStock.WarehouseID = -4
      SET @wh4Val = $SetStock.Count
    ELSE IF $SetStock.WarehouseID = -5
      SET @wh5Val = $SetStock.Count
    ELSE
    BEGIN
      SET @error = 'Non-existent warehouse specified'
      RAISERROR (50001, @error, 1)
      RETURN
    END;

    IF EXISTS(SELECT SKU FROM LegacyInventoryItems WHERE
➡SKU = $SetStock.SKU)
    BEGIN
      UPDATE LegacyInventoryItems SET
        Warehouse1Count = COALESCE(@wh1Val, Warehouse1Count),
        Warehouse2Count = COALESCE(@wh2Val, Warehouse2Count),
        Warehouse3Count = COALESCE(@wh3Val, Warehouse3Count),
        Warehouse4Count = COALESCE(@wh4Val, Warehouse4Count),
        Warehouse5Count = COALESCE(@wh5Val, Warehouse5Count)
      WHERE SKU = $SetStock.SKU
    END
    ELSE
    BEGIN
      IF NOT EXISTS(SELECT SKU FROM ItemTypes WHERE SKU =
➡$SetStock.SKU)
      BEGIN
        SET @error = 'No details for that S'
        RAISERROR (50001, @error, 1)
        RETURN
      END;

      INSERT INTO LegacyInventoryItems(
        SKU, ItemCategory, ItemType,
        Warehouse1Count, Warehouse2Count,
        Warehouse3Count, Warehouse4Count,
        Warehouse5Count)
      SELECT SKU, Category, Type,
        @wh1Val, @wh2Val, @wh3Val, @wh4Val, @wh5Val
      FROM ItemTypes
      WHERE SKU = $SetStock.SKU;
    END
  END;
END;
```

Following that, I need a way to get all of my inventory items out of the Facade database, shown in the following example.

```
CREATE PROCEDURE $GetAllInventoryItems
AS
BEGIN
  SELECT *
  FROM
  (
  /*
  Explode legacy warehouse rows into correct shape.
  I snipped this for brevity; look at companion code for details.
  */
  UNION ALL
  (SELECT
    s.SKU AS $GetAllInventoryItems.ResultSKU,
    it.Category AS $GetAllInventoryItems.ResultCategory,
    it.Type AS $GetAllInventoryItems.ResultType,
    s.WarehouseID AS $GetAllInventoryItems.ResultWarehouseID,
    s.Count AS $GetAllInventoryItems.ResultCount
  FROM Stock AS s
  INNER JOIN ItemTypes AS it ON s.SKU = it.SKU)) v
  ORDER BY
    v.$GetAllInventoryItems.ResultSKU,
    v.$GetAllInventoryItems.ResultWarehouseID DESC
END
```

If I strictly adhere to this process, I will soon have a clean, test-driven database that completely hides the existence of my old, dirty database design from its clients.

Compositional Alternative

When using the façade-and-strangle technique, I prefer to keep my façade and my legacy database as separate as possible. This is partly to prevent changes in one from accidentally affecting the other but mostly to establish in any developers' minds a firm separation of concerns.

The legacy database is a bad thing. It's something with which you ultimately want to dispense. The façade is a good thing. It's something you want to grow into a primary source of record.

To Encapsulate or Not

Façades might facilitate controlled rewrites, but even a controlled rewrite is still a rewrite. My experience has shown me that rewrites are expensive. If any chance exists that you can enlist a database design into your TDD process without rewriting it, I very highly recommend you go that way. Even for object-oriented code in a middle-tier environment, you should treat a rewrite as a last resort. Rewriting a database should only ever be done when you have no other alternatives.

> **Note**
>
> By the way, this entire chapter and Chapter 12 are both predicated on there being some value to a legacy system. If there is truly and honestly no value in it in the form of meaningful functionality or knowledge, then get rid of it and starting writing a new thing against new requirements. The façade pattern and the technique shown in Chapter 12 are for successful database designs being used in production.

Strangling the Old Interface

If I choose to façade a legacy system, I'm deciding that it must go away. I'm at least tentatively committing to a path on which coupling to the old database design should only ever stay the same or decrease and coupling to the new database design should stay the same or increase.

The nature of databases and how they are used actually provides some distinct advantages in this endeavor. Much of the time, a database is accessed using many different credentials. That gives you the ability to constrain each set of credentials' access to exactly those things they are already doing as soon as you decide to façade and strangle a legacy database. Doing so will discourage coupling to a legacy database over time.

Something you can do with any system, including a database, is refuse to add any new behavior or interface to the legacy system. After you've locked down the permissions to the old database, only relax them under the most extreme circumstances. To support that policy, make sure that you quickly turn around changes to the façade database.

Do not duplicate behaviors. Instead, transfer behaviors that need to change from a legacy system into the new test-driven system and change the legacy system to delegate to the new system. In this way, the legacy system will "hollow out" and become nothing more than an adapter allowing old systems to access your new database design.

Transferring Changing Behaviors to Façade

You will from time to time need to change a behavior that lives in your legacy database. Before changing such a behavior, create a test that accesses it through your façade as well as a test that specifies how the behavior looks when accessing it through the legacy database. Next, refactor your two systems so that the behavior lives in the façade and the legacy system delegates to it, and then change the behavior. This is the one way that you should ever change the apparent behavior of your legacy database.

Imagine the design of the façade database has evolved to contain a table that backs a messaging feature. Let's further stipulate that I want to add a notifications feature to my database. Whenever a new shipment is inserted or updated, I want to add a new message to the `ShipmentMessages` table.

The first step is to move the add `Shipment` and update `Shipment` features to the façade database design.

I would start by adding pinning tests showing how the current add and update `Shipment` feature works. You've already seen how to do that in other contexts, so I leave it to you to imagine how it might be done in this one.

I would also add tests showing how those features work when accessed through my façade. Again, you already know how to write pinning tests that show the behavior of a façade, so I leave that as an exercise for the reader as well.

When dealing with the façade pattern, there is a really interesting demonstration of the relationship between patterns and tests. The façade is all about slowly transferring behaviors from one set of design elements to another. Tests are about providing feedback for you while you are changing design. As a result, you want tests that touch a façade pattern to cover both the old and the new design so that they will be resilient when you move a feature.

After running the tests and seeing them fail, I could change the assertions to make them pass. The next step would be to determine how best to make a change while keeping the tests passing. One option in this case would be to create a view that pretends to be a table; that is, one that accepts INSERT and UPDATE statements.

That view could then communicate with the stored procedures on a corresponding façade database to get, add, and update shipments. Will this have a performance impact? Probably. Do I care? Kind of. It won't be a big performance cost to be sure and the small cost it represents provides a little bit of pressure for people to start using my new, test-driven database.

In any event, the implementation details for this vary too much from one platform to another for me to include it in this book. Consult your favorite "how to do neat things with your database platform" book for details on implementing a view that delegates to stored procedures or views on another database.

Removing Access and Features When No Longer Needed

Over time, the developers who maintain clients to your database will transition away from the legacy database and toward the new database. As soon as you find out a privilege is no longer used, remove it.

If the person who maintains clients to your databases is you, you'll know exactly when to remove a permission because you're the one taking advantage of the new stuff. If other parties are responsible for developing database clients, keep in touch with them so you know when they are no longer using a particular privilege. If people are recalcitrant, take whatever measures you must in order to get this vital information. One thing that comes to mind is tracing the actions taken by a particular actor and reviewing a report periodically, and then using that report to force a conversation.

Ideally and probably, a time will come when no remaining clients with permissions to a legacy structure exist. This means that the structure is no longer needed. If no knowledge is stored in the structure, as would be the case with an adaptor that forwards requests to a non-legacy database, get rid of it. If the structure still contains valuable data, you probably won't want to delete it outright, but you can at least archive it and remove it from your legacy database, or move it to your primary database.

Test-Driving Behaviors in the Façade Database

The other aspect I haven't touched on is how you deal with adding new behaviors to your façade and how you grow it into something with enough functionality to deprecate your legacy database. The process is mostly the same as building a new database class with just a few variations.

Forces exist in this kind of problem that mandate providing multiple access-points for the same behavior. You also want clients to be unaware of whether a behavior lives in the new or old database. This means that you need a test for each of those access points and that those tests must not know whether the behavior they specify lives in the legacy or the new database. It also means that you will probably need at least one test that shows a cause in one database design yields an effect in the other. It's an unfortunate but necessary duplication.

Another small distinction is that you have two kinds of behavior to add: exposure of behaviors available in a legacy database and new behaviors not available in the legacy database. Tests that touch a legacy behavior will need to ensure that a legacy database is available. Ones that don't touch a legacy database need not bother.

Finally, certain circumstances exist under which you simply cannot easily test the integration between a façade and its underlying legacy database. Under those conditions, you have to mock out a legacy database when testing your façade database.

Exposing Legacy Behaviors

Especially early in a façade database's life, you will find yourself exposing the behavior of a legacy database a great deal. This is because a wealth of value is already in that system. Maybe it's in the form of functionality. Maybe it's in the form of data. Whatever the case, you might be unhappy with the design, but you have a reason you aren't throwing it away and writing a new one.

Depending on the complexity of the legacy database, you will want to go one of two ways while test driving the exposure of an existing feature. One option is to simply test the existing feature. The other is to mock out the interface of the legacy database and test *that* your façade delegates to the legacy database without testing *what* the legacy database does.

The more complex the legacy feature, the more you're going to want to mock it out. Simple features with few dependencies, however, you are going to want to test indirectly via your façade. I'll show you why shortly.

Another Way to Do It

I'm a very mocking-friendly guy. Objects and classes as design constructs come very naturally to me. Not everyone is like that. Also there are people who espouse reasons why mocking is bad, but I'm pretty sure those arguments are contrived so that mocking opponents won't have to admit they don't like it because it's hard for them.

While I'm very pro-mocking in the general case, I can accept some of the arguments against it in the case of a façade and its underlying legacy database. One argument, which I think is kind of weak, is that there is no guarantee of integration. You should have integration tests for that anyway, so I'm not buying it.

Another argument, which is much stronger, is that tests specify behaviors and that a very special relationship exists between a façade and the things it encapsulates that requires behaviors to move more freely between classes than in most other arrangements.

In other words: The façade pattern is largely about *not knowing* where exactly a behavior lives and, therefore, testing a behavior into one class or another is anathematic.

An alternative that I think works pretty well is to factor the setup, trigger, and assertion parts of a test into reusable components and then create variants of each for both the legacy and façade database interfaces. You can then define the same specification and run it several times with different combinations of variants. Figure 13.8 shows the design for such a test.

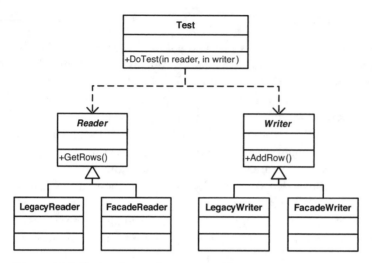

Figure 13.8 *Design for an abstract reusable test*

In this way, you write one test that serves as an abstract specification for a behavior and then by running that abstract specification in several different contexts, you specify how it is exposed to developers.

New Behaviors

Development of new behavior in a façade database works just like developing new behavior in any other test-driven database with one small exception: You might have to incorporate legacy behaviors into the new behaviors.

In that case, I highly recommend mocking instead of testing how the two classes integrate with one another. Specifying a behavior without specifying where it lives is one thing. Specifying that a behavior delegates to another behavior without mocking the dependency is quite another. If you try to integrate a bunch of behaviors together in the course of regular unit testing, you will quickly get to the point where your unit test suite is as interconnected and unmaintainable as the legacy database you are trying to rewrite.

Summary

The façade pattern allows you to have the "best of both worlds" when bringing a formerly unregulated database into the test-driven process. You can get as much of the existing value out of your legacy system as you like and you can expose it to as many new clients as you please. You can do all of this without allowing an untamed wilderness of coupling to grow up around your legacy database.

The process begins by creating an encapsulating entity for your database to which public access is freely or easily granted. This means that all new coupling to your legacy database is funneled through a single thing.

If existing behaviors need to be accessed through the new interface, test-drive how you expose them by mocking out your legacy database. If new behaviors are needed, add them to the façade whenever possible and do so in a test-driven way.

This allows you to "strangle" the old interface—removing privileges as they are no longer needed. Eventually, there will be little enough coupling to a behavior that you can move it into the façade. This, too, can be done under the protection of tests. Pinning tests ensures that existing behaviors are preserved, and unit tests allow you to make additions.

This and the content of Chapter 12 complete the legacy database TDD picture. In Chapter 14, I switch gears a little and look at some variations I've seen used on what I've prescribed up to this point.

Chapter 14

Variations

When I help people implement test-driven database development, I get something like this a lot: "This sounds great, but we can't really have a linear growth model for design." Most of the time, that's actually false, but some of the time it is true. It's a frequent enough question that it warrants addressing.

In this book, I've given you a way to grow databases over time that works in most cases, but it is really just an example. The key to test-driven database development is having a class of databases that you can test. You need a place that defines your design and documents how databases grow. That you do it is imperative. How you do it is not as important.

In discussing this topic with a number of folks, one of them mentioned what he perceived to be a problem. For very large databases, numerous incremental changes can take too long to deploy. In production environments, transitions need to be "rolled up" and optimized for speed. To make matters worse, many different deployments were releasing on different schedules.

The solution that person came up with was to define a single database design and maintain it using test-driven development. That served as the "gold standard" against which a per-customer database design was measured with tests.

Another problem I've run into, which I suspect is much more common, is customer resistance to accepting new versions of a database while still wanting small "maintenance changes." The solution for this problem was to have a single master database design that is developed in a linear way and then a special class for each variant deployment path, ensuring parity at certain "checkpoints" with tests.

A common thread runs through this and, as near as I can tell, all problems where you need to deviate from the linear growth model of database design. Regardless of the way you need to adapt this process, it seems like there is always the option of having your first-class design comply with the process laid out in this book and then deriving second-class designs from the first using tests to enforce parity between the second- and first-class designs.

Having a Class Is Important—Implementation Is Not

I want to start with a reminder.

Fundamentally, the problem is ensuring that all deployment paths produce exactly the same result. That's what having a class gives you in the object-oriented programming world. That's what it gives you in the database world. Having a single source of record for design from which instances are derived is the key to enabling test-driven development.

How you do it isn't nearly as important. I've given you a way to do it that works in almost all the cases I've seen. I'm about to give you another way that adapts this process to work in all the other cases I've seen. Yet, even if you cannot take the process as is and cannot use the adaptation demonstrated in this chapter, you can still probably find another way to solve the problem.

Scenario: Skipping Steps

Imagine a situation in which the amount of data is gargantuan, even by data warehousing standards. Each site hosts its own gigantic database and accepts updates to design on its own schedule, but the design they are updating is shared across all sites. The time needed to perform even simple refactors like moving a column from one table to another table is substantial, so you want to skip any steps that have been rendered unnecessary by subsequent transitions.

One solution to the problem is to pretend it isn't there while defining design. That is, you act like you can build a production database in small, linear increments while specifying and implementing behavior. You can then build a different class of databases for each release schedule.

In this scenario, unit tests for the master design specify what its behavior should be and transition tests document the ideal transformative path a database would take. The same unit tests can be used to verify the behavior of a derivative design as that of a particular version. The transition tests for a derivative design then populate an instance of the master design and an instance of the derivative design with the exact same data, transition them both to the target version, then test that the derivative database instance has the exact same data as it would if it had taken the long path through the master design.

The amount of extra work demanded by this process is, I believe, pretty close to the minimum amount of work that could possibly address the special problem.

Problem

Let's take a moment to delve into the problem a little more deeply. Let's say you have a database that you've developed in five versions. Because there are five versions, that means there have been five releases. In this scenario, they've been divvied among three deployment sites, as shown in Figure 14.1.

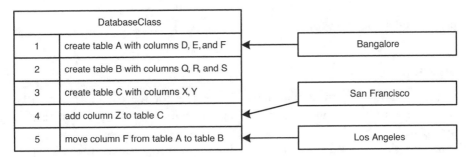

Figure 14.1 *Five versions with various deployments*

Up to this point, there has been no cost to deploying these increments. That is, no version obviated the need for a change made in a prior version. At version 5, the design of a database looks like Figure 14.2.

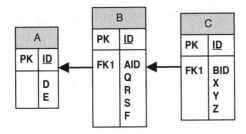

Figure 14.2 *Design as of version 5*

Version 5 moved the F column from A to B. However, in developing version 6, you realize that you really need the design from Figure 14.3 wherein F actually should be moved to C.

That means that the move of F from A to B is unnecessary when transitioning from version 4 to version 6, which will happen for two of the three deployments. If that move takes a half hour, there is a real value to avoiding the change: A half hour of downtime can be avoided.

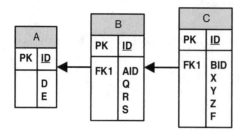

Figure 14.3 *Version 6 design*

Solution

In this situation, encapsulation makes it possible for the column move to be transparent to clients, making this change a refactor. A suite of unit tests is assumed.

First, write the transition test for version 6 as you've seen already in Chapter 4, "Safely Changing Design." After seeing it fail, add the corresponding transition. Now the master database class is updated to have the new design.

When the time comes to deploy to the San Francisco site, you can create a San Francisco deployment class. You do that by creating a database class called SanFranciscoData, which takes as an input a version 4 master database. To make this work, moving the interface stuff for new versions (at least) into an abstraction and coupling your code to that abstraction is also necessary. Because the interface isn't changing, just moving, this should be a very low-cost and low-risk change.

After that is in place, make a new version of the San Francisco database that implements version 6 of the interface class. This version can skip over the unwanted move and minimize downtime for the San Francisco office. Figure 14.4 depicts this scenario.

The transition test for this version is as follows:

```
[Test]
public void VersionFourToSixMatch()
{
    standardInstantiator.UpgradeToSpecificVersion(standardConnection, 4);
    standardInstantiator.UpgradeToSpecificVersion(variantConnection, 4);

    PopulateDatabaseWithSampleData(standardConnection);
    PopulateDatabaseWithSampleData(variantConnection);

    standardInstantiator.UpgradeToSpecificVersion(standardConnection, 6);
    variantInstantiator.UpgradeToSpecificVersion(variantConnection, 2);
```

```
var standardRows = GetSnapshotOfDatabaseData(standardConnection);
var variantRows = GetSnapshotOfDatabaseData(variantConnection);

Assertions.AssertRowsAreEqual(standardRows, variantRows);
}
```

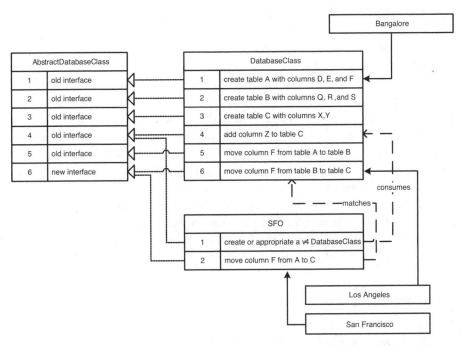

Figure 14.4 *Branching SFO and possibly Bangalore onto their own deployment type*

As I suggested earlier, the transition test populates an instance of Database-Class at version 4. It then transitions that database to version 6. That database represents how every derivative design should transform. So, you populate a version 1 SFO database with the exact same input and transition it to version 2 as well. Comparing that the two databases precisely match is then pretty simple.

The Right Amount of Work

If you don't have to deal with a problem like the one in this section, it looks like a lot of extra work. If, however, you work under these kinds of circumstances, you will recognize these steps as not requiring any more effort than what you were doing before.

Scenario: Deviations

I imagine many software development organizations are in the kind of situation described in this section. A company sells software to several large customers. Each customer wants support for the version they bought and doesn't want to upgrade to the latest version whenever they need a problem fixed.

If they don't get patches, customers' responses will range from dropping vendors to sending a couple hulking tow-truck drivers to people's houses for "tune ups." Patches are not just something that is hard to talk people out of—they are a reality of the business climate in which this company exists.

One solution to this problem is to apply the same trick as was used on the previous scenario. Create a master class then create a custom class for each deployment path. Patches can then be added to the relevant derivative deployment paths as new versions. Any time you want to upgrade a particular deployment path to a revision that exists in the master design, you can use transition tests to drive out variation between the two lineages.

Another way to handle the patch problem is to promote it to a first-class part of your database class design. Part of a version's definition is the set of patches that might have gone out against it. Reconciliations for the deviation created by that patch are then added to the subsequent versions.

Problem

Imagine you have a database with three versions (see Figure 14.5). You also have a different customer that has deployed each version.

No customer wants to accept any of the software changes that correspond to upgrading to the latest version, but they've all noticed that the performance of queries for resorts by price are very slow and demand a patch to fix it.

You've discovered that adding an index on the MinimumRoomPrice column will solve the problem for each of them. As a result, you've decided that version 4 should have that index.

However, you need to update all the customers with a patch. This is complicated by the fact that MinimumRoomPrice was named MinRoomPrice in version 1. The patch for version 1 follows:

```
CREATE INDEX Patch_RoomsMinRoomPrice ON Rooms(MinRoomPrice)
```

The patch for versions 2 and 3 are as follows:

```
CREATE INDEX Patch_RoomPriceMinimumPriceIndex
ON RoomPricingConstraints(MinimumRoomPrice)
```

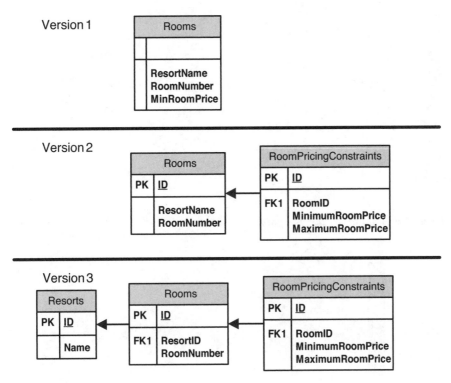

Figure 14.5 *Three versions of a database design*

The problem then becomes clear: find a way to introduce these patches into customer environments that degrades the processes outlined in the previous chapters as little as possible.

Solution

The best solution, as I see it, is to extend the concept of a class of databases to incorporate the notion of a patch. If you imagine that a database class represents a linear growth pattern (see Figure 14.6) for instances of a class of databases, then a patch would represent a branch that departs from that path, creating an alternative path (see Figure 14.7).

Worse still, two patches create not two additional paths, but three because both patches could conceivably be needed at the same time (see Figure 14.8). The result is that the number of configurations you have to support doubles every time you add a patch, and that number never goes back down. In actuality, it's even worse than that because there could be variation that creeps in based on when a patch is applied as well as which patches are applied.

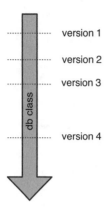

Figure 14.6 *A database class is a path*

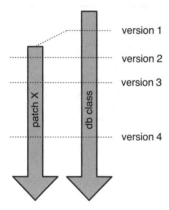

Figure 14.7 *Patches represent alternative paths*

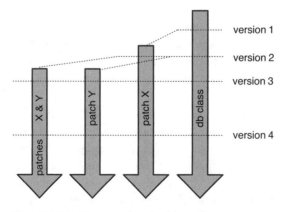

Figure 14.8 *New patches double paths*

You can solve this problem by having the alternate path, embodied in a patch, rejoin the "main" path. To limit the amount of variation a patch creates, have it rejoin the main path of a database class's growth as soon as it possibly can (see Figure 14.9).

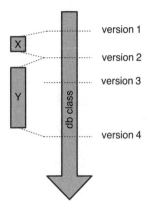

Figure 14.9 *Limit variation by merging paths*

Now let's take a look at how to take this theoretical concept and apply it to the problem set up in the previous subsection.

Solution Applied

You're changing the design of a database in a controlled way. I hope that, by now, you've guessed the first step is to write a transition test. The transition test for the version 1 patch would look like the following:

```
[Test]
public void Version1RoomPricePatchCreatesIndex()
{
    instantiator.UpgradeToSpecificVersion(connection, 1);

    instantiator.ApplyPatch(connection, "RoomPriceSpeedUp1");

    Assert.That(IndexExists("Patch_RoomsMinRoomPrice"));
}
```

In the setup, you upgrade to a particular version and populate with data. In the trigger, instead of transitioning to a subsequent version, you apply a patch transition. Your assertions then ensure that the corresponding index exists. Up next is the transition test for the `MinimumRoomPrice` patch. The transition test for the v3 patch looks exactly the same:

```
[Test]
public void Version2RoomPricePatchCreatesIndex()
{
  instantiator.UpgradeToSpecificVersion(connection, 2);

  instantiator.ApplyPatch(connection, "RoomPriceSpeedUp2");

  Assert.That(IndexExists("Patch_RoomsMinRoomPrice"), Is.False);
  Assert.That(IndexExists("Patch_RoomPriceMinimumPriceIndex"));
}
```

Those failing drive the creation of the patches to be applied as needed. The following example shows what the patches look like. The scripts to build a "normal" database instance as well as the code to apply a patch are available in the companion zip file:

```
<Version Number="1">
  <Script>
    <!-- snipped -->
  </Script>
  <Patch Id="RoomPriceSpeedUp1">
    <Apply>
      <Script>
        <![CDATA[
CREATE INDEX Patch_RoomsMinRoomPrice ON Rooms(MinRoomPrice)
        ]]>
      </Script>
    </Apply>
  </Patch>
</Version>
<Version Number="2">
  <Script>
    <!-- snipped -->
  </Script>
  <Patch Id="RoomPriceSpeedUp2">
    <Apply>
      <Script>
        <![CDATA[
CREATE INDEX Patch_RoomPriceMinimumPriceIndex ON
➡RoomPricingConstraints(MinimumRoomPrice)
        ]]>
      </Script>
    </Apply>
  </Patch>
</Version>
```

You'll also need a transition test for version 4.

```
[Test]
public void Version4AddsRealRoomPriceIndex()
{
  instantiator.UpgradeToSpecificVersion(connection, 3);
  Assume.That(IndexExists("RoomPriceConstraintsMinimumRoomPriceIndex"),
    Is.False);

  instantiator.UpgradeToSpecificVersion(connection, 4);

  Assert.That(IndexExists("RoomPriceConstraintsMinimumRoomPriceIndex"));
}
```

That test drives the creation of a new version.

```
<Version Number="4">
  <Script>
    <![CDATA[
CREATE INDEX RoomPriceConstraintsMinimumRoomPriceIndex
ON RoomPricingConstraints(MinimumRoomPrice)
    ]]>
  </Script>
</Version>
```

The final step for building this patch is to include the reconciliation for it. You would start with transition tests for it.

```
[Test]
public void Version1RoomPricePatchResolvedInVersion4()
{
  instantiator.UpgradeToSpecificVersion(connection, 1);

  instantiator.ApplyPatch(connection, "RoomPriceSpeedUp1");

  instantiator.UpgradeToSpecificVersion(connection, 4);

  Assert.That(IndexExists("Patch_RoomsMinRoomPrice"), Is.False);
  Assert.That(IndexExists("Patch_RoomPriceMinimumPriceIndex"),
➥Is.False);
  Assert.That(instantiator.PatchIsApplied(connection,
➥"RoomPriceSpeedUp1"),
    Is.False);
}

[Test]
public void Version2RoomPricePatchResolvedInVersion4()
{
  instantiator.UpgradeToSpecificVersion(connection, 2);

  instantiator.ApplyPatch(connection, "RoomPriceSpeedUp2");
```

```
  instantiator.UpgradeToSpecificVersion(connection, 4);

  Assert.That(IndexExists("Patch_RoomsMinRoomPrice"), Is.False);
  Assert.That(IndexExists("Patch_RoomPriceMinimumPriceIndex"),
➥Is.False);
  Assert.That(instantiator.PatchIsApplied(connection,
➥"RoomPriceSpeedUp2"),
    Is.False);
}

[Test]
public void Version3RoomPricePatchResolvedInVersion4()
{
  instantiator.UpgradeToSpecificVersion(connection, 3);

  instantiator.ApplyPatch(connection, "RoomPriceSpeedUp2");

  instantiator.UpgradeToSpecificVersion(connection, 4);

  Assert.That(IndexExists("Patch_RoomsMinRoomPrice"), Is.False);
  Assert.That(IndexExists("Patch_RoomPriceMinimumPriceIndex"),
➥Is.False);
  Assert.That(instantiator.PatchIsApplied(connection,
➥"RoomPriceSpeedUp2"),
    Is.False);
}
```

Those tests would fail because the transition for version 4 tries to create an index that already exists. To make them pass, all you have to do is make the creation of the index conditional.

```
<Version Number="2">
  <Script>
    <!-- snipped -->
  </Script>
  <Patch Id="RoomPriceSpeedUp1">
    <Resolve>
      <Script>
        <![CDATA[
DROP INDEX Patch_RoomsMinRoomPrice ON Rooms
        ]]>
      </Script>
    </Resolve>
  </Patch>
  <Patch Id="RoomPriceSpeedUp2">
    <!-- snipped -->
  </Patch>
</Version>
<Version Number="4">
  <Script>
    <!-- snipped -->
  </Script>
  <Patch Id="RoomPriceSpeedUp2">
```

```
   <Resolve>
     <Script>
       <![CDATA[
DROP INDEX Patch_RoomPriceMinimumPriceIndex ON
RoomPricingConstraints
       ]]>
     </Script>
   </Resolve>
  </Patch>
</Version>
```

This allows you to define when a patch can be applied, when it transforms alongside other designs, and when it merges back in to the main flow of design.

If necessary, you could also make certain steps only run when a patch was run previously. The implementation of that feature is left as an exercise for you, should the need ever arise.

Common Solution

The common thread in all the solutions to each kind of variation I have seen is having a linear "master path" toward which you are constantly driving all of your variant deployments. Doing this won't create uniformity. Variation in your deployed environments exists for a reason, and if you want uniformity, you will have to address that reason using techniques outside the scope of this book. However, driving everything back toward a master path minimizes variation by coercing conformity wherever variation is no longer necessary.

Summary

This book is not about converting you to my religion. It is about showing you how my religion can help you. It is improbable in the extreme that test-driven development cannot help you at all, but if TDD the way I've described doesn't help you, then my recommendation is to do it some other way.

This chapter showed two examples of how to do this. One involved creating a "master" database design and then creating "slave" classes that were proven by tests to produce the exact same effect as the master, but skipped certain transitions that were deemed unnecessary in their context. The other involved creating a branching mechanism within a class of databases so that patches could be applied and then resolved patches against the main course of database growth as soon as possible.

In both of these cases, a common theme exists—defining a single course of development as "ideal" and then doing everything in your power to match all of your deviant courses as closely to that ideal as possible. I have yet to observe a successful deviation from the main test-driven database development process I've shown in this book that does not follow that pattern.

Needing to deviate from a tightly controlled test-driven database development process is not to be confused with adapting or evolving the TDD database process. I am *deadly certain* that someone will come up with improvements on this process and would be disappointed if that didn't end up happening.

This chapter covers one of the interesting "side topics" pertaining to test-driven database development by answering the question, "What if this doesn't work for me exactly as you prescribe?" Chapter 15, "Other Applications," address the other interesting question I've been asked several times: "Can this be applied to things other than databases?" (HINT: The answer is, "Yes.")

Chapter 15

Other Applications

If it can be persisted, you can apply this discipline to it. I focused mainly on databases for two reasons.

The main reason is this: Until very recently, nobody has ever said to me, "We've got agility down but this darn XML format keeps slowing us down." The fact that databases are large objects that store many, many units of knowledge makes them a much more pressing problem for the software development industry at the time of this writing.

A secondary reason is that it allowed for a certain consistency in the conversation. By focusing on databases, then tacking on that this could be applied to anything later, I could focus on the processes and the various applications separately.

In any case, I regularly get asked about applying these techniques to three other major categories of data.

The first is XML. It's very natural to wonder about applying these techniques to XML because it's a highly structured data format with a rich set of tools built around it. The XML documents controlled this way could be configuration files, data records stored on disk, or anything else. Applying this process to any XML is easy.

Another case where this applies well is hierarchical directory of relatively small objects. File systems, registry trees, and LDAP servers are all examples of the kind of thing you can govern with this kind of process.

Finally, there are data objects in an object-oriented design. It is not an uncommon decision for people to use a platform's serialization format to create blobs of data that are tightly coupled to a particular version of a class's design. Such objects can also be wrangled and brought under control by this process.

XML

The classic thorn in the side of anyone who has ever tried to write a piece of shrink-wrap software is the configuration file that can be edited by a customer but for which the format must evolve over time. Developer response has always been to just live with a format even when it ceases to be natural to a problem or a design.

It doesn't have to be that way. It's very easy to inject into an XML document a single attribute on the root node that declares the version of a format and to use the host of XML tools to create natural transitions from one format to another.

Encapsulation

I've found that creating good encapsulation in an XML document is hard but, then again, XML is pure data with no behavior, so it's not that important anyway. The main kinds of encapsulation I end up creating are the classic sorts of things such as keeping unrelated data in separate elements.

Of course, you can always encapsulate an XML format in whatever code manipulates documents in that format, and you probably should.

XSD Schemas

XML has a widely accepted schema definition language in the form of XSD (XML Schema Definition). It is an optional part of any XML format and, choosing to use it tends to complicate things a little bit. Consider the following schema-less document, which represents a configuration file for a company that sells bedding sets:

```
<?xml version="1.0" encoding="utf-8" ?>
<Inventory>
  <Sheet Name="Egyptian Cotton" ThreadCount="300" />
  <Sheet Name="Georgia Cotton" ThreadCount="180" />
  <Sheet Name="K-Mart" ThreadCount="10" />
</Inventory>
```

Reverse-engineering a schema for this is easy and accessing the data without a schema definition wouldn't be hard for a program. However, let's say that you want to use a schema definition for whatever reason. It would probably look like the following:

```
<?xml version="1.0" encoding="utf-8"?>
<xs:schema id="SheetsAndThreadCountSchema"
  targetNamespace=
```

```
     "http://schemas.hexsw.com/examples/tddd/sheets-and-threadcount"
   elementFormDefault="qualified"
   xmlns="http://schemas.hexsw.com/examples/tddd/sheets-and-threadcount"
   xmlns:xs="http://www.w3.org/2001/XMLSchema"
>
   <xs:element name="Inventory">
     <xs:complexType>
       <xs:sequence>
         <xs:element minOccurs="0" maxOccurs="unbounded" name="Sheet">
           <xs:complexType>
             <xs:attribute name="Name" type="xs:string" />
             <xs:attribute name="ThreadCount" type="xs:int" />
           </xs:complexType>
         </xs:element>
       </xs:sequence>
     </xs:complexType>
   </xs:element>
</xs:schema>
```

To make your document use the XSD, you would change it as follows:

```
<?xml version="1.0" encoding="utf-8" ?>
<Inventory
   xmlns="http://schemas.hexsw.com/examples/tddd/sheets-and-threadcount"
>
   <Sheet Name="Egyptian Cotton" ThreadCount="300" />
   <Sheet Name="Georgia Cotton" ThreadCount="180" />
   <Sheet Name="K-Mart" ThreadCount="10" />
</Inventory>
```

The problem this introduces is that there is no notion of versioning built into the XSD standard. So, if you change your schema in any substantive way, either old documents or new documents will probably not be compliant. The solution is to keep a distinct schema document with its own namespace for each version of your schema. Following is a new version of an XSD and a corresponding XML document:

```
<?xml version="1.0" encoding="utf-8"?>
<xs:schema id="SheetsAndThreadCountSchema"
   targetNamespace=
     "http://schemas.hexsw.com/examples/tddd/sheets-and-threadcount/2"
   elementFormDefault="qualified"
   xmlns="http://schemas.hexsw.com/examples/tddd/sheets-and-threadcount/2"
   xmlns:xs="http://www.w3.org/2001/XMLSchema"
>
   <xs:element name="Inventory">
     <xs:complexType>
       <xs:sequence>
         <xs:element minOccurs="0" maxOccurs="unbounded" name="Vendor">
           <xs:complexType>
             <xs:sequence>
```

```
                <xs:element minOccurs="0" maxOccurs="unbounded"
name="Sheet">
                    <xs:complexType>
                      <xs:attribute name="Name" type="xs:string" />
                      <xs:attribute name="ThreadCount" type="xs:int" />
                    </xs:complexType>
                  </xs:element>
                </xs:sequence>
              </xs:complexType>
            </xs:element>
          </xs:sequence>
        </xs:complexType>
      </xs:element>
</xs:schema>
```

This solution ends up being an extremely minor complication because creating a new schema any time there is a breaking change for an XSD that has a lot of documents in production is a common practice.

If you create an XSD for each version of your XML format, even when there isn't a breaking change, then a natural way exists to determine the version of any given document. All you have to do is apply all the transitions between that version and the target version and you'll have a document with the right format.

XSLT Transitions

The question then ends up being, "How do I define a transition?" If you are a proficient programmer, you could use a language such as C#, Java, or C++. Another option, which I think is easier than writing code in this case, is to use XSLT transformations to represent a transition from one design to another.

Given the two previous XSD formats, you could define an XSLT document that transitions between them as follows:

```
<?xml version="1.0" encoding="utf-8"?>
<xsl:stylesheet
  version="1.0"
  xmlns:xsl="http://www.w3.org/1999/XSL/Transform"
  xmlns:src="http://schemas.hexsw.com/examples/tddd/sheets-and-
threadcount"
  xmlns:trg=
    "http://schemas.hexsw.com/examples/tddd/sheets-and-
threadcount/2"
>
  <xsl:output method="xml" indent="yes"/>

  <xsl:template match="/src:Inventory">
    <xsl:element name="trg:Inventory">
      <xsl:element name="trg:Vendor">
        <xsl:attribute name="Name">Default</xsl:attribute>
        <xsl:apply-templates select="*" />
```

```
      </xsl:element>
    </xsl:element>
  </xsl:template>

  <xsl:template match="/src:Inventory/src:Sheet">
    <xsl:element name="trg:Sheet">
      <xsl:attribute name="Name">
        <xsl:value-of select="@Name" />
      </xsl:attribute>
      <xsl:attribute name="ThreadCount">
        <xsl:value-of select="@ThreadCount" />
      </xsl:attribute>
    </xsl:element>
  </xsl:template>
</xsl:stylesheet>
```

Granted, it looks like you have to do a lot of work just to change versions. Hand typing something like that would be a huge hassle. So I guess it's a good thing you don't have to. Think about how trivial it is to write a tool that generates an XSLT document that does nothing but change the schema of a document. It should only take minutes and that's a one-time investment.

For a non-breaking change in design, you would literally need to run only the tool to create the identity transformation from version x to version x + 1. The only code that has to be written by hand is the additional template invocation in the following sample.

You would also need a tool that decides which transitions need to be applied. I'll leave building that tool as an exercise for you if you happen to end up in a situation where you need to manage the designs of XML documents over time. It would look like the tool I've included in the sample code except that it would be a lot simpler because XML naturally declares its schema (including version), and a single XSL transformation does all the work you could need for a single transition.

Now all you need is a way to ensure that data aren't lost in the shift from one version to another. The obvious thing to do is to set up a safety net that causes old configuration files to be renamed rather than wholly replaced.

Transition Test XSLT Changes

A clown on a tightrope is perfectly in control. That's one of my favorite lines from *Ed Parker's Infinite Insights into Kenpo: Mental Stimulation*, and it's hard to overstate how happy I am that I could find a way to use it in this book.

Ed Parker meant something different but not too dissimilar from what I mean when I bring it into this context. He was talking about maintaining the element of surprise by creating an illusion of incompetence. I am trying to point out that the best use for a safety net is no use at all. Of course, you want something there in case disaster strikes, but what you really want is to drive the probability of disaster so far down toward zero that you barely even consider it as a real possibility.

So, even when not dealing with vital data in a database and even when a fairly-easy-to-employ safety net exists in the form of a backup of a small file, I think that the right thing to do is to transition test all of your XSLT transformations.

Let's think about the transition in the previous section for a moment. How would you test it? Here's how I would do it:

```
[Test]
public void TransformInput()
{
  var transform = new XslCompiledTransform();
  transform.Load("V1ToV2.xslt");
  var stringWriter = new StringWriter();
  var writer = XmlWriter.Create(stringWriter);
  transform.Transform("SheetsAndThreadCount.xml", writer);
  writer.Flush();

  Console.WriteLine(stringWriter.GetStringBuilder());

  Assert.That(
    stringWriter.GetStringBuilder().ToString(),
    Is.EqualTo(TRANSFORMED_XML));
}
```

In some ways, the transition tests for XML transitions are much easier to write than for databases, because the entirety of an XML document before or after a transformation is easily codified—just type up the document. Better still, they run in a tiny fraction of the time that a database test takes.

File Systems and Other Object Directories

Another common thing that you might want to bring this discipline to is hierarchies of data blobs. File systems are, by far, the most frequently used persistence mechanism in this category. They are trailed by things such as Windows registry entries and LDAP deployments, but file systems are so prolific and so frequently changed that they can't even see the dust cloud kicked up by those other things in the rear-view mirror.

They are typically another kind of thing that is hard to create encapsulation in because they are pretty much purely data. I suppose there are structures such as soft links that one might think of as behavior, but I'm not going to waste your time discussing that. Again, because this discussion is about pure data, this really isn't much of a weakness.

Much like XML, directories of objects have a very mature host of tools built around them. In the case of file systems, many of those tools existed back when I didn't. This will make building a class of file systems very easy.

Transition Test File System Manipulations

Let's get right into it. Let's say I've deployed an application with the file system described in Figure 15.1. I'll call that version 1 of the `GameDeployment` class of file systems.

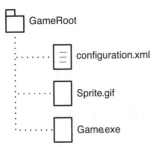

Figure 15.1 *A class of file systems*

In version 2, I need to make the following changes (also depicted in Figure 15.2):

- Upgrade the `configuration.xml` file to match its new format

- Replace `Game.exe` with a new version

- Create an `Images` folder

- Move `Sprite.gif` to the `Images` folder

- Add `Background.png` to the `Images` folder

- Move all the `.sav` files from the base folder into a newly created `SaveGames` folder

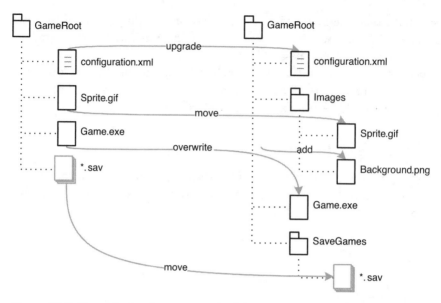

Figure 15.2 *Transitioning from version 1 of the* GameDeployment *class to version 2*

Following is a transition test that demands all the .sav files are moved to the right place in version 2 of this file system:

```
[Test]
public void V1ToV2MovesSavFiles()
{
  const string sourceFile1Name =
    TEST_FOLDER + @"\" + FILE1_BASENAME + ".sav";
  const string sourceFile2Name =
    TEST_FOLDER + @"\" + FILE2_BASENAME + ".sav";
  var deployment = GameDeployment.GetInstance();
  deployment.UpgradeToSpecificVersion(TEST_FOLDER, 1);
  File.WriteAllText(sourceFile1Name, FILE1_CONTENT);
  File.WriteAllText(sourceFile2Name, FILE2_CONTENT);

  deployment.UpgradeToSpecificVersion(TEST_FOLDER, 2);

  Assert.That(File.Exists(sourceFile1Name), Is.False);
  Assert.That(
    File.ReadAllText(TEST_FOLDER + @"\SaveGames\" +
      FILE1_BASENAME + ".sav"),
    Is.EqualTo(FILE1_CONTENT));
  Assert.That(File.Exists(sourceFile2Name), Is.False);
  Assert.That(
    File.ReadAllText(TEST_FOLDER + @"\SaveGames\" +
      FILE2_BASENAME + ".sav"),
    Is.EqualTo(FILE2_CONTENT));
}
```

As you can see, that test mimics a database transition test by creating the version 1 file system, populating it with .sav files, moving to version 2, and measuring that the .sav files were appropriately moved. That test could be used to drive the transition in the next subsection.

Shell Script Transitions

You have many, many options as to how to codify a transition. I'm going to use pseudo-code that looks shockingly like DOS's command prompt syntax. This example has a test failing because of a couple missing files in the Images folder:

```
setlocal
set Source=%1
set Target=%2

md %Target%\SaveGames
move %Target%\*.sav %Target%\SaveGames
```

That code makes the transition test pass. I can then repeat the process, writing more transition tests and expanding on my transition logic. Eventually, I would end up with something like this:

```
setlocal
set Source=%1
set Target=%2

rem Move the .sav files
md %Target%\SaveGames
move %Target%\*.sav %Target%\SaveGames

rem Move Sprite.gif
md %Target%\Images
move %Target%\Sprite.gif %Target%\Images

rem Add Background.png
copy /b /y %Source%\Background.png %Target%\Images

rem Upgrade configuration.xml
%Source%\UpgradeConfiguration.exe %Target%\configuration.xml

rem Replace Game.exe
copy /b /y %Source%\Game.exe %Target%\Game.exe
```

That code would make all tests pass and meet all the upgrade requirements.

Data Objects

The serialized data object is the format to beat when it comes to invasive perniciousness. It makes me tear up a little even when I'm writing about it. Nevertheless, it's a fact of life. People do stuff like use Java or .NET serialization formats to persist objects for long periods of time with shocking consistency. I used to do it, and every time I lie awake in bed underneath a slow-turning ceiling fan, it takes me back to the terrors I've inflicted and seen.

If you're stuck with a design that relies on serialized objects from an object-oriented system, then you might feel like the design of your data storage cannot change. Fortunately, these techniques can even be applied to the horror that is the serialized data object, giving you the ability to periodically revise the design of that tiny knowledge container.

Class Definitions Are Schemas

It's not a bad thing when an object is serialized in a transient way—for example, transmitting it from one process to another. When an instance of a class is serialized in a persistent way—as would be the case if you save it off to a file for later use—it becomes a data container. When you release that class into the wild, it becomes a historical fact. You can't introduce a breaking change to that class's contents ever again. You can, however, expose data and introduce new classes with totally different designs.

Consider the design represented by Figure 15.3.

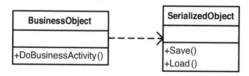

Figure 15.3 A `BusinessObject` *uses a serialized object*

A few small changes put you in a position to start applying the techniques from this book to `SerializedObject`. First, you have to hide from `Business Object` how `SerializedObject` is stored and saved. You can't change how it is stored and saved, but you can move where it is persisted to another class (see Figure 15.4).

When the time comes to introduce a breaking change, you can add a new type (`SerializedObject2`) and couple `BusinessObject` to it instead of `SerializedObject`. The only problem left is figuring out how to convert instances of

`SerializedObject` into instances of `SerializedObject2`. That problem can be solved by creating something that knows how to do exactly that and delegating to it from `Persister`. Figure 15.5 shows the design for this.

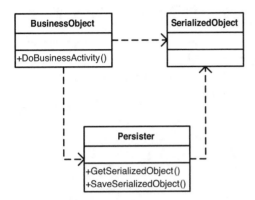

Figure 15.4 *Persistence factored into its own class*

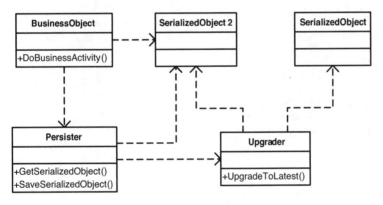

Figure 15.5 *Adding upgrader and a new version*

`Persister` saves and loads objects more or less blindly. On read, it takes whatever it loads and delegates to `Updater`. `Updater` knows that, if it is handed an instance of `SerializedObject`, it should create a `SerializedObject2` and populate it with the contents of the original object.

Eventually, it will be time to introduce another breaking change. When this happens, it's time to create a `SerializedObject3` and update `Upgrader` so that it knows how to turn `SerializedObject2` instances into the new format. If you stick to this pattern, no matter how long a saved object lay dormant, it can always be loaded and upgraded to the current format.

Transition Test the Ugrader Class

Construction logic in this kind of context is one of the easiest things to test in the world. Your Upgrader class takes a data object in and spits out a different data object. All you have to do is send in an old version and test that it is upgraded to the target version.

Suppose you have four versions of a data type. The first three represent non-breaking changes; you are just adding fields. However, as complexity grows, things start to get unruly and your only choice is to make a breaking change in version 4, as shown in the following example:

```
[Serializable]
public class FVSerializedObject1
{
  public string Name { get; set; }
}


[Serializable]
public class FVSerializedObject2
{
  public string Name { get; set; }
  public string HomeAddress { get; set; }
}


[Serializable]
public class FVSerializedObject3
{
  public string Name { get; set; }
  public string HomeAddress { get; set; }
  public string BusinessAddress { get; set; }
}


[Serializable]
public class FVSerializedObject4
{
  public enum AddressType
  {
    Home,
    Business,
    Mailing
  }

  [Serializable]
  public class Address
  {
    public AddressType Type { get; set; }
    public string Label { get; set; }
  }

  public string Name { get; set; }
  public Address[] Addresses { get; set; }
}
```

Following is a suite of transition tests that takes you all the way through version 4:

```
[Test]
public void UpgradeToVersion2PreservesName()
{
  var v1 = new FVSerializedObject1
  {
    Name = NAME_DATA,
  };

  var v2 = new FVUpgrader().UpgradeToV2(v1);

  Assert.That(v2.Name, Is.EqualTo(NAME_DATA));
}

[Test]
public void UpgradeToVersion3PreservesNameAndHomeAddress()
{
  var v2 = new FVSerializedObject2
  {
    Name = NAME_DATA,
    HomeAddress = ADDRESS1_DATA
  };

  var v3 = new FVUpgrader().UpgradeToV3(v2);

  Assert.That(v3.Name, Is.EqualTo(NAME_DATA));
  Assert.That(v3.HomeAddress, Is.EqualTo(ADDRESS1_DATA));
}

[Test]
public void UpgradeToVersion4PreservesNameAndAddresses()
{
  var v3 = new FVSerializedObject3
  {
    Name = NAME_DATA,
    HomeAddress = ADDRESS1_DATA,
    BusinessAddress = ADDRESS2_DATA
  };

  var v4 = new FVUpgrader().UpgradeToV4(v3);

  Assert.That(v4.Name, Is.EqualTo(NAME_DATA));
  Assert.That(v4.Addresses.Length, Is.EqualTo(2));
  Assert.That(v4.Addresses[0].Type,
    Is.EqualTo(FVSerializedObject4.AddressType.Home));
  Assert.That(v4.Addresses[0].Label, Is.EqualTo(ADDRESS1_DATA));
  Assert.That(v4.Addresses[1].Type,
    Is.EqualTo(FVSerializedObject4.AddressType.Business));
  Assert.That(v4.Addresses[1].Label, Is.EqualTo(ADDRESS2_DATA));
}
```

```
[Test]
public void UpgradeToVersion4DoesNotGenerateEmptyAddressEntities()
{
  var v3 = new FVSerializedObject3
  {
    Name = NAME_DATA,
    HomeAddress = ADDRESS1_DATA,
  };

  var v4 = new FVUpgrader().UpgradeToV4(v3);

  Assert.That(v4.Name, Is.EqualTo(NAME_DATA));
  Assert.That(v4.Addresses.Length, Is.EqualTo(1));
  Assert.That(v4.Addresses[0].Label, Is.EqualTo(ADDRESS1_DATA));
}
```

Implementing the transitions is about as hard. That is: not at all.

Code Transitions

Generalizing something like the Upgrader class mentioned previously the same way you would with any other system makes sense. We'll start with a generic upgrader design (see Figure 15.6).

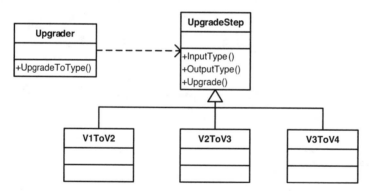

Figure 15.6 *A generic data object upgrader design*

In this design, an Upgrader has a collection of UpgradeStep objects. Each upgrade step declares its source object type and has a Translate method that converts objects of the source type into some other type. The code for Upgrader is pretty simple, then:

```
public class Upgrader
{
  private readonly List<UpgradeStep> steps;
  private Upgrader(UpgradeStep[] steps)
```

```
{
  this.steps = new List<UpgradeStep>(steps);
}

public static Upgrader GetInstance(
  params UpgradeStep[] steps)
{
  return new Upgrader(steps);
}

public IEnumerable<UpgradeStep> Steps
{
  get
  {
    return steps.AsReadOnly();
  }
}

public object UpgradeToType(object input, Type target)
{
  var result = input;

  foreach (var step in Steps)
  {
    if (result == null)
    {
      return null;
    }

    if (Equals(result.GetType(), step.InputType))
    {
      result = step.Upgrade(result);

    }

    if (Equals(step.OutputType, target))
    {
      break;
    }
  }

  if (!Equals(result.GetType(), target))
  {
    throw new InvalidOperationException(
      "Could not convert from " + input.GetType() + " to " + target);
  }

  return result;
}
}
```

The code for each UpgradeStep represents a single transition.

```
public abstract class UpgradeStep
{
  public abstract Type InputType { get; }
  public abstract Type OutputType { get; }
  public abstract object Upgrade(object input);
}

public abstract class UpgradeStep<I, O> : UpgradeStep
{
  public sealed override Type InputType { get { return typeof(I); } }
  public sealed override Type OutputType { get { return typeof(O); } }

  public sealed override object Upgrade(object input)
  {
    return (O)Upgrade((I)input);
  }

  public abstract O Upgrade(I input);
}

public class UpgradeV1ToV2 :
  UpgradeStep<FVSerializedObject1, FVSerializedObject2>
{
  public override FVSerializedObject2 Upgrade(FVSerializedObject1
➡input)
  {
    return new FVSerializedObject2()
    {
      Name = input.Name
    };
  }
}

public class UpgradeV2ToV3 :
  UpgradeStep<FVSerializedObject2, FVSerializedObject3>
{
  public override FVSerializedObject3 Upgrade(FVSerializedObject2
➡input)
  {
    return new FVSerializedObject3()
    {
      Name = input.Name,
      HomeAddress = input.HomeAddress
    };
  }
}

public class UpgradeV3ToV4 :
  UpgradeStep<FVSerializedObject3, FVSerializedObject4>
{
  public override FVSerializedObject4 Upgrade(FVSerializedObject3 v3)
```

```
  {
    var addresses = new List<FVSerializedObject4.Address>();

    if (v3.HomeAddress != null)
      addresses.Add(MakeAddress(
        FVSerializedObject4.AddressType.Home, v3.HomeAddress));

    if (v3.BusinessAddress != null)
      addresses.Add(MakeAddress(
        FVSerializedObject4.AddressType.Business, v3.BusinessAddress));

    return
      new FVSerializedObject4
      {
        Name = v3.Name,
        Addresses = addresses.ToArray()
      };
  }

  private static FVSerializedObject4.Address MakeAddress(
    FVSerializedObject4.AddressType type, string label)
  {
    return new FVSerializedObject4.Address
    {
      Type = type,
      Label = label
    };
  }
}
```

Note how this enables you to reform the transition tests so that they don't even use `Upgrader` (following):

```
[Test]
public void UpgradeToVersion2PreservesName()
{
  var v1 = new FVSerializedObject1
  {
    Name = NAME_DATA,
  };

  var v2 = new UpgradeV1ToV2().Upgrade(v1);

  Assert.That(v2.Name, Is.EqualTo(NAME_DATA));
}
```

Then the only test that you have to have for `Upgrader` is that it has the right steps in the right order.

```
[Test]
public void UpgraderHasRightSteps()
{
  Assert.That(
```

```
FVUpgraderFactory.GetInstance().Steps
  .Select(s => s.GetType()).ToArray(),
Is.EqualTo(
  new[] {
    typeof(UpgradeV1ToV2),
    typeof(UpgradeV2ToV3),
    typeof(UpgradeV3ToV4)
  }));
}
```

You could go as far as you want with it, but this should at least get you started.

Summary and Send Off

The answer to the questison, "Can this be done with things other than databases?" is a resounding, "Yes!" In fact, it should. The truth is that this process is about any data, not just databases. However, databases are where the vast majority of the intractable seeming problems live.

I've given you three examples of applying this process to other domains. The first was XML using XSL transformations. Next, it was a file system using batch files. Finally, I brought it full circle and showed you how to apply this process at the most microscopic of levels in the application programming domain.

You should now be armed with everything you need to go out into the world and start writing test-driven databases that are as flexible, maintainable, and easy to update as any other class of objects.

This process should not be confused with the tools surrounding it. I've written a couple tools for the process already. At the time of this writing, there is the tool that I built in the companion code for this book and a commercial tool I've written called "dataclass." The tools are already there, and, if developers do the process, the tools will get better and better until using them is second nature.

Finally, I would like to thank you for taking the time to read this book and investigate a new way of dealing with data.

Index

A

abstraction, 160

  composition type relationships, 178-179

  database classes, linking, 178-179

  dependencies, allowing variation in, 185-186

  implementation and interface, synchronizing, 186-189

  low-risk refactoring operations, 222-223

access to façade database, removing, 263-264

advantages of TDD, 27

aggregation, 160, 167, 172-174

  mocking, 203, 210

  reuse, 177

allowing variation in dependencies, 185-186

applications, coupling to database instances, 66

applying

  changes to incremental builds, 16

  façade pattern to legacy databases, 254-261

    old interface, strangling, 262-264

  patches, 274-281

    linear growth pattern of database class, rejoining, 275-281

    resulting variation, limiting, 277

    transition testing, 277-281

  safeguards to upgrades, 60

  TDD

    to data objects, 292-300

    to databases, challenges in, 3

    to file systems, 288-291

    to XML, 284-288

assembly language, suitability for TDD, 160-162

auditing current uses of legacy databases, 232-233

avoiding requirements forecasting, 111-112

B

backups, importance of, 156

bad errors

  released errors, 150-157

    documenting, 154-157

    unreleased errors, 147-150

behaviors, 102-106

  controlling through mocking, 194-195

301

X-Y-Z

REGISTER

THIS PRODUCT

informit.com/register

Register the Addison-Wesley, Exam Cram, Prentice Hall, Que, and Sams products you own to unlock great benefits.

To begin the registration process, simply go to **informit.com/register** to sign in or create an account. You will then be prompted to enter the 10- or 13-digit ISBN that appears on the back cover of your product.

Registering your products can unlock the following benefits:

- Access to supplemental content, including bonus chapters, source code, or project files.
- A coupon to be used on your next purchase.

Registration benefits vary by product. Benefits will be listed on your Account page under Registered Products.

About InformIT — THE TRUSTED TECHNOLOGY LEARNING SOURCE

INFORMIT IS HOME TO THE LEADING TECHNOLOGY PUBLISHING IMPRINTS Addison-Wesley Professional, Cisco Press, Exam Cram, IBM Press, Prentice Hall Professional, Que, and Sams. Here you will gain access to quality and trusted content and resources from the authors, creators, innovators, and leaders of technology. Whether you're looking for a book on a new technology, a helpful article, timely newsletters, or access to the Safari Books Online digital library, InformIT has a solution for you.

THE TRUSTED TECHNOLOGY LEARNING SOURCE

Addison-Wesley | Cisco Press | Exam Cram
IBM Press | Que | Prentice Hall | Sams

SAFARI BOOKS ONLINE

informIT.com THE TRUSTED TECHNOLOGY LEARNING SOURCE

 InformIT is a brand of Pearson and the online presence for the world's leading technology publishers. It's your source for reliable and qualified content and knowledge, providing access to the top brands, authors, and contributors from the tech community.

⋀Addison-Wesley   **Cisco Press**   EXAM/**CRAM**   **IBM** Press.   **que˙**   ⠿ **PRENTICE HALL**   **SΛMS** | **Safari˚** Books Online

LearnIT at InformIT

Looking for a book, eBook, or training video on a new technology? Seeking timely and relevant information and tutorials? Looking for expert opinions, advice, and tips? **InformIT has the solution.**

- Learn about new releases and special promotions by subscribing to a wide variety of newsletters. Visit **informit.com/newsletters**.

- Access FREE podcasts from experts at **informit.com/podcasts**.

- Read the latest author articles and sample chapters at **informit.com/articles**.

- Access thousands of books and videos in the Safari Books Online digital library at **safari.informit.com**.

- Get tips from expert blogs at **informit.com/blogs**.

Visit **informit.com/learn** to discover all the ways you can access the hottest technology content.

Are You Part of the IT Crowd?

Connect with Pearson authors and editors via RSS feeds, Facebook, Twitter, YouTube, and more! Visit **informit.com/socialconnect**.

informIT.com THE TRUSTED TECHNOLOGY LEARNING SOURCE   PEARSON

⋀Addison-Wesley   **Cisco Press**   EXAM/**CRAM**   **IBM** Press.   **que˙**   ⠿ **PRENTICE HALL**   **SΛMS** | **Safari˚** Books Online

Get Agile with AW and PH!

The Agile Software Development Series	Robert C. Martin Series	Addison-Wesley Signature Series	The Net Objectives Lean-Agile Series

Addison-Wesley   **PRENTICE HALL**   **informIT.com**

For a complete list of titles, special offers, pod casts, articles and more please visit **informit.com/agile**

Addison-Wesley and **Prentice Hall Professional** are the leading publishers on agile methods and software engineering. With series from the thought leaders in the industry including Mike Cohn, Kent Beck, Bob C. Martin, Alistair Cockburn and Jim Highsmith, Alan Shalloway, and Martin Fowler, our titles cover everything you need to know about agile methods, technologies, tools, and leadership principles.

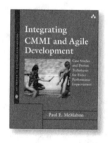

PEARSON

Addison-Wesley   **Cisco Press**   **EXAM/CRAM**   **IBM Press.**   **QUE**   **PRENTICE HALL**   **SAMS**   **Safari** Books Online

Try Safari Books Online FREE for 15 days

Get online access to Thousands of Books and Videos

Safari Books Online

FREE 15-DAY TRIAL + 15% OFF*
informit.com/safaritrial

> **Feed your brain**
> Gain unlimited access to thousands of books and videos about technology,
> digital media and professional development from O'Reilly Media,
> Addison-Wesley, Microsoft Press, Cisco Press, McGraw Hill, Wiley, WROX,
> Prentice Hall, Que, Sams, Apress, Adobe Press and other top publishers.

> **See it, believe it**
> Watch hundreds of expert-led instructional videos on today's hottest topics.

WAIT, THERE'S MORE!

> **Gain a competitive edge**
> Be first to learn about the newest technologies and subjects with Rough Cuts
> pre-published manuscripts and new technology overviews in Short Cuts.

> **Accelerate your project**
> Copy and paste code, create smart searches that let you know when new
> books about your favorite topics are available, and customize your library
> with favorites, highlights, tags, notes, mash-ups and more.

* Available to new subscribers only. Discount applies to the Safari Library and is valid for first
12 consecutive monthly billing cycles. Safari Library is not available in all countries.

Safari
Books Online

FREE
Online Edition

Your purchase of **Test-Driven Database Development** includes access to a free online edition for 45 days through the **Safari Books Online** subscription service. Nearly every Addison-Wesley Professional book is available online through **Safari Books Online**, along with thousands of books and videos from publishers such as Cisco Press, Exam Cram, IBM Press, O'Reilly Media, Prentice Hall, Que, Sams, and VMware Press.

Safari Books Online is a digital library providing searchable, on-demand access to thousands of technology, digital media, and professional development books and videos from leading publishers. With one monthly or yearly subscription price, you get unlimited access to learning tools and information on topics including mobile app and software development, tips and tricks on using your favorite gadgets, networking, project management, graphic design, and much more.

Activate your FREE Online Edition at
informit.com/safarifree

STEP 1:   Enter the coupon code: CZGMPEH.

STEP 2:   New Safari users, complete the brief registration form. Safari subscribers, just log in.

If you have difficulty registering on Safari or accessing the online edition, please e-mail customer-service@safaribooksonline.com

 Addison Wesley
 Adobe Press
 ALPHA
 Cisco Press
 FT Press
 IBM Press
 Microsoft Press
 New Riders
 O'REILLY

 Peachpit Press
 PRENTICE HALL
 que
 Redbooks
 SAMS
 sas Publishing
 vmware PRESS
 WILEY
wrox